普通高等学校"十四五"规划旅游管理类精品教材
旅游管理双语系列教材
总主编◎史 达

CHINESE
CULTURE
AND TOURISM

中国 旅游文化
（双语版）

CHINESE CULTURE AND TOURISM (BILINGUAL EDITION)

主　编◎石芳芳
副主编◎史　达
参　编◎季少军　白　薇　周　姝
　　　　赵　硕　张　琳

华中科技大学出版社
http://press.hust.edu.cn
中国·武汉

内容提要

本书用英文介绍了中国文化和文化旅游资源,包括中国旅游发展历史、文化遗产、历史建筑、文学艺术、书法绘画、节事庆典、传统工艺、饮食文化、中国武术和中医中药,以及它们与旅游之间的关系。每章开始的部分列出了本章的生词和中文释义,展示了本章的知识图谱,文中穿插了丰富的图片、案例、可扫码播放的有声资料和视频资料,每章的结束部分提供了主题案例和延展阅读书单。同时,本书也为教师提供了课件和习题库。

Abstract

This book provides an introduction to Chinese culture and cultural tourism resources in China. The topics include the history of tourism development in China, cultural heritage, architecture, literature, Chinese calligraphy and painting, festivals and events, traditional crafts, Chinese cuisine, martial arts and Chinese traditional medicine. Their relationships with tourism have also been discussed. The technical terms and the Chinese translation are presented at the beginning of each chapter to facilitate reading. A knowledge graph is illustrated to show the structure of the chapter. A lot of photos, cases, and further reading materials have been provided in the text. Readers may also access additional audio and video materials by scanning the QR codes in the text. A major case study in the form of China Story and a recommended reading list are put at the end of each chapter. Lecture slides and a test bank are available for teachers to use.

图书在版编目(CIP)数据

中国旅游文化:双语版:汉、英 / 石芳芳主编 . —武汉:华中科技大学出版社,2023.5
ISBN 978-7-5680-8941-8

Ⅰ.①中… Ⅱ.①石… Ⅲ.①旅游文化-中国-汉、英 Ⅳ.①F592

中国国家版本馆 CIP 数据核字(2023)第 088673 号

中国旅游文化(双语版) 石芳芳 主编
Zhongguo Lüyou Wenhua (Shuangyu Ban)

策划编辑:王　乾
责任编辑:王　乾
封面设计:高　鹏　原色设计
责任校对:张会军
责任监印:周治超

出版发行:华中科技大学出版社(中国•武汉)　　电　话:(027)81321913
　　　　　武汉市东湖新技术开发区华工科技园　　邮　编:430223
录　　排:孙雅丽
印　　刷:武汉科源印刷设计有限公司
开　　本:787mm×1092mm　1/16
印　　张:16
字　　数:436千字
版　　次:2023年5月第1版第1次印刷
定　　价:59.80元

本书若有印装质量问题,请向出版社营销中心调换
全国免费服务热线:400-6679-118　竭诚为您服务
版权所有　侵权必究

总序

华中科技大学出版社出版的旅游管理类专业的双语教材，首套包含《旅游消费者行为》《旅游学概论》《旅游目的地管理》《中国旅游文化》《旅游资源学》五本教材，由分别来自东北财经大学、山东大学、云南大学、西安外国语大学、北京第二外国语学院等多所在旅游管理国际化办学方面有较多经验积累的高校的三十多名教师合作完成。

我们都知道，旅游业是中国1978年改革开放后，较早对外开放的一个行业。旅游业的特性也决定了它始终具有国际化发展的元素和内在动因。从行业发展和顾客服务的角度来看，这个行业与人，比如国际游客的直接接触频率很高；对英文信息，比如各境外旅游目的地或英文版的旅游网站的搜索量很大。从语言要求上来看，英语是为大多数国际游客所能听懂的语言。在国内的很多知名旅游景点，我们会经常看到用熟练的外语给外国游客介绍中国历史文化景点的导游；在很多城市的街头巷角，会有一些当地居民用外语为外国旅客指路或者推介家乡的风土人情。他们亲切友善的表达，不仅传递了信息，还展现了一个国家的包容度和自信。所以，与其他服务业业态和商业业态相比，旅游业的国际化程度相对较高，对国际化人才的需求也更多。要想做到准确地把握不同国家旅游者的行为，达意地传递旅游和文化信息，就需要旅游业的从业者能够掌握和使用专业外语。

高等教育机构作为人才的提供者，要想满足行业对于国际化人才的需求，就需要从教师国际化和课程国际化等方面提供支撑。从目前高校发展的情况看，在经过多年教育国际化发展后，越来越多的教师已经具备较强的国际化视野和国际化沟通能力。但是课程国际化的关键环节——教材国际化却成为木桶上的短板。在国际化教材的使用方面，高校主要通过中国图书进出口(集团)有限公司来引进教材,或者由教师自制课程讲义和幻灯片。引进的教材几乎都为国外学者所著,里面的案例多以国外企业为样本,中国学生甚至教师对很多国外企业并不了解。特别是在新的旅游业态方面,中国的旅游业有着其他一些国家所没有的运营形态,比如数字化等,在这个层面上,中国的旅游业与国外存在较大程度的差异性。

而教师自制的讲义对于学生而言,其在课后很难进行阅读和复习。此外,随着中国教育改革和对外开放的不断深入,越来越多的国际留学生选择来华学习。这个时候再拿着境外的教材讲中国企业的案例,就显得有点不合时宜了。因此,由中国教师编著一套讲述"中国故事"的双语教材,让境外的读者也能更便捷地了解中国旅游业的实践与发展,就成为一项非常紧迫且有意义的工作了。首套五本教材涵盖了旅游管理类专业的三门核心课程,同时还包括"中国旅游文化""旅游资源学"两门非常有特点的课程,希望能够满足大多数读者的需求。

华中科技大学出版社是国内在旅游管理类教材出版方面的佼佼者。因为工作的关系,编者与李欢社长、王乾编辑在多次交流中碰撞出火花,并很快确定出版书目,组建写作团队。从筹备到五本教材全部完稿用时一年半。经历了严肃的周例会讨论、外审等多个环节,克服了各种困难,该系列教材终于能够与读者见面了,编者在内心充满了喜悦的同时,也有担心不能如读者所愿的不安。

因此,也希望读者在阅读过程中,如发现其中的问题或不足之处,能及时与我们进行沟通。编者将不断吸取读者的意见和建议,不断完善本套教材,以便能为旅游管理教育提供更多、更好的教材。

史达

2023年3月19日

前言

读万卷书,行万里路。旅游是了解、学习文化的有效途径之一。文化是一个国家独特的旅游资源。中华文化历史悠久,灿烂辉煌,是中华民族的骄傲,也是世界文化的瑰宝。习近平总书记在党的二十大报告中作出"推进文化自信自强,铸就社会主义文化新辉煌"的重大部署,提出"增强中华文明传播力影响力"的任务要求,为新时代新征程提升国家文化软实力、加强国际传播能力建设、推动中华文化更好地走向世界,指明了前进方向,提供了根本遵循。文化自信的建立源自对本国文化的了解,文化交流的条件是能够用通用语言来表述文化的内容。本书旨在用英文介绍中国文化和文化旅游资源,让读者在学习中国文化发展历史、文化思想、文化元素的同时,认识文化与旅游的关系和文化旅游发展的基础,掌握用英文表达、传播中国旅游文化的方法。

本书共十一章,第一章为绪论,介绍了文化和旅游的概念、二者的关系、中国文化的特点、核心元素,以及中国旅游文化的作用;第二章介绍了中国旅游的历史,丝绸之路和中华人民共和国成立以后中国旅游的发展;第三章对中国文化遗产及其作为旅游资源的价值做了阐述,并分析了发展有形和无形文化遗产旅游的方法和需要注意的问题;第四章的主题是建筑,介绍了中国历史建筑的发展、文化内涵,以及著名的建筑类景点;第五章从中国文学的发展讲起,讨论了旅游与文学的关系,并介绍了与文学密切相关的景区;第六章介绍了中国书法和绘画的特点、历史发展,以及与书画相关的著名旅游吸引物;第七章的主题是节庆活动,内容包括中国节庆的起源和演变、旅游节庆活动的概念、特点和种类,以及旅游节庆的发展路径;第八章介绍了中国工艺的起源、发展、分类和特征,中国工艺与旅游的关系，以及在旅游景区常见的几种中国工艺；第九章的内容是中国饮食文化，探讨了餐饮文化和旅游的关系，介绍了中国餐饮文化和茶文化及其特点；第十章的主题是中国武术，涵盖了武术的发展历史、主要种类、武术思想，以及和中国武术有关的旅游景点；第十一章介绍了中医，包括中医理论、诊治方法、保健方法以及中医旅游。

　　为了让本书更加生动、有趣、易读，每章开始的部分列出了本章的生词和中文释义，展示了本章的知识图谱，文中穿插了丰富的图片、案例、可扫码播放的有声资料，每章的结束部分提供了主题案例和延展阅读书单。同时，本书也为教师提供了课件和习题库。

　　本书由七位作者通力合作完成。东北财经大学石芳芳老师担任主编，负责第一章和第六章的编写以及全书统稿工作；第二章由东北财经大学史达老师编写；第三章和第七章由北京联合大学季少军老师编写；第四章和第五章由沈阳师范大学白薇老师编写；第八章由东北财经大学张琳老师编写；第九章由东北财经大学周姝老师编写；第十章和第十一章由东北财经大学赵硕老师编写。

　　本书的出版得益于多方的支持的帮助。感谢华中科技大学出版社王乾老师在编写过程中的悉心指导，感谢中国书法家协会石岱老师提供的书法作品图片，感谢东北财经大学本科教材建设项目的资助。尽管书稿经过多次修改和审校，但难免还有疏漏和不足之处，恳请广大读者批评指正，在此表示诚挚的谢意。

石芳芳

目 录
Contents

Chapter 1 Introduction — 001

1.1 Tourism and culture — 002
1.1.1 Definitions of tourism and culture — 002
1.1.2 The relationships between culture and tourism — 003

1.2 Cultural tourism — 005
1.2.1 Definitions of cultural tourism — 005
1.2.2 Types of cultural tourism — 005
1.2.3 Types of cultural tourists — 011
1.2.4 The impacts of cultural tourism — 011

1.3 Cultural tourism in China — 015

Chapter 2 The History of Chinese Tourism — 018

2.1 An Overview of the History of Travel and Tourism — 020
2.1.1 Travel for Business Purposes — 020
2.1.2 Travel for Education — 020
2.1.3 Travel for Leisure — 021
2.1.4 Travel to Visit Families and Friends — 021

2.2 Travel in Different Historical Periods in China — 021
2.2.1 Travel Before the Qin Dynasty — 021
2.2.2 The Qin Dynasty and the Han Dynasty — 022
2.2.3 The Wei, Jin, and Northern and Southern Dynasties — 024
2.2.4 The Sui and Tang Dynasties — 025
2.2.5 The Song and Yuan Dynasties — 026

2.2.6 The Ming Dynasty and the Qing Dynasty　026
2.2.7 Between 1840 and 1949　027
2.2.8 Between 1949 and 1978　027
2.2.9 After 1978　028

2.3 The Driving Force of Tourism Development　029

2.3.1 Development of Tourism Transportation Facilities　029
2.3.2 Refinement of the Tourism Market　030

2.4 Tourism Along the Silk Road　032

2.4.1 The Origin of the Silk Road　033
2.4.2 Travellers on the Continental Silk Road　033

Chapter 3　Cultural Heritage　037

3.1 Introduction to cultural heritage　039

3.1.1 Definitions and characteristics of cultural heritage　040
3.1.2 Categories of cultural heritage　042

3.2 Cultural heritage as a tourism resource　043

3.2.1 Value of cultural heritage as a tourism resource　043
3.2.2 Current cultural heritage tourism resources in China　046

3.3 Tourism development of tangible cultural heritage　048

3.3.1 Relationship between protection and tourism development　048
3.3.2 Problems in tourism development of tangible cultural heritage　048
3.3.3 Paths for the tourism development of tangible cultural heritage　049

3.4 Tourism development of intangible cultural heritage　051

3.4.1 Relationship between preservation and tourism development　051
3.4.2 Problems in the development of intangible cultural heritage tourism　051
3.4.3 Paths for tourism development of intangible cultural heritage　052

Chapter 4　Architecture　056

4.1 General History of the Development of Ancient Chinese Architecture　058

4.1.1 The founding stage　059
4.1.2 The forming stage　059
4.1.3 The maturity stage　060
4.1.4 Further development stage　060

4.1.5 Improvement and perfection stage　061

4.2 The cultural connotations of ancient Chinese architecture　063

4.2.1 Harmony between man and nature　063
4.2.2 Strict system of hierarchy　064

4.3 Historical architecture attractions in China　070

4.3.1 Imperial Palaces　070
4.3.2 Imperial Mausoleum　074
4.3.3 Sacrificial altar and memorial temple　077
4.3.4 Other types of traditional architectures　079

Chapter 5　Literature　083

5.1 General History of The Developmentof Ancient Chinese Literature　085

5.2 Tourism and Tourism Literature　087

5.3 Famous Scenic Spots and Relevant Literary Works　088

5.3.1 Poetry　088
5.3.2 Lyric　093
5.3.3 Prose　099
5.3.4 Antithetical couplets　105

Chapter 6　Chinese Calligraphy and Painting　111

6.1 Chinese Calligraphy　113

6.1.1 Calligraphy scripts　114
6.1.2 Historical development of Chinese calligraphy　116
6.1.3 Calligraphy and tourist attractions　118

6.2 Traditional Chinese Painting　121

6.2.1 Features of traditional Chinese painting　121
6.2.2 Techniques of traditional Chinese painting　123
6.2.3 Types of Chinese painting　124
6.2.4 Historical development of Chinese painting　126
6.2.5 Chinese paintings as tourist attractions　129

Chapter 7 Festivals and Events — 133

7.1 Introduction to Chinese festivals and events — 134
    7.1.1 Origin of traditional Chinese festivals and events — 134
    7.1.2 Evolution of Chinese festivals and events — 136

7.2 Festivals and events as tourism resources — 137
    7.2.1 Concepts of tourism festivals and events — 137
    7.2.2 Characteristics of tourism festivals and events — 139
    7.2.3 Types of tourism festivals and events — 140

7.3 Development of tourism festivals and events — 146
    7.3.1 Current status of tourism development of festivals and events in China — 146
    7.3.2 Paths for tourism development of festivals and events — 147

Chapter 8 Chinese Crafts — 150

8.1 Overview of Chinese Crafts — 152
    8.1.1 The Origins and Development of Chinese Crafts — 153
    8.1.2 Features and Categories of Chinese Crafts — 156
    8.1.3 Chinese Crafts and Tourism — 157

8.2 Chinese Paper Cutting — 158
    8.2.1 The Origin and Development of Chinese Paper Cutting — 158
    8.2.2 Categories and Themes of Chinese Paper Cutting — 159
    8.2.3 Chinese Paper Cutting in Different Places — 161

8.3 Chinese Ceramics — 162
    8.3.1 The Origin and Development of Chinese Ceramics — 163
    8.3.2 Well-known "Capitals of Porcelain" in China — 164

8.4 Chinese Carving — 166
    8.4.1 The Origins and Development of Chinese Carving — 166
    8.4.2 Features and Categories of Chinese Carving — 167

Chapter 9 Chinese Food Culture — 172

9.1 Overview of Chinese Cuisines — 174
    9.1.1 The Emergence and Development of Chinese Food Culture — 174
    9.1.2 Philosophy of Chinese Food Culture — 178

9.1.3 Food Culture and Tourism	182

9.2 Chinese Cuisine · 185

9.2.1 Eight Regional Cuisines	185
9.2.2 Local Specialties	190

9.3 Tea Culture · 192

9.3.1 History and Development	193
9.3.2 Categories of Tea	194
9.3.3 Chinese Tea Culture	195
9.3.4 Tea Culture and Tourism	196

Chapter 10 Martial Arts · 198

10.1 The origins and development of Chinese martial arts · 201

10.1.1 Origin	201
10.1.2 The formative stage	203
10.1.3 The mature stage	205
10.1.4 The modern stage	207

10.2 Influential Chinese martial arts styles · 208

10.2.1 Taijiquan	208
10.2.2 Shaolin Kung Fu	210

10.3 The philosophy of Chinese martial arts · 211

10.3.1 Harmony	212
10.3.2 Yin-yang	215

10.4 Martial art-related tourist attractions · 216

10.4.1 Shaolin Temple	216
10.4.2 Wudang Mountains	217

Chapter 11 Traditional Chinese Medicine · 220

11.1 Theories of traditional Chinese medicine · 222

11.1.1 Theory of yin-yang	222
11.1.2 Theory of five elements	224

11.2 Diagnosis and treatment · 225

11.2.1 Four examinations	225
11.2.2 Acupuncture	227
11.2.3 TCM massage - manipulation treatment	228

11.3 The promotion and maintenance of good health — 230
11.3.1 The role of diet in nurturing good health — 230
11.3.2 Solar Terms and health promotion — 231
11.4 TCM health tourism — 232
11.4.1 Trends in TCM health tourism — 233
11.4.2 TCM tourism attractions — 235

Chapter 1
Introduction

Learning Objectives

After reading this chapter, you should have a good understanding of:
1. The definitions of culture and tourism as well as their relationships;
2. The definition of cultural tourism and its types;
3. The impacts of cultural tourism;
4. Cultural tourism development in China.

Technical Words

English Words	中文翻译
culinary	食物的, 烹饪的
heritage	遗产
integration	整合
tangible	有形的
intangible	无形的
intellectual	知识的
spiritual	精神的
plurality	多元性
popularity	大众性
diffusion	扩散
comprehensiveness	综合性
continuity	连续性
evolution	进化
acculturation	文化互渗
ethnicity	民族性
preservation	保护
couplets	楹联

续表

English Words	中文翻译
inscriptions	碑刻
yurt	蒙古包
Confucian culture	儒家文化
Taoist culture	道家文化

Knowledge Graph

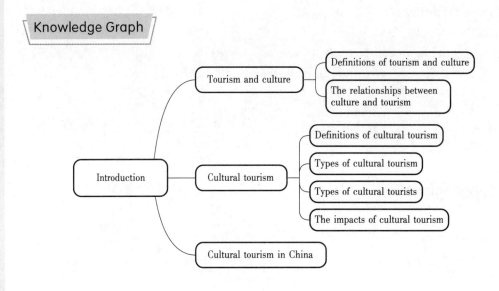

1.1 Tourism and culture

1.1.1 Definitions of tourism and culture

Tourism and culture have become intricately intertwined with the growth of interest in culture, the increasing accessibility of cultural assets and experiences, and the expansion of the tourism market. Tourism is a social, cultural, and economic phenomenon that entails the movement of people to countries or places outside their usual environment for personal or business/professional purposes①. Culture is the most unique tourism resource for destinations in the international tourism market. It gives a local

---

① UNWTO. (2008). Glossary of tourism terms. (Accessed 3 August 2022) https://www.unwto.org/glossary-tourism-terms

identity to the destination in this increasingly globalized world. Culture can be defined as the patterns of thoughts, feelings, and behaviors shared by a group of people. The key elements of culture include values and beliefs, customs and traditions, language, music, art, crafts, food and drink, and social norms. Culture is passed down through the generations via traditions and customs. At the same time, it can be disseminated to other societies via cross-cultural communication and contact.

1.1.2 The relationships between culture and tourism

Culture and tourism are closely linked. On the one hand, unique cultural resources can be a competitive advantage for a tourist destination; on the other hand, tourism can be a vehicle for cultural dissemination and preservation.

(1) Culture is one of the most valuable tourism resources.

Cultural resources are the foundation of numerous types of tourism product, including religious tourism, ethnic tourism, folklore tourism, heritage tourism, culinary tourism, and film tourism. For example, the top three Chinese tourist attractions for international tourists are the Great Wall of China, the Forbidden City, and the Terracotta Army, all of which are heritage sites embodying different cultural elements of China, including architecture, art, traditions, and history. While one can easily find similar beach holidays, ski resorts, and entertainment parks in different places of the world, these cultural sites are irreplaceable due to their uniqueness and significant cultural value.

(2) Tourism is a way to learn about culture.

There is a Chinese saying that "it is better to travel ten thousand miles than to read ten thousand books," showing the importance of learning through travelling. The best way to learn about a different culture is to spend time in it. One can only appreciate another culture in any real sense by seeing the place, eating the local food, talking to local people, participating in their events, and experiencing their everyday life. Not all travel can facilitate cultural learning. Staying at an all-inclusive resort with sparse contact with local people provides limited understanding of the culture of the destination. In comparison, less institutionalized travel can be more informative if a tourist chooses to stay with a local host, eat with the family or in local restaurants, attend a local festival, and shop in the open market. The knowledge obtained from organic personal experience is more comprehensive and authentic than that learned from the media and textbooks. At the same time, immersing oneself in another culture also provides an opportunity to reflect on one's own culture in terms of similarities and differences, which may lead to sympathy and tolerance. Domestic travel can help to expand one's knowledge of his or her own culture and stimulate a sense of pride.

(3) Tourism can contribute to the preservation of traditional culture.

The UNWTO 2001 report on Cultural Heritage and Tourism Development stated that: "Culture and tourism have a symbiotic relationship. Arts and crafts, dances, rituals, and legends which are at risk of being forgotten by the younger generation may be revitalized when tourists show a keen interest in them. Monuments and cultural relics may be preserved by using funds generated by tourism. In fact, those monuments and relics which have been abandoned suffer decay from lack of visitation."[①] An example is the work songs that have long been sung by fishermen in various situations to coordinate collective effort, to relax, or to wish one another good luck. Very few fishermen from the younger generation know the work songs today. The Changhai fisherman's work song (长海渔民号子), which was designated an intangible national heritage in 2010, gained more awareness and attention due to tourism development in Changhai County. Tourists may enjoy the work songs at local festivals and events in the form of singing performances by former fishermen. Thanks to tourist demand, the fisherman's work songs have been passed on to the next generation for preservation and commercial purposes. In addition, the income generated via tourism through admissions, retail trade, food, and accommodation expenses can be used to finance the preservation of cultural relics and the maintenance of heritage sites.

(4) Tourism may lead to cultural commoditisation.

Due to the economic value of cultural resources, they are subject to a process of commoditisation, which means the packaging of cultural activities and artifacts for sale in the tourism market. The effect of such commoditisation is ambivalent. On the one hand, cultural commoditisation may lead to change in the meaning of rituals, a simplifying of the design of cultural objects, and eventually a loss of the authenticity of the local culture.[②] Commoditisation may result in conflicts between local people, who prefer to maintain their original culture, and tourism businesses, who tend to sell cultural experiences and products for profit.[③] On the other hand, those engaged in the production and trade of

---

① World Tourism Organisation. (2001). *Cultural Heritage and Tourism Development*, UNWTO, Madrid.
② MacCannell, D. Staged authenticity: Arrangements of social space in tourist settings[J]. *American Journal of Sociology*, 1973(79).
③ Steiner, C. J., &. Reisinger, Y. Reconceptualising object authenticity[J]. *Annals of Tourism Research*, 2006(33).

cultural performance and goods find it beneficial, as it brings income, enhances their cultural identity, and improves the livelihood of the local community.[①]

1.2 Cultural tourism

1.2.1 Definitions of cultural tourism

Cultural tourism is one of the biggest and fastest-developing products in international tourism. It is estimated that 40 percent of tourists select their destination based on its cultural offering.[②] Cultural tourism refers to "a type of tourism activity in which the visitor's essential motivation is to learn, discover, experience and consume the tangible and intangible cultural attractions/products in a tourism destination. These attractions/products are related to a set of distinctive material, intellectual, spiritual and emotional features of a society that encompasses arts and architecture, historical and cultural heritage, culinary heritage, literature, music, creative industries and the living cultures with their lifestyles, value systems, beliefs and traditions."[③] People engage in cultural tourism to satisfy a need for diversity, learning and self-development. As can be seen from the above definition, both tangible and intangible heritage and contemporary culture are components of cultural tourism: it pertains to almost all aspects that represent the overall way of life of a population both in the past and in the present. Cultural tourism shows how tourism is closely linked to various elements of a culture. This book explains how tourism is related to history (Chapter 2), heritage sites (Chapter 3), architecture (Chapter 4), literature (Chapter 5), Chinese calligraphy and painting (Chapter 6), festivals (Chapter 7), crafts (Chapter 8), cuisine (Chapter 9), martial arts (Chapter 10), and traditional Chinese medicine (Chapter 11).

1.2.2 Types of cultural tourism

Cultural tourism is practically as diverse as culture itself. It is an umbrella term that encompasses a broad range of products and activities connected to a destination's cultural

---

① Mbaiwa, J. E., & Sakuze, L. K. Cultural tourism and livelihood diversification: The case of Gcwihaba Caves and XaiXai Village in the Okavango Delta, Botswana[J]. *Journal of Tourism and Cultural Change*, 2009(7).

② World Tourism Organisation. (2018). *Tourism and culture synergies*. UNWTO, Madrid.

③ World Tourism Organisation. (2022). *Tourism and culture*. (Accessed 3 August 2022) https://www.unwto.org/ethics-culture-and-social-responsibility

landscape and its people, including art, cinema, language, religion, architecture, gastronomy and folklore. There are a wide range of activities that can be engaged in as part of a cultural tourism experience. Here are a few examples:

Staying with a local family in a homestay.

Taking a tour around a village or town.

Taking a course such as cooking, art, embroidery, etc.

Visiting a museum.

Visiting a religious building, such as a mosque.

Socializing with members of the local community.

Visiting a local market or shopping area.

Trying the local food and drink.

Going to a cultural show or performance.

Visiting historic monuments.

Cultural tourism includes various subcategories and practices ranging from heritage tourism to festival and event tourism, gastronomic tourism, and creative tourism.① In addition, there are niche forms of cultural tourism, such as study trips, film tourism, and martial arts tourism.② The following section introduces some major forms of cultural tourism.

(1) Heritage tourism

Heritage tourism is a core category of cultural tourism. It involves "travelling to experience the places, artifacts, and activities that authentically represent the stories and people of the past and present. It includes visitation to cultural, historic, and natural resources."③ Cultural heritage can be tangible, in the form of monuments, sites, and buildings, and intangible, in the form of legends, rituals, and music. As such, visiting museums, archaeological sites, or indigenous settlements is heritage tourism, as is tourism associated with attending traditional festivals and appreciating traditional performance. Chapter 3 provides further details about cultural heritage tourism and cultural heritage resources in China.

① Richards, G. Cultural tourism: A review of recent research and trends[J]. *Journal of Hospitality and Tourism Management*, 2018(36).

② Pawelec, P., Świder, P., & Cynarski, W. J. Martial arts tourism: Meta-analysis of publications from 2005 – 2020 [J]. *Sustainability*, 2020(12).

③ The National Trust for Historic Preservation. (2022). Today's word: Heritage tourism. (Accessed 3 August 2022)https://savingplaces.org/stories/preservation-glossary-todays-word-heritage-tourism#.YJftArVKhPY

(2) Religious tourism

Religious tourism involves visits to religious sites for various reasons, ranging from faith-related motivation such as pursuit of blessings, worship, seeking forgiveness for sins, and being closer to divinity, to secular motives, such as learning, social gathering, and leisure. Many religious sites are also heritage sites of historic, artistic, and aesthetic value, so they attract a diverse range of visitors, from the most pious pilgrims to the most profane tourists. In China, the Four Sacred Mountains, Wutai, Putuo, Emei, and Jiuhua, are popular pilgrimage destinations for Buddhists. The Potala Palace also attracts thousands of pilgrims and tourists every year for its religious significance as well as for its architectural beauty. A more detailed introduction to the Potala Palace's architecture can be found in Chapter 4. Other forms of religious tourism include visits to religious grottoes. There are four important Buddhist grottoes in China: Mogao, Yungang, Longmen, and Maiji Mountain. The murals depicting religious stories and Buddha sculptures in these grottoes are of great religious, historical, and artistic value. For more information about the murals in the Mogao grottoes, please refer to Chapter 6.

(3) Ethnic tourism

Ethnic tourism is the practice of visiting locations where indigenous or minorities live.[①] Tourists are motivated to engage in ethnic tourism to get insights into the culture of a specific group or tribe and understand their way of life. With 25 minority ethnic groups, Yunnan Province is one of the most popular destinations for ethnic tourism in China. The distinct dress, traditions, festivals, and way of life arouse tourists' interest in learning about a new culture and meet their needs for novelty and learning. Engaging tourists in ethnic festivals is a common practice intended to create authentic experiences, though some may argue that such authenticity is "staged" rather than genuine.[②] An example is the Water Splashing Festival of the Dai ethnic minority. An important part of the festival is the cleaning of Buddha statues with water to obtain a blessing and then participants splashing water on each other, signifying the rinsing away of sickness and fatigue. Hundreds of tourists are attracted to the Water Splashing Festival to experience Dai culture every year. For more information about the Water Splashing Festival and other ethnic festivals, please refer to Chapter 7.

---

① Li, X., Xie, C., Morrison, A. M., & Nguyen, T. H. H. Experiences, motivations, perceptions, and attitudes regarding ethnic minority village tourism[J]. *Sustainability*, 2021(13).

② MacCannell, D. Staged authenticity: Arrangements of social space in tourist settings[J]. *American Journal of Sociology*, 1973(79).

(4) Literary tourism

Literary tourism, a type of niche cultural tourism, refers to travel inspired by literary works or their authors. Tourists visit literary sites such as writers' homes or graves, bookshops, literature festivals, literary settings, and literature-themed attractions.① Many attractions and destinations have become famous because they were depicted or featured in literary works such as poems and novels. An example is the West Lake, which was compared to the Lady of the West in Su Shi's poem "Drinking at a Lake on a Clear Day Followed by Rain." Another example is the Yueyang Tower, which has featured in the works of a number of poets, including Liu Yuxi, Du Fu, and Fan Zhongyan. Chapter 5 has more on Chinese literature and literary tourism attractions in China.

(5) Creative tourism

Creative tourism is a dynamic form of cultural tourism that allows participants to boost their creative potential by engaging in interactive and meaningful activities that appeal to all the senses and create authentic and memorable experiences.② As such, it involves active participation in hands-on or kinetic activities that stimulate the imagination and bolster dexterity, such as traditional crafts, drawing, perfume-making, porcelain painting, dancing, acting, or pottery crafting. Moreover, creative practices such as crafts entertainment, cultural appreciation, and self-development as tourists closely interact with locals and learn about traditional practices and culture at the destination.③ Being personally involved in the creative process provides a deeper understanding of the specific aspects of the local lifestyle and traditions and thus results in a greater sense of authenticity and satisfaction with the trip. For this reason, more and more destinations view the development of creative spaces as an important asset that can significantly increase their competitive advantage and attract the "creative class" of visitors.④ In Shanghai, for example, Tianzifang Alley（田子坊）houses numerous arts and crafts, it also provides places where tourists can take courses in traditional and contemporary arts, such as stage drama, traditional musical instruments, art appreciation, pottery, and ceramics.

---

① MacLeod, N., Shelley, J., & Morrison, A. M. The touring reader: Understanding the bibliophile's experience of literary tourism[J]. *Tourism Management*, 2018(6).

② Li, P. Q., & Kovacs, J. F. Creative tourism and creative spectacles in China[J]. *Journal of Hospitality and Tourism Management*, 2021(49).

③ Ali, F., Ryu, K., & Hussain, K. Influence of experiences on memories, satisfaction and behavioural intentions: A study of creative tourism[J]. *Journal of Travel & Tourism Marketing*, 2016(33).

④ Richards, G. Designing creative places: The role of creative tourism[J]. *Annals of Tourism Research*, 2020(85).

Similarly, in Jingdezhen, tourists can learn about various ancestral ceramic-painting techniques from local experts while exchanging ideas with other pottery enthusiasts in the workshops. Chapter 8 introduces the features and development of Chinese crafts, and their role in tourism in China.

(6) Food tourism

Food tourism, or culinary tourism, is "visitation to primary and secondary food producers, food festivals, restaurants and specific locations for which food tasting and/or experiencing the attributes of specialist food production region are the primary motivating factor for travel."[①] The activities may include preparing dishes, attending food events, visiting food-themed museums, and eating local food. For instance, visitors may learn the history of the development of Hangzhou cuisine, appreciate the Man-han Overall Feast (满汉全席) and other famous local dishes, and taste authentic Hangzhou cuisine in the restaurants at the Chinese Hangzhou Cuisine Museum. Local food is a key element of the local culture and can be an important attraction for a destination. Roast duck, for example, has become an iconic item of Beijing cuisine, a must-eat dish for tourists visiting the city. Quanjude (全聚德) (Photograph 1.1) is one of the most famous fine dining restaurants known for its roast duck and has a long culinary heritage, established in 1864. The technique of roasting duck in hanging ovens was designated a national intangible cultural heritage in 2008. Chinese cuisine is one of the three greatest cuisines in the world. Chapter 9 introduces Chinese food culture, famous Chinese cuisines, and their relationships with tourism.

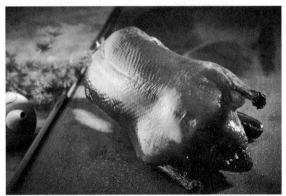

Photograph 1.1　Beijing Roast Duck

(Source: https://pixabay.com/zh/photos/peking-duck-roast-duck-meal-6826022/)

---

① Hall, C. M., & Sharples, L. The consumption of experiences or the experience of consumption? An introduction to the tourism of taste[J]. In C. M. Hall, L. Sharples, R. Mitchell, N. Macionis, & B. Cambourne (Eds.), *Food tourism around the world*[M]. New York: Routledge, 2023.

(7) Martial arts tourism

Martial arts tourism entails travelling to destinations to practice, learn, and compete in martial arts-related events.① It is a niche-type tourism combining educational, cultural, and sports tourism that appeals to combat practitioners and enthusiasts who may wish to meet experts, share experiences with other enthusiasts, and visit the location where the art originated. In addition, martial arts tourists can receive unique learning from their masters regarding philosophy and ancient practices that can bolster their self-cultivation. In this way, visiting martial arts destinations can provide travellers with a sense of authenticity and self-realisation through obtaining new skills and knowledge. The Shaolin temple in Henan Province is one of the most popular destinations among martial arts tourists interested in improving their skills as well as learning about the history of the millennial practice of Shaolin kung fu and the technique of the Shaolin fist.② Other heritage sites, such as the Wudang Mountains in Hubei and Mount Qingcheng and Mount Emei in Sichuan, also attract visitors who gain insights into the cultural significance of the locations while enjoying martial arts activities and the landscape. Chapter 10 provides an introduction to traditional Chinese martial arts and their philosophies, an overview of their historical development, and martial arts-related tourist destinations in China.

(8) Medical tourism

Medical tourism, also known as health tourism or wellness tourism, refers to travelling to a place outside one's country of residence to improve/maintain one's health by obtaining medical, therapeutic, or surgical care. Tourists may be motivated to engage in medical tourism due to the price of treatment, its quality, or in the search of procedures that are not available in their home country. It is usually not considered part of cultural tourism. However, unlike general medical tourism, traditional Chinese medicine tourism blends wellness and heritage learning, providing tourists with a cultural experience as they learn about traditional Chinese health philosophy and herbal medicine uses besides treatment (e.g., acupuncture, moxibustion, cupping). The Shengu Chinese Medicine Hospital is a designated National Traditional Chinese Medicine Culture Education Base. In addition to medical services, the hospital offers lessons on traditional Chinese medicine

---

① Cynarski, W. J., & Johnson, J. A. North Korea's emerging martial arts tourism: A Taekwon-Do case study [J]. *International Journal of Culture, Tourism and Hospitality Research*, 2019.

② Wang, Z., Yang, P., & Li, D. The influence of heritage tourism destination reputation on tourist consumption behavior: A case study of world cultural heritage Shaolin temple[J]. *SAGE Open*, 2021(11).

and treatment, medicated diets, and herbal cuisine. Chapter 11 provides an introduction to the theories and treatments of traditional Chinese medicine and how it is linked to tourism.

1.2.3 Types of cultural tourists

Based on tourists' different levels of motivation, Bywater (1993) differentiated tourists according to whether they were interested in, motivated by, or inspired by culture. Culturally interested tourists demonstrate a general interest in culture and consume cultural attractions casually as part of a holiday rather than consciously planning to do so. Culturally motivated tourists consume culture as a major part of their trip, but do not choose their destination on the basis of specific cultural experiences. For culturally inspired tourists, culture is the main goal of travel.

A more complex typology was proposed by McKercher and Du Cros (2002), who defined tourists based upon the depth of the cultural experience sought. They suggested five hierarchical categories of tourist. The first is the purposeful cultural tourist, for whom cultural tourism is the primary motive for travel. These tourists have a very deep cultural experience. The second category is the sightseeing cultural tourist, for whom cultural tourism is a primary reason for visiting a destination, but the experience is shallower in nature. The third category is called the serendipitous cultural tourist, who does not travel for cultural reasons, but after participating in cultural activities, ends up having a deep cultural tourism experience. The fourth category is the incidental cultural tourist, who does not travel for cultural tourism but nonetheless participates in some activities and has shallow cultural experiences. The fifth category is the casual cultural tourist, who is weakly motivated by culture and subsequently has a shallow experience.

1.2.4 The impacts of cultural tourism

Cultural tourism has economic, social, and cultural impacts on both destinations and visitors, by generating income, inspiring local pride, promoting intercultural understanding, facilitating personal growth. At the same time, there can be unfavorable consequences, such as loss of authenticity and originality.

(1) Positive impacts of cultural tourism

Economic contribution

Cultural tourism, like any other type of tourism, can make an economic contribution to the destination by generating income, creating employment, and attracting investment. For example, in Yanyuan County, Sichuan Province (四川省盐源县), where the Mosuo people live, ethnic tourism has seen rapid development. The Mosuo, a branch of the Naxi ethnic minority, are known for their unique culture, including their matriarchal system, nail-free wooden architecture, their elegant traditional costumes, their ancient music, and the Sanduo Festival. Local people engage in the tourism business by running inns, restaurants, shops, performing ethnic dances, serving as tour guides, or working in scenic spots and museums. The tourism income of Yanyuan County in 2019 reached CNY 1.11 billion.①

Cultural tourism can be a useful vehicle for poverty alleviation and sustainable development, as it supports economic growth by empowering locals to run their own businesses while preserving their culture. An example is from Haiyuan County, Ningxia Hui Autonomous Region(宁夏回族自治区海原县), where 1,800 low-income families from the Hui minority reported overcoming poverty thanks to the sale of Hui embroidery (e.g., silk scarfs, wallets, and blessing bags) and papercuts that local women produce for tourists in the Intangible Cultural Heritage Incubation Centres.② Similarly, residents from Yuanjia Village in Shanxi Province(陕西省袁家村)benefit from food tourism, as tourists travel there to purchase and observe how traditional Chinese food products like tofu, jellied bean curd, and vinegar are produced. In addition, family-run hotels and collective cooperatives attract visitors who can learn about traditional cooking methods and local cultural practices, creating permanent and seasonal jobs for locals.③

Cultural confidence and community pride

Cultural tourism can also bolster local residents' confidence in their own culture and inspire community pride when they realize that their traditions, arts, and lifestyles are valuable and of interest to people beyond their own community. This can trigger positive emotions that nurture cultural appreciation and a sense of belonging. Consequently, they are more likely to engage in cultural preservation, as they feel personally responsible for destination development. For instance, residents in Badaling(八达岭)and Mutianyu(慕田峪), two well-known tourist villages located close to the Great Wall in Beijing, find that living near the heritage attraction is a source of pride due to the political and cultural significance of the site, which is why they are keen to learn about the history of the place and educate visitors on its value.

---

① Yanyuan Government. (2020). 2019 Financial report. (Accessed 3 August 2022) http://www.yanyuan.gov.cn/zt/czyjsgk/xjbmdwyjs/lszmsjyjlghlyjqglj/js_9387/202009/t20200927_1709981.html

② Su, M. M., Wall, G., Ma, J., Notarianni, M., & Wang, S. Empowerment of women through cultural tourism: Perspectives of Hui minority embroiderers in Ningxia, China. [J]. *Journal of Sustainable Tourism*, 2020.

③ Gao, J., & Wu, B. Revitalizing traditional villages through rural tourism: A case study of Yuanjia Village, Shaanxi Province, China [J]. *Tourism Management*, 2017(63).

Similar feelings are shared among locals in the Panyu district of Guangzhou (广州市番禺区), home of ancient towns with rich architectural styles. Cultural tourism has heightened community pride by showing residents the importance of the Lingnan heritage, as reflected by the increasing numbers of tourists who visit the area, attend festivals, consume local specialties, and explore the local lifestyle.① By instilling cultural confidence and pride, cultural tourism reinforces residents' identity and sense of ownership of the local culture. For example, cultural rural tourism has empowered residents in Chongdu Valley in Luoyang (洛阳市重渡沟) to embrace their origins and unique intangible heritage. In this way, residents no longer describe themselves as peasants but as entrepreneurs, destination ambassadors, and protectors of the local culture and traditional practices (e.g., the art of cultivating crops in mountainous areas) who find it attractive to communicate and share their time with visitors.②

Cross-cultural understanding and personal growth

Cultural tourism can facilitate cross-cultural understanding through exploration and firsthand experience. Host-guest communication can foster cultural appreciation and emotional solidarity, reducing discrimination, stereotypes, and misunderstandings. These positive outcomes are even more evident in ethnic tourism, where individuals travel to discover and understand other cultures and embrace their differences. For instance, the Naxi people find it rewarding to explain to visitors the significance of the cultural artifacts (e.g., wooden plates bearing Dongba hieroglyphics and ethnic dress) in their houses and discuss the possible meaning of the ancient language.③ For visitors, it is an authentic learning experience as they get to know the Naxi heritage directly from the Naxi people.

Other forms of special interest cultural tourism, such as traditional medicine tourism and martial arts tourism, can provide an educational experience for visitors to learn about a place's tangible and intangible heritage while improving their skills in a certain area. For example, tourists who visit Guangdong Province to learn martial arts can obtain a combination of educational, cultural, and entertainment experiences as they improve their technique, share with other practitioners, and learn martial arts philosophies, enhancing

---

① Butler, G., Szili, G., & Huang, H. Cultural heritage tourism development in Panyu district, Guangzhou: Community perspectives on pride and preservation, and concerns for the future[J]. *Journal of Heritage Tourism*, 17(1).

② Xue, L., Kerstetter, D., & Hunt, C. Tourism development and changing rural identity in China[J]. *Annals of Tourism Research*, 2017(66).

③ Zhang, J., Xu, H. G., & Xing, W. The host-guest interactions in ethnic tourism, Lijiang, China[J]. *Current Issues in Tourism*, 20(7).

their well-being and cultural capital.① Similarly, Chinese wine enthusiasts who visit rural wine cellars in Xinjiang, Yunnan, and Shangdong describe their experiences as educational and entertaining as they learn about wine production while enjoying the landscape of the vineyards.②

(2) Negative impacts of cultural tourism

While cultural tourism can prompt the development of impoverished areas thanks to the flood of visitors and investors, studies show that touristification has brought several problems for locals, such as the loss of cultural identity, commoditisation, and lifestyle transformation. Members of the Mosuo minority, for example, have changed their daily habits, abandoning chatting with family members while cooking, performing religious rituals, and raising livestock to run BBQ restaurants until late and perform for tourists. Tourist destinations in urban areas, such as Nanluoguxiang in Beijing（北京南锣鼓巷）, face similar problems, and tourism is blamed for the increasing pollution, insecurity, congestion, and environmental degradation.

Yet, as tourism becomes central to the economy of many areas, locals are forced to compromise their values and beliefs and shift toward staging behaviors to attract tourists, leading to a surge in contested attractions, rituals, and practices. This is the case of the bamboo-beating folk dance performed by the Li people in Hainan, which has been rebranded from a funerary ritual to a touristic performance that reflects the joy of the locals, taking away its religious meaning and reducing its sense of objective authenticity by presenting a modified version of the original ritual. Similarly, the Shaolin Temple reflects commoditisation, defined as transforming a cultural site into a leisure-oriented commercial attraction offered to tourists. In the monastery, tensions arise as commercial facilities (e.g., souvenir stalls and restaurants) and donation boxes create the atmosphere of a folk fair, diminishing the cultural and religious value of the site and significantly reducing the authenticity of visitors' experience.

Commodification has not only led to the loss of authenticity but also to the loss of cultural diversity and the appearance of cultural homogeneity where cultural attractions and communities are losing their unique value in the pursuit of profit maximization. Indeed, the fierce competition among cultural attractions has created a culture of

---

① Ye, G. Canton kung fu: The culture of Guangdong martial arts[J]. *Sage Open*, *9*(3).

② Duan, B., Arcodia, C., Ma, E., & Hsiao, A. Understanding wine tourism in China using an integrated product-level and experience economy framework[J]. *Asia Pacific Journal of Tourism Research*, 23(10).

McDonaldization, in which sites offer standardized products and services to make the most profit. The term McDonaldization, coined by Ritzer, describes a society in which businesses operate under the Fordist paradigm and the principles of efficiency (i.e., most output for the least cost), calculability (i.e., quality control), predictability (i.e., standardized production), and control of the workforce by technological means[①]. Wuzhen (乌镇)(Photograph 1.2 left), is an ancient riverine town in Zhejiang Province known for its historic houses, traditional crafts, and waterside lifestyle. Gubei Water Town (古北水镇)(Photograph 1.2 right), located in the Miyun district of Beijing, is a purpose-built attraction. It is called "Wuzhen in Beijing" for its clear resemblance to Wuzhen in architecture, landscape, and crafts. The lack of uniqueness can be rather disappointing for those who are seeking novelty and authentic experiences.

Photograph 1.2　Wuzhen (left) and Gubei Water Town (right)
Source: https://unsplash.com/photos/O9wF7LNnOGE (Wuzhen) and author (Gubei Water Town)

1.3 Cultural tourism in China

The Chinese government has been promoting the integration of culture and tourism since 2009, when the former Ministry of Culture and the former National Tourism Administration jointly issued the Guidance on Promoting the Integration of Culture and Tourism. After this, 25 local integration policies were formulated to facilitate

---

①Crossman, A. edit an article McDonaldization: Definition and Overview of the Concept. Available at: https://www.thoughtco.com/mcdonaldization-of-society-3026751

implementation at provincial level. In 2018, the China National Tourism Administration and the Ministry of Culture were merged into the Ministry of Culture and Tourism. The integration of culture and tourism can help to establish cultural brands in tourism projects, create competitive advantage,① and preserve the originality of tourism projects.②

China is rich in cultural tourism resources. According to the Ministry of Culture and Tourism, by the end of 2021, there were 5,772 museums in China with 46.65 million objects; there were 108 million movable cultural relics and 767,000 immovable cultural relics across China. By the end of 2022, China had 43 items on UNESCO's Intangible Heritage List, and 56 places on the World Heritage Site List. In addition, there were 7,526 galleries in China, receiving 35.16 million visitors in 2021.

According to the 2019 Culture and Tourism Integration Development Report released by the Chinese social travel platform Mafengwo and the People's Cultural Tourism Research Institute, 80 percent of respondents indicated that they had experienced cultural tourism during vacations, and that culturally inspired tourists mainly live in first-tier cities, including Beijing, Shanghai, and Guangzhou. Beijing was ranked as the most popular cultural tourism destination, followed by Shanghai, Chengdu, and Hangzhou in Zhejiang Province and Xi'an in Shanxi Province. The most popular cultural tourist destination was the Palace Museum in Beijing, followed by Shanghai Disney Resort, Chengdu Research Base of Giant Panda Breeding, and Chongqing's Hongya Cave scenic spot.

Chapter Summary

In this chapter, we have introduced definitions of tourism and culture, and discussed the relationships between them. Then we explained the definition of cultural tourism, and introduced several types of cultural tourism. Next the positive and negative impacts of cultural tourism were elaborated. Lastly, we traced cultural tourism's development in China.

China Story

Does this museum have China's coolest gift shop?

①Richards, G., & Wilson, J. Developing creativity in tourist experiences: A solution to the serial reproduction of culture?[J]. *Tourism Management*, 27(6).

②Zhang, C. & Zhu, M. The integration of culture and tourism: Multi-understandings, various challenges and approaches[J]. *Tourism Tribune*, 35(3).

Issues for Review and Discussion

1. Discuss the relationship between culture and tourism with examples.
2. Discuss the impacts of cultural tourism with examples and ways to minimize the negative impacts.

Exercises

Recom-
mended
Reading

Chapter 2
The History of Chinese Tourism

Learning Objectives

After reading this chapter, you should have a good understanding of
1. The purpose of ancient travel;
2. Chinese culture and travel in different historical periods;
3. The development of tourism transportation facilities;
4. The refinement of the tourism culture market;
5. Tourism along the Silk Road.

Technical Words

English Words	中文翻译
Confucius	孔子
commerce and trade	经贸
humanism	人文主义
religious	宗教信仰
sacrifice	牺牲
historiography	史学
Fengshanpay homage to Heaven and Earth at Mount Taishan	封禅
national integration	民族融合
reclusiveness	隐居
landscape poetry	山水诗词
Buddhism	佛教
confrontation	对抗
feudal society	封建社会
Taoism	道教
capitalist countries	资本主义国家

Chapter 2   The History of Chinese Tourism

续表

English Words	中文翻译
elite scholars	精英学者
merchant	商人
implementation	贯彻、实施
the Reform and Opening Up	改革开放
refinement	改进、改善
diplomatic envoy	外交使节
the Third Plenary Session of the 11th CPC Central Committee	十一届三中全会

Knowledge Graph

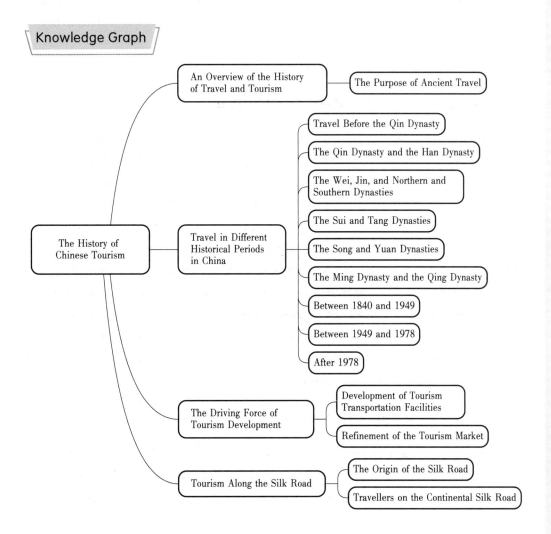

2.1 An Overview of the History of Travel and Tourism

Tourism is part of our daily life. In today's highly competitive society, people view travelling as a leisure and entertainment approach to alleviating stress and enjoying a moment of relaxation. Did the ancients have so-called tourism activities? If they did, what were their travel activities like, and how did those ancient tourism activities evolve into the current ones? This chapter will focus on those issues to offer a clear understanding of ancient tourism.

What was the purpose of Ancient Travel?

2.1.1 Travel for Business Purposes

Due to the limitations of road infrastructure and transportation capabilities two millennia ago, the ancients could only travel very short distances. Meanwhile, because their living depended entirely on farming or fishing, the ancients had to spend most of their time farming in the fields to ensure that there would be enough harvest to feed the family. Therefore, only a few individuals could travel, and the minority tourism activities at the time were devoted to various political, diplomatic, and educational purposes, such as diplomatic visits to foreign countries, hunting tours to the empire's hunting fields, study tours to exam venues, and other related activities. Travel didn't exist by itself and was mostly associated with various practical needs. Therefore, ancient tourism activities were targeted primarily at business purposes, whereas most modern tourism activities are for leisure. Individuals today are freed from farming and have both the economic ability and the leisure time to engage in true tourism activities.

2.1.2 Travel for Education

Because travelling was not easy in ancient times, only people in the upper classes who could pay for transportation and accommodations travelled. Aside from merchants' travel "hustling and bustling for profits", travel historically included study tours conducted by professionals to promote political ideas and educational travel conducted by people to increase their knowledge. Study tours were usually engaged in by educated professionals. For example, during his travels across the different kingdoms, Confucius took advantage of study tours to educate his students and followers.

2.1.3 Travel for Leisure

Festival touring was an important content for folk tourism, and indeed, festivals have always been tightly bound to tourism. During festivals, people would hold reunions and dine together, sing, dance, and play, go for an outing, climb mountains, or organize boat racing or lantern competitions, enjoying themselves to their heart's content with happiness knowing no bounds. There were already festivals carrying features of tourism in the Xia, Shang, and Western Zhou periods (2100BC-771BC).

In the seasons with beautiful scenery, ladies and gentlemen would walk toward the banks of rivers and the undulating green waves of open fields, enjoying the charming scenery and the beauty of nature to their heart's content. They chatted about their feelings and gave each other gifts for the sake of friendship and love. Such festival touring was to please the eyes and minds and cultivate a positive temperament.

2.1.4 Travel to Visit Families and Friends

The term "wanderer" is a general expression for people who are away from home. Even though they may live in a foreign land, they are still spiritually affected by blood ties to home and by homesickness. Especially for the ancient traditional society, with people's strong ethical sensitivities, it was very difficult for them to travel back home, and the sadness of leaving home was very strong.

Tours featuring a local connection had fewer utilitarian characteristics; they were simple and brought a breeze of love and nostalgia to the travelling culture in the ancient period. In addition, such emotions have been passed down even to current society and have had an impact on scholars and poets who are far away from their hometowns.

2.2 Travel in Different Historical Periods in China

2.2.1 Travel Before the Qin Dynasty

The beginning stage of the travelling culture was during the pre-Qin Period, which had three phases: ancient times (before 2070BC), the Xia (2070BC - 1600BC), Shang

(1600BC - 1046BC), and Western Zhou (1046BC - 771BC) Dynasties, and the Spring and Autumn (770BC - 476BC) and Warring States Periods (475BC - 221BC).

In terms of forms of travel, in ancient times there were journeys for survival in the forests, and travellers relied on instinct in an age of savagery and barbarism. Eventually, in the Xia Dynasty, there were people travelling for commerce and trade. During the Shang period and the Western Zhou period, travel had a strong sense of humanism and was entering the age of civilization. During that time there were ritual travels (such as a pilgrimage to present himself before an overlord) and travelling for marriage between the two royal families of the Qin and Jin kingdoms during the Spring and Autumn period and the Warring States period. There were people also travelling for sightseeing and entertainment (hunting trips and sightseeing adventures), and travelling for cultural reasons (e.g., study tours and lobbying).

The people who travelled ranged from monarchs and dukes in ancient times and the Xia, Shang, and Western Zhou Dynasties, to slave owners, nobles, the emperor, princes, and the class of scholar-officials in the Spring and Autumn and Warring States periods. It is worth noting that the class of scholar-officials were the social-intellectual elites and travelled actively, with many attendants. In travelling, they developed a trend of standing up to the leading classes such as the Sons of Heaven and dukes, and that trend changed the pattern of people who travelled.

Business travel activities were also very active during this period. The Shang Dynasty was the prosperous period in China's slave economy, and slave merchants travelled all over the world. By the Spring and Autumn Period, merchants had been recognised by the rulers as one of the "Four occupations" of scholars, farmers, workers and merchants. During the Warring States Period, long-distance business travel was very popular.

2.2.2 The Qin Dynasty and the Han Dynasty

The Qin (221BC - AD 207) and Han Dynasties (202BC - AD 220) were the period of the establishment and development of China's centralized feudal state system. Qin Shi Huangdi unified the six kingdoms, and the strength of the two Han Dynasties provided a safety guarantee for travel activities. The main travel activities during the period included the emperor's sacrificial paying homage to Heaven and Earth at Mount Taifengshan tours, academic study tours, and foreign adventure travel. Before Qin Shi Huangdi unified the six kingdoms, the vassal states of Qi and Yan on the southeast coast had already developed a class of "alchemists" who sought immortality and medicines. After Qin Shi Huangdi unified the six kingdoms, he built a carriageway centred on the capital, Xianyang

(咸阳), that led across the whole country. Qin Shi Huangdi used the carriageway to make five tours during his 12-year reign and travelled all over the country seeking the elixir of immortality. He also went to Mount Tai (泰山) to hold fengshanthe worship event. Paying homage to Heaven and Earth at Mount Tai(Feng Shan)Fengshan is essentially a sacrificial activity with a political purpose and requiring travel, but also with a mysterious and religious nature. "Feng" means building the earth as an altar of sacrifice to the sky. The ancients believed that Mount Tai in Dongyue (东岳) was the top of the mountains, and emperors went to Mount Tai to sacrifice to the sky to show that they were approved by the sky. "Shan" means sacrifice to the earth. Sacrifices of this kind were held on Tingting Mountain, Liangfu Mountain, Sheshou Mountain, and others. Legend has it that fengshanthis event was also practiced in the Xia, Shang, and Zhou Dynasties, but there is no historical evidence to support this claim. In addition to Qin Shi Huangdi, Emperor Wu of the Western Han Dynasty and Emperor Guangwu of the Eastern Han Dynasty also went to Mount Tai to enshrine fengshan.

During this period, academic research activities were also quite common. To pursue their hopes of mapping the world, the literati not only read thousands of books but also walked thousands of miles to expand their horizons, broaden their knowledge, and display their talents. They also frequently went places to investigate and learn, so that the science, technology, historiography, and literature of this period were improved. Sima Qian, a great historian and writer of the Western Han Dynasty, was the most outstanding representative of the academic expedition in this period. At the age of 20, he began to travel and inspect the whole country. He went to the "Southwest Yi" ("西南夷") to ask for help, later accompanying Emperor Wu of the Han Dynasty fengshanto pay homage to Heaven and Earth at Mount Tai, and going to other places to explore historical sites. All of these activities enabled him to obtain a large amount of information that could not be found in archives. These real and vivid historical experiences laid a solid foundation for him to write his *Records of the Grand Historian of China* (《史记》).

Another important tourist activity during the Han Dynasty was foreign adventure travel. The most famous figures were Zhang Qian in the Western Han Dynasty and Ban Chao and Gan Ying in the Eastern Han Dynasty. In 139 BC and 119 BC, Zhang Qian went to the Western Regions twice, opened up the "Silk Road," and established friendly relations with countries in the Western Regions. Ban Chao joined the army and worked in the Western Regions for 31 years and was returned by Gan Ying as an envoy to Daqin (大秦) (the Roman Empire) and Tiaozhixihai (条支西海) (now the Persian Gulf). Gan Ying was the first Chinese traveller to reach Arabia. During the Qin and Han Dynasties, fengshan worship, academic investigations, and foreign adventure travel expanded the field of tourism activities in this period, deepened the understanding of natural landscapes.

2.2.3 The Wei, Jin, and Northern and Southern Dynasties

The Wei (AD 220 - AD 266), Jin (AD 266 - AD 420), and Northern and Southern Dynasties (AD 420 - AD 589) were a period of great divisions in China's feudal society and also a period of great national integration. These dynasties caused great chaos in the world, and the conflicts between ethnic groups and classes were sharp and complex. Due to the brutal political power struggle in these dynasties, some upper-level figures had to consider protecting themselves and staying away from conflict. Most of the intellectuals also preferred passivity and reclusiveness; with no intention of having official careers, they turned their attention to nature and embarked on a roaming road of expressing their love for landscapes, enjoying the natural scenery, and pursuing pleasure. According to the records of *A New Account of Tales of the World* (《世说新语》), Ruan Ji, Ji Kang, and five other people during the Wei and Jin Dynasties, because they were dissatisfied with current affairs, often gathered from thousands of miles, travelled together and roamed in the bamboo forest to drink Chinese Baijiu; they were called "The Seven Sages of the Bamboo Forest." Wang Xizhi of the Eastern Jin Dynasty also created *At the Orchid Pavilion* (《兰亭集序》), which has survived for centuries. Tao Yuanming in the late Eastern Jin Dynasty voluntarily resigned from office, retired to the countryside, and wrote *A Tale of the Fountain of the Peach Blossom Spring* (《桃花源记》). After being dismissed from office during the Northern and Southern Dynasties, Xie Lingyun also travelled indigently in the mountains and rivers and noted the aesthetic qualities of landscapes, becoming the originator of landscape poetry in China.

In addition to roaming scholars, tourism for religious purposes was also very popular. During this period, China's Buddhism and Taoism developed rapidly. In pursuit of immortality, Taoists went to caves, remote mountains and valleys, secluded seasides, and remote islands to explore immortality. Famous figures include Ge Hong, Lu Xiujing, and others. Ge Hong visited the strange mountains and different bodies of water between Xu (徐), Yu (豫), Jing (荆), Xiang (襄) and Guang (广). Lu Xiujing travelled around China and visited Bashan (巴山), Shushui (蜀水), Ouyue (瓯越), Jinou (金瓯), and Yue (越国). Due to the social turmoil of that time, Buddhism won the faith of people in all strata of society and travel became fashionable, especially in Chinese and foreign tourism for teaching and learning scriptures and achieved remarkable results. During this period, there was Zhu Shixing in the Wei Dynasty, Fotucheng and Kumarajiva in the Northern Dynasty, and many others. The most famous, however, is Fa Xian of the Eastern Jin

Dynasty, who was known as a great traveller in the early 5th century, and with his immortal masterpiece *Buddha Kingdom*(《佛国记》).

During this period, travel was prevented due to the division of the world and the confrontation between the north and the south of China. Therefore, most of the tourism activities during this period were short-distance and attached to the mountains and rivers near a person's place of residence, or were gatherings of relatives and friends. But some travellers were not afraid of hardships and dangers in far-flung places. In addition to Fa Xian and others, Li Daoyuan of the Northern Wei Dynasty was a national researcher of waterways. His *Shui Jing Zhu*(《水经注》) is a famous Chinese masterpiece of geography.

2.2.4 The Sui and Tang Dynasties

The Sui (AD 581 - AD 618) and Tang Dynasties (AD 618 - AD 907) were the heyday of Chinese feudal society. With the unification of China in the Sui Dynasty and the prosperity of the Tang Dynasty, China's economy and culture showed unprecedented prosperity. The excavation of the Grand Canal led to it becoming the main artery of north-south waterway traffic. The land routes took the capital as their centre, forming a transportation network extending in all directions. In terms of external traffic, the maritime traffic between China and Japan developed unprecedentedly; at the same time, travel could also reach Persia (波斯), Dashi (大石), and the Mediterranean Sea in the west, and the Nanyang (南洋) Islands in the south, as far as India and Arabia. Political stability, economic and cultural development, and smooth traffic laid a solid foundation for the prosperity of domestic and foreign tourism activities during this period. The main tourist activities at the time included imperial tours, scholarly excursions, religious tours, international tours, and outings for the common people.

The Tang Dynasty followed the Sui system in terms of its political system and implemented the imperial examination system, which also greatly mobilized the enthusiasm of the middle and lower intellectuals to engage in politics. As a result, scholars travelled far and wide, and outstanding scholars such as Li Bai, Du Fu, Cen Shen, and Zhang Ji (poet and traveller) appeared. Li Bai took roaming as the leading motif of his career. He travelled all over the famous mountains and rivers of the motherland and wrote poems such as "Flying down three thousand feet" (飞流直下三千尺) and "The water of the Yellow River rising from the sky" (黄河之水天上来).

This period was also the heyday of Chinese Buddhism and Taoism. During this period, Buddhism formed eight major sects, including the Tiantai School, Mi School, and Jing School. Religious activities in this period were valued and funded by the imperial court, and outstanding religious travellers like Xuanzang and Jianzhen appeared. Xuanzang sought the law in Tianzhu(天竺), and after his return, he wrote *The History of the Western Regions of the Tang Dynasty* 《大唐西域记》. To promote Buddhism and Chinese civilization, Jianzhen travelled to Japan despite untold hardships.

During this period, due to the development of the economy, the travel activities of the people were also very prosperous. On the third day of the third lunar month in Chang'an(长安), the capital of the Tang Dynasty, people rushed out of the city to be in the countryside①. The Dragon Boat Festival, Double Ninth Festival, and others were also popular times for the common people to go on outings. Built in various places were not only capitals but also public scenic spots. For example, when Liu Zongyuan was exiled to Yongzhou(永州), he built eight scenic spots in Yongzhou for ordinary people to visit.

2.2.5 The Song and Yuan Dynasties

The Song (AD 960 – AD 1279) and Yuan (AD 1271 – AD 1368) Dynasties were a period of continuous development in Chinese feudal society, with remarkable achievements in science and technology, literature, and medicine. In particular, the invention of the compass and its application in navigation followed by its spread to the West made a significant contribution to promoting the development of the maritime cause of various countries, the opening of the "Silk Road", and the strengthening of trade and tourism exchanges with Western countries. During this period, the tourism service industry also developed. In the early Song Dynasty, government funding appeared, and ministers' treasuries were set up in various places to entertain former officials. There were also inns with elegant names for travellers to live in. In this period, tourism literature and tourism theory developed more than during the Tang Dynasty, and many famous travellers appeared, including Fan Zhongyan, Su Shi, Lu You, and Fan Chengda. These travellers wrote *The Story of Yueyang Tower*《岳阳楼记》, *Entering Shu Ji*《入蜀记》 and *Wu Chuan Lu*《吴船录》, all of which are travel masterpieces that have been passed down through the ages.

2.2.6 The Ming Dynasty and the Qing Dynasty

The Ming (AD 1368 – AD 1644) and Qing Dynasties (AD 1644 – AD 1912) were a peak period followed by a decline in Chinese culture. During this period, tourism activities

---

①上巳节。唐朝,上巳成为当时隆重的节日之一。节日的内容除了休禊之外,主要是春游踏青、临水宴饮。宋吴自牧在《梦粱录·卷二》中写道:"唐朝赐宴曲江,倾都禊饮踏青",说的正是彼时上巳当日,长安城内男女老少盛服而出,在曲江畔宴饮、郊游的景象。杜甫的《丽人行》对此盛况亦有描写:"三月三日天气新,长安水边多丽人……"。中唐诗人白居易在《三月三日谢恩曲江宴会状》一文中也详细记载了盛会的情况。

were prosperous and continued to develop. Compared with the Tang and Song Dynasties, more attention was paid to the appreciation of natural landscapes and the summarization of the tourism experience. In particular, domestic scientific discoveries flourished in the Ming Dynasty and the academic works were outstanding. The most outstanding travellers are Zheng He, Xu Xiake, and Li Shizhen. Zheng He led the ocean-going fleet to the South China Sea seven times, as far as the Red Sea coast and the east coast of Africa, commanding the largest and most advanced fleet in the world. In 38 years, Xu Xiake visited today's equivalent of 19 provinces and autonomous regions and left the first-hand inspection report *Xu Xiake's Travel Notes*(《徐霞客游记》). Li Shizhen read medical records, made field investigations, and travelled across the country. It took him 27 years to complete *Chinese Herbal Medicine* (《本草纲目》), which is the most complete and comprehensive medical book ever written in the history of traditional Chinese medicine.

After the middle of the Ming Dynasty, due to the economic aggression of Western capitalist countries, the pattern of isolation of Qing Dynasty was broken, the influence of Western culture gradually changed the Chinese people's concept of tourism, and the space for tourism was further expanded.

2.2.7 Between 1840 and 1949

The First Opium War from 1840 to 1842 marked the starting point of China's modern history and ushered in a period of transformation in Chinese culture. At first, Wei Yuan, Lin Zexu, and others studied advanced Western science and technology, and later the Qing government imitated the West by creating a whole set of Western-style schools. That educational system was followed by elite scholars studying Western social science theories and cultural influences, including Marxism and Leninism. This process is aligned with the four-level structure of culture (low, high, shallow and deep), and it is still going on today. A major historical issue that confronts us today is how to combine learning from the West with the preservation and inheritance of traditional Chinese culture's essence.

2.2.8 Between 1949 and 1978

During the first 30 years after the founding of the PRC, tourism culture showed the characteristics of politics and diplomacy. Because of a variety of reasons tied to the nation's economic shortages and limited productivity, not only were serious restrictions placed on the Chinese demand for travel and vacation, but also the scope of travel activity was simultaneously limited. Tourism culture was not a high priority at this stage, and the tourism market was not prosperous. During this period, people's main cultural tourism activities were mainly short trips in the suburbs to visit the natural scenery.

Due to the international political environment at that time, the task of China's tourism department was mainly to serve the needs of the nation's diplomatic work and to undertake the political task of receiving international friends when they visited China. Therefore, the tourism after the founding of PRC was not "tourism" in the real sense. During this period, tourism mainly served the international activities of the central and local governments, and focused on receiving foreign guests in China, foreign delegations in China, and foreign tourists. Tourism resources were also used as a diplomatic means to deepen exchanges with people around the world and establish New China's image of friendly diplomacy. The work carried out by the tourism department served as political reception rather than as a commercial operation.

2.2.9 After 1978

In 1978, with the implementation of the Reform and Opening Up policy, China's tourism industry began to get on track and gradually entered a period of rapid development. After the Third Plenary Session of the 11th CPC Central Committee, the revitalization and development of the tourism industry therefore received the attention of the State Council and governments at all levels, as the focus of national work had shifted to economic construction.

During this period, Chinese cultural tourism activities became more and more frequent, and the tourism culture at that time showed the characteristics of leisure travel. People actively sought opportunities to travel, hoping to relax and return to nature. The industrial revolution (driven by modern science and technology) accelerated the process of urbanization, which shifted the focus of people's work and life from the countryside to the city. This change ultimately led to the need for people to escape from the tense rhythm of urban life and the pressure of crowded and noisy environments, generating the motivation to return to free and quiet nature. Driven by this motivation, tourism became a way for people to take the initiative and go out to relax their bodies and minds.

In this period of development, the Chinese government's national policy of opening to the outside world on the one hand promoted mass commercial tourism to the world and let the world understand Chinese culture through tourism. On the other hand, it created a fashion of studying abroad, giving Chinese students the opportunity to learn about different cultures in other countries. Therefore, academic tourism was also developed to a certain extent.

2.3 The Driving Force of Tourism Development

2.3.1 Development of Tourism Transportation Facilities

The advancing progress of transportation has expanded the scope of travel available to tourists. After the founding of the PRC, air transportation, water transportation, and land transportation have been rapidly developing.

(1) Air Transport

In terms of air transportation, state-owned airlines such as Air China, China Southern Airlines and China Eastern Airlines, as well as local airlines such as Hainan Airlines, compete to introduce aircraft made by Boeing and Airbus. Airports have blossomed everywhere. Large airports have been built in provincial capitals, and passenger transport capacity has increased year by year. By the end of 2021, China had 248 mainland transport airports, 275 runways, 7,133 parking stands, and a terminal area of 17.879 million square meters. China's civil aviation transport airports handled 907 million passengers in 2021 (1.352 billion passengers in 2019).[①]

(2) Water Transport

In terms of water transportation, sea ferries have opened along the eastern coast of China. There are ferries from Shanghai(上海) to Qingdao(青岛), Tianjin(天津), Dalian(大连), or from Guangzhou Huangpu to Shanghai, and even to Southeast Asia and Europe and other parts of the world. Inland river traffic is also very busy, such as the tourist trips on the Yangtze River. China's water transportation handled 163 million passengers in 2021[②].

---

① 2021年民航行业发展统计公报,(Accessed: 12th November 2022)http://www.caac.gov.cn/XXGK/XXGK/TJSJ/202205/t20220518_213297.html

② 交通发布,(Accessed: 12th November 2022)https://baijiahao.baidu.com/s?id=1733776590515764606&wfr=spider&for=pc

(3) Land Transport

In terms of land transportation, expressways have developed rapidly and now extend in all directions. By the end of 2021, 117,000 kilometres of national expressways and 257,700 kilometres of national highways were completed and opened to traffic, which provided great convenience for self-driven tours①. Simply speaking, national highways cover administrative regions that are at the county level and above as well as border ports that are open all year round, effectively connecting important towns, industrial parks, transportation hubs, and tourist attractions. In 2021, a total of 5.087 billion commercial passengers were transported on expressways and national highways②.

In addition, another mode of transportation that people are choosing more is by train. By the end of 2021, the operating mileage of national railways reached 150,000 kilometres, including 40,000 kilometres of high-speed railways(Photograph 2.1). In 2021, 2.612 billion railway passengers were transported across the country.③

Photograph 2.1　A Picture of China High-speed Railway
(Source:https://pixabay.com/zh/photos/train-railway-speed-travel-fast-6177793/)

2.3.2 Refinement of the Tourism Market

In recent years, along with the leapfrog improvement in development levels and the change of people's living demands, China's tourism industry has rapidly developed,

---

①中国新闻网,(Accessed: 12th November 2022)https://baijiahao.baidu.com/s?id＝1739293803704635561&wfr＝spider&for＝pc

②交通发布,(Accessed: 12th November 2022) https://baijiahao.baidu.com/s?id＝1733776590515764606&wfr＝spider&for＝pc

③国家铁路局《2021年铁道统计公报》,(Accessed: 12th November 2022) https://zwfw.nra.gov.cn/art/2022/4/28/art_62_6493.html

continuously expanded its scale, and improved its quality. Tourism has become an important indicator of the improvement of living standards and an important way of living in a well-off society.

(1) Expanding Scale of Tourism Industry

Since 2012, China's domestic tourism revenue has grown by an average of 10.6% annually. In 2019, the total revenue reached 6.63 trillion yuan, and the added value of tourism and related industries reached 4.5 trillion yuan, accounting for 4.56% of GDP[①]. Despite the impact of the epidemic, although the tourism industry has experienced great fluctuations, its pillar position in the national economic structure has not changed.

(2) Abundant Supply of Tourism Products

The number of A-level tourist attractions increased from 6,042 in 2012 to 14,332 in 2021. In addition, by the end of 2021, China had about 42,000 travel agencies and 8,771 star-rated hotels[②], 671 national and provincial tourism resorts, 1,299 national key villages and towns for rural tourism, and 300 national dark-tourism scenic spots[③]. Basically, it has formed a tourism product supply system with extensive coverage, rich formats, and diversified choices.

With the continuing expansion of tourism, the tourism market has been constantly subdividing, from the initial urban tourism to rural tourism, exhibition tourism, ecological tourism, industrial heritage tourism, dark tourism, sport tourism, leisure tourism, study tours, cruise tours, and various other new tourism formats.

(3) Cultural and Tourism Integration

The integration of cultural and tourism industries has become a new driving force and engine for economic growth. For example, the combination of tourism and cultural elements, combined with endowment of local cultural resources and in-depth exploration of regional culture, historical culture, intangible culture, red culture, and other cultural sections; the integration of tourism and public cultural facilities as well as the conversion of public cultural facilities such as libraries, art galleries, museums into tourist districts, scenic spots, parks, and other tourist sites to increase the cultural attributes of tourism activity spaces; the integration of tourism and public cultural services, introducing public

---

①腾讯网,(Accessed: 12th November 2022) https://new.qq.com/rain/a/20220818A047Z200
②人民网,(Accessed: 12th November 2022) https://baijiahao.baidu.com/s?id=1742091197185843017&wfr=spider&for=pc
③腾讯网,(Accessed: 12th November 2022) https://new.qq.com/rain/a/20220818A047Z200

cultural activities such as intangible cultural heritage displays, art exhibitions, art performances, and so on in the tourism activity space, thus improving the cultural atmosphere of tourism sites; the combination of tourism and cultural products, and the development of tourism cultural and creative products.

As the cultural connotations of tourism are continuously enriched, the number of historical and cultural scenic spots has nearly doubled from 2,064 in 2012 to 4,111 in 2021[①].

2.4 Tourism Along the Silk Road

The ancient Silk Road was the most dazzling stage for the exchange and integration of civilizations in human history (Photograph 2.2). It condensed the evolution of the economy, politics, culture, and society in the long historical period of development of the Eurasian continent, and it witnessed the exchange and integration of the material and spiritual civilizations of the East and the West. The tourism and cultural resources along the Silk Road are very rich, with numerous historical relics, historic sites, magnificent natural scenes, and distinctive ethnic customs, attracting thousands of tourists from all over the world. In ancient times, camels used to be the main means of transportation on the Silk Road, but now tourists can travel along the Silk Road by plane, train, and car, making travel along it fast, convenient, comfortable, and safe. Today, the Silk Road is pushing international tourism cooperation to a new stage with the integration and development of Eastern, Western, ancient, and modern cultures.

Photograph 2.2 The Silk Road
(Source:https://pixabay.com/zh/photos/camels-sunset-caravan-desert-5750126/)

---

① 腾讯网,(Accessed: 12th November 2022) https://new.qq.com/rain/a/20220818A047Z200_

2.4.1 The Origin of the Silk Road

Silk is one of China's greatest inventions and embodies many characteristics of Chinese civilization. China was the first country in the world to raise silkworms and make silk. Silk provides people with comfortable clothes and beautiful decorations, so it is popular with the local people when it is available, and it is sold everywhere. From the Han Dynasty to the Ming and Qing Dynasties, silk was one of the most popular Chinese products exported worldwide.

The name "Silk Road" was first used by German geographer and geologist Ferdinand Richthofen.[①] In the late 1860s, he went to China as an explorer and wrote the results of his travels into *"China, the Results of My Travels and the Studies Based Thereon"*. He believed that during the Han Dynasty of China, a transportation route existed between China and Central Asia, and also between China and India, that was dominated by the silk trade and also handled many other commodities. He called this transportation route the "Seidenstrassen," or "Silk Road" in English. Later, Albert Herrmann, a German orientalist, extended one of the ends of the Silk Road from Central Asia to Syria. The so-called Silk Road, in short, was a large transportation corridor that wound across Eurasia and connected the East and the West.

2.4.2 Travellers on the Continental Silk Road

For thousands of years, the Silk Road was travelled by people of different nationalities and for different reasons. Some were engaged in long-distance trade for profit, some were forced to emigrate for living, some travelled for the faith in their hearts to spread the Gospel, or to seek the truth, and some were on an official mission to make contact with friends or wage war, or even for the simple purpose of travel, and to see the world. However, no matter what kind of people they were, no matter what kind of mission they were undertaking, they were all cultural emissaries, following the same cause — they were all making their own contributions to the exchange and communication of ethnic cultures, and to the integration and common prosperity of human civilizations.

Who left their footprints on the Silk Road?

(1) Merchants

The largest and most persistent groups of merchants from different countries routinely travelled along the Silk Road. Material and cultural exchanges were the most

---

①武斌. 丝绸之路史话[M]. 沈阳:沈阳出版社, 2018.

important, basic, and common of all of the exchanges that the road facilitated. The Silk Road was originally opened up by merchants for international silk trade, and was first and foremost a route for trade, business travel, and material and cultural flows. The official trading of successive dynasties was called "tribute trade," and apart from that official trade, the folk trade was also very active throughout all ages and never stopped. Through those direct and indirect trade relations, abundant Chinese products, such as silk, porcelain, lacquerware, iron and other production tools, tea, various items of traditional Chinese medicine, and arts and crafts, were continuously exported to foreign countries in large quantities. In addition, a large number of products from other ethnic groups and countries were also imported into China through these channels, thereby enriching the daily life of the Chinese people.

(2) Diplomatic Envoys

Some of the people using the Silk Road were diplomatic envoys sent by the Chinese government. They established diplomatic relations with countries or regimes outside the region and exchanged diplomatic envoys, creating an important channel for cultural exchanges. Following Zhang Qian's delegation to the Western Regions in the Western Han Dynasty, Chinese dynasties gradually established official relationships with many countries and exchanged envoys. In addition to settling disputes between countries and strengthening bilateral relations, the exchanges of official envoys also enhanced mutual understanding. Zhang Qian, an official and diplomat for Emperor Wu of Western Han, not only opened up the official communication route with the Western regions, but also developed an intuitive and detailed understanding of the politics, human relations, customs, and cultures of the Western regions through field investigation, and provided the emperor with a detailed report on his mission. This was the first time that the Chinese had a relatively accurate knowledge of the Western regions. Since then, a number of foreign official envoys have returned home with reports and travel notes. At the same time, a large number of foreign envoys also came to China.

(3) Foreign Students

Some of the people who travelled along the Silk Road were foreign students studying Chinese culture. During the Tang Dynasty, the prefect of Chang'an accepted a large number of foreign students, including students from Silla, Japan, and the Western regions. They studied Chinese cultural classics and books in China, received formal Chinese education, and some of them even took part in the imperial examination of China. After the Tang Dynasty, some countries still sent students to study in China.

(4) Religious People

Among the multitude of people who walked along the Silk Road were many religious pilgrims. In the Han and Tang Dynasties, Chinese monks travelled west to India for Buddhist scriptures and Dharma in order to pursue the truth of Buddhism, which became a magnificent scene in the history of the Silk Road. At the same time, many monks from India and the Western regions came to the East to spread Buddhism and translate Buddhist Scripture, making great contributions to the spread of Buddhism in the East[①]. During the Ming and Qing Dynasties, the Catholic Church in Western Europe sent a large number of missionaries to China in order to spread the church's "Gospel." It is worth noting that, among the travellers in all of the dynasties, religious figures have been a group with a high level of culture. Whether they were Chinese or foreign eminent monks, or Catholic missionaries, they were bearers of the science and culture of their times, and they were people who had studied and learned a great deal. In addition to spreading their beliefs, they also undertook the important mission of cultural exchange. Therefore, throughout history, they have been primary channels of cultural communication, involving science, art, academia, and even the culture of daily life.

(5) Immigrants

Many immigrants also made their way along the Silk Road. Human migration is a primary form of cultural exchange, and especially in ancient times, the spread of culture on the Eurasian continent was mainly realized through the migration of various ethnic groups. In more recent times, foreigners moved into China and even settled down there. From the Han Dynasty to the Southern and Northern Dynasties, there were continuous records of the horse-riding nomads from the north and west of China, called the "Hu people." In the Tang Dynasty and the Yuan Dynasty, a large number of foreign immigrants came to China. At the same time, many Chinese people emigrated to other countries, like Japan.

(6) Travellers

Travellers from other, more distant countries also used the Silk Road — notably, Marco Polo, Ibn Battuta, and Friar Odoric. They came to China and recorded their experiences in China into books that then became important resources from which foreigners could gain an understanding of China and Chinese culture. Among these travellers, Venetian Marco Polo was the most famous and influential, living in China for

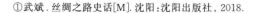

① 武斌. 丝绸之路史话[M]. 沈阳:沈阳出版社,2018.

Recommended Video

Decoding the history of the Silk Road

China Story

The Travels of Marco Polo

Exercise

Recommended Reading

17 years and travelling most of the country, from south to north. The book known in English as "The Travels of Marco Polo" recorded Marco Polo's accounts of his travels along the Silk Road and praised China's vast territory, abundant resources, and flourishing culture and education, and systematically introduced the glorious culture of China to the Western world.

We can see that in the long history of cultural exchanges between China and foreign countries, there were many well-known people, and even more lesser-known ones, who made outstanding contributions via the encounters, acquaintances, and communications between Chinese and Western cultures. Some official envoys played important roles in the diplomatic relations and cultural exchanges that took place throughout the succession of Chinese dynasties, and the contributions of Chinese and foreign monks, missionaries, students, travellers, and businessmen were particularly valued. Those individuals were the messengers of cultural exchange, and also the creators and inspirers of culture.

Chapter Summary

This chapter first introduces the history of travel and tourism, including the purpose of ancient travel and Chinese travel culture in different historical periods. This part helps readers to have a general understanding of the development of Chinese tourism and culture from ancient times to the present. Secondly, this chapter introduces the development of tourism infrastructure and improvement of the tourism market to help readers understand the driving forces behind tourism development. Finally, this chapter introduces the Silk Road, which is very important for the development of Chinese tourism culture and cultural exchanges between China and the West.

Issues for Review and Discussion

1. During what time periods did the emergence and development of Chinese tourism culture occur?
2. In what ways can culture and tourism be integrated?
3. Why is the Silk Road not only for China, but also for the world?

Chapter 3
Cultural Heritage

Learning Objectives

After reading this chapter, you should have a good understanding of
1. The definitions, characteristics, and categories of cultural heritage;
2. The cultural heritage resources of China;
3. The value of cultural heritage as a tourism resource;
4. The paths towards tourism development with regard to cultural heritage.

Technical Words

English Words	中文翻译
cultural heritage	文化遗产
ethnic group	民族
Song dynasty porcelain	宋代瓷器
Convention concerning the Protection of the World Cultural and Natural Heritage	保护世界文化和自然遗产公约
the United Nations Educational, Scientific, and Cultural Organization (UNESCO)	联合国教育、科学及文化组织
living fossil	活化石
intangible cultural heritage	非物质文化遗产
natural heritage	自然文化遗产
mixed cultural heritage	自然和文化双遗产
the World Heritage List	世界文化遗产名录
tangible cultural heritage	物质文化遗产
movable cultural relics	可移动文物

续表

English Words	中文翻译
immovable cultural relics	不可移动文物
China's Protection of Cultural Relics Law	中国文物保护法
Standing Committee of the Twelfth National Peoples Congress	第十二届全国人民代表大会常务委员会
Convention for the Safeguarding of the Intangible Cultural Heritage	保护非物质文化遗产公约
Intangible Cultural Heritage Law of the People's Republic of China	中华人民共和国非物质文化遗产法
Banpo village relic site	半坡遗址
Humble Administrator's Garden	拙政园
Liuyuan Garden	留园
Hongcun Village	宏村
Confucius Temple	孔庙
ownership value	所有权价值
price of managerial authority	经营权价格
aggregate value	总体性价值
the third national survey of cultural relics	第三次全国文物普查
the first national survey of movable cultural relics	第一次全国可移动文物普查
Daming Palace Heritage Park	大明宫遗址公园
the National Cultural Heritage Administration	国家文物局
the Ministry of Housing and Urban-Rural Development of the People' Republic of China	中华人民共和国住房和城乡建设部
the State Council of China	中华人民共和国国务院
Beijing Opera	京剧
Kunqu Opera	昆曲

Knowledge Graph

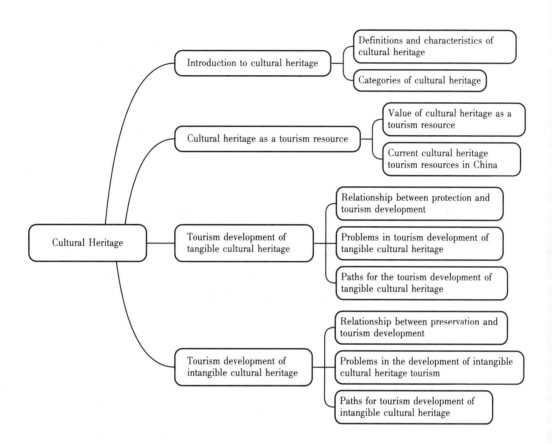

3.1 Introduction to cultural heritage

Cultural heritage is a term that cannot be easily defined, because its two components, culture and heritage, are both rich in meaning. When culture is considered as a common memory of a nation or an ethnic group, cultural heritage refers to the degree of civilization of that nation or ethnic group relating to a particular historical period and containing the cultural cues and values of that period. In this sense, cultural heritage is a material symbol and a remnant of the collective memory of the civilization of an era. For example, the Song dynasty (AD 960-AD 1279) porcelain we see today is not a simple material artefact; rather, it is a historical remnant that reflects the aesthetic interest, spiritual pursuit, and level of craft-making of the Song Dynasty and represents the level of material and spiritual civilization of that period. Alternatively, when culture is understood as the embodiment of the ideology of a certain period of social development, it involves multiple fields of literature, art, science, philosophy, religion, education, customs, politics, and law. In this sense, cultural heritage refers to ideological products created by humans during a particular period, and each piece or form of cultural heritage is linked to the creators, producers, and inheritors of the time it was created and has its own unique history and lineage of inheritance. In this regard, the Song porcelain we see today not only has a specific craft form and cultural style representing the aesthetic preference of the Song Dynasty, but at the time it was made, it also had a practical material function—to serve the needs of people's daily lives.

3.1.1 Definitions and characteristics of cultural heritage

The term cultural heritage was first introduced in the Convention Concerning the Protection of the World Cultural and Natural Heritage, adopted by the United Nations Educational, Scientific, and Cultural Organization (UNESCO) in 1972. According to the Convention Concerning the Protection of the World Cultural and Natural Heritage, cultural heritage consists of:

— *Monuments: architectural works, works of monumental sculpture and painting, elements or structures of an archaeological nature, inscriptions, cave dwellings and combinations of features, which are of outstanding universal value from the point of view of history, art or science;*

— *Groups of buildings: groups of separate or connected buildings which, because of their architecture, their homogeneity or their place in the landscape, are of outstanding universal value from the point of view of history, art or science;*

— *Sites: works of man or the combined works of nature and man, and areas including archaeological sites which are of outstanding universal value from the historical, aesthetic, ethnological or anthropological point of view.* (p.2, Article 1)

With growing awareness of the role of cultural heritage in socio-economic development and its importance to the identity of the nation state, cultural heritage has witnessed growth in many of its categories, expanding from the initial categories of tangible cultural heritage to those of intangible cultural heritage, and has become a term with rich connotations. In general, cultural heritage is the legacy of history in physical or non-physical form. As a human creation with widely recognised values, cultural heritage can be seen as a "living fossil" that records the long-term activities and historical footprints of humans, and acts as an important symbol of different time periods.

As a term with rich connotations, cultural heritage has the following characteristics. Firstly, cultural heritage encompasses multiple values in economic value, cultural value, artistic and aesthetic value, and scientific research value. In comparison to the economic value, other values of cultural heritage tend to be more appreciated. For example, intangible cultural heritage such as folk legends and folk performing arts provide few opportunities for economic and commercial development, but are of great importance to cultural inheritance and national identity establishment, and are valuable remnants of the common memory of a nation.

Secondly, cultural heritage encompasses the wealth of knowledge and skills transmitted from generation to generation. It is witness to human history and can reproduce the historical characteristics of the past, a "living fossil" of a specific historical period, representing creative achievements and human values. Throughout human history, the social structures and lifestyles of people of a certain period are difficult to reproduce, but the culture of that time can leave memories for future generations through its cultural heritage. In a sense, human creation is built on the inheritance of the cultural wisdom of the past. The value of cultural heritage lies in the cultural memory passed down from one generation to the next. When a social structure disappears, the legacy of the memory through its cultural heritage becomes particularly important.

Thirdly, cultural heritage has a certain form or shape. At the macro level, cultural heritage can be abstractly expressed as a national treasure or a cultural tradition shared by a nation; while at the micro level, each piece of cultural heritage is preserved in the form of concrete cultural existence. Tangible objects of cultural heritage are typically preserved in the form of cultural objects with material carriers and stylised structures, such as artifacts obtained from archaeological excavations. Intangible cultural heritage tends to be passed on, presented, and remembered through successors, legends, performances, such as folklore, crafts, and performing arts.

Fourthly, cultural heritage (tangible or intangible) is produced or created by humans and does not include pure natural heritage. However, some cultural heritage resources, known as mixed cultural heritage, have components of both cultural and natural heritage. For example, Mount Taishan in Shandong province has breath taking natural scenery as well as cultural relics such as rhetoric and inscriptions left by ancient literary writers. There are four mixed cultural heritage sites in China (see table 3.1 on the UNESCO World Heritage List.

Table 3.1 Mixed cultural heritage sites in China

Site name	Year of inclusion in the World Heritage List of the UNESCO
Mount Wuyi	1999
Mount Emei Scenic Area, including Leshan Giant Buddha Scenic Area	1996
Mount Huangshan	1990
Mount Taishan	1987

(Source: https://whc.unesco.org/en/statesparties/cn)

Fifthly, cultural heritage is irreproducible. Cultural heritage is the accumulation of history and culture in the process of human adaptation to nature and continuous self-improvement, and is also the inheritance of the cultural texture of a nation. Once the uniqueness of a cultural heritage resource is destroyed, part of the witness of human history is lost. For example, when the city wall of Nanjing（南京）built in the Ming Dynasty (AD 1368-AD 1644) was demolished, part of the very charm of the city was lost.

3.1.2 Categories of cultural heritage

The most common way of classifying cultural heritage is to look at whether a cultural heritage resource has a visible physical carrier. Accordingly, cultural heritage is classified into two types: tangible cultural heritage and intangible cultural heritage.

(1) Tangible cultural heritage

Tangible cultural heritage refers to cultural relics. Based on the characteristics of the carrier, tangible cultural heritage can be further divided into two categories: movable cultural relics and immovable cultural relics. Movable cultural relics are those that can be moved by external forces, and the movement does not change its value and performance. According to China's Protection of Cultural Relics Law (revised at the 30th Meeting of the Standing Committee of the Twelfth National People's Congress on November 4, 2017), movable cultural relics include important objects, works of art, documents, manuscripts, books, and typical material objects, dating from various historical periods (Article 3). Immovable cultural relics refer to those that cannot be moved by external forces, and their value and performance would be damaged if moved. Immovable cultural relics include sites of ancient culture, ancient tombs, ancient architectural structures, cave temples, stone carvings and murals, as well as important modern and contemporary historic sites and typical buildings.

(2) Intangible cultural heritage

According to the Convention for the Safeguarding of the Intangible Cultural Heritage *(Article 2)* adopted by the 32nd session of the General Conference of UNESCO in 2003, intangible cultural heritage refers to

the practices, representations, expressions, knowledge, skills – as well as the instruments, objects, artefacts and cultural spaces associated therewith – that communities, groups and, in some cases, individuals recognise as part of their cultural heritage.

In the Intangible Cultural Heritage Law of the People's Republic of China, intangible cultural heritage is defined as various traditional cultural expressions that have been passed down from generation to generation by people of all ethnic groups and are considered part of their cultural heritage. It includes physical objects and places related to traditional cultural expressions, categorised as: ① traditional oral literature and language; ② traditional arts, calligraphy, music, dance, drama, opera, and acrobatics; ③ traditional skills, medicine, and calendars; ④ traditional rituals, festivals, and other folklore; ⑤ traditional sports and amusement; ⑥ other intangible cultural heritage.

3.2 Cultural heritage as a tourism resource

3.2.1 Value of cultural heritage as a tourism resource

Cultural heritage resources have unique values, such as historical value, artistic value, and aesthetic value, which are suitable for tourism development. Some cultural heritage resources have become tourism products with distinctive regional characteristics and cultural characteristics enhanced through tourism planning and development. However, not all cultural heritage resources have the potential for tourism use. Those that bring economic, social, and ecological benefits by means of tourism development without breaking the loop of the cultural heritage itself, can be regarded as suitable tourism resources. Specifically, the value of cultural heritage as a tourism resource can be evaluated from three perspectives of resource elements, resource property rights, and resource markets.

(1) The perspective from the resource elements

a. Historical value

Cultural heritage is an important carrier of history and culture, and is a product of a specific historical period, carrying cultural information about the unique architectural style, dress and manners, folk customs and aesthetic characteristics of a particular period, and therefore has a very high historical value. For example, the Banpo village relic site(半坡遗址), located in the eastern suburb of Xi'an(西安) on the eastern bank of the Chan River(浐河) is the first documented Neolithic settlement site in China with oracle bone inscriptions and archaeological excavations, and is an important place for future generations to understand the matrilineal clans of the Yangshao(仰韶) culture of the Neolithic period.

b. Ornamental value

Cultural heritage is attractive to tourists because of its exquisite artistic craftsmanship, unique aesthetic features, or ingenious expressions, and therefore has ornamental value. For example, Suzhou's(苏州) Humble Administrator's Garden(拙政园) and Liuyuan Garden(留园) are famous for their unique spatial layout and elegant artistic style, enabling visitors to sense the philosophical thoughts and aesthetic pursuits of the Ming (AD 1368 - AD 1644) and Qing dynasties (AD 1644 - AD 1911).

c. Scientific and educational value

Cultural heritage provides a window for people to learn of the history and culture of their ancestors, and so has scientific and educational value. These values are mainly realised through scientific investigation and education and science popularization. The former refers to scientific research and study, while the latter refers to historical, cultural, and patriotic education. For example, the "bull" structure of Hongcun Village(宏村), an ancient village of the Ming and Qing dynasties in Anhui(安徽), has very high scientific research value. Another example is Xibaipo(西柏坡), which contains rich cultural resources and is a patriotic educational base.

d. Social value

Cultural heritage is culture crystallization left by our ancestors. When visiting cultural heritage tourism sites, people can understand the wisdom of their predecessors, and increase their sense of national belonging and identity with Chinese civilization. In this regard, cultural heritage tourism resources have social value. For example, when visiting the Confucius Temple(孔庙)in Qufu(曲阜), Shandong Province, people can increase their understanding of Confucius and the doctrine of Confucianism.

e. Environmental value

As a scarce resource, cultural heritage can undoubtedly bring significant benefits to a place. Accordingly, governments at all levels attach importance to the protection and utilization of these resources, and maintain and manage the infrastructure and environment relating to cultural heritage sites to enhance the overall competitiveness of local development.

(2) The perspective from the resource property rights

a. Ownership value

Cultural heritage resources are valuable assets inherited from previous generations and to a certain extent their property rights belong to the public. However, the property rights of some cultural heritage resources belong to particular groups of people. The following list indicates the various cultural heritage rights and the attribution of ownership of cultural heritage resources.

-Right of use: the right to access, appreciate, and use cultural heritage.

-Right of authorship: the rights of the groups or communities to which a cultural heritage resource belongs to signify their identity as the source of that cultural heritage by attributing names to specific cultural heritage resources.

-Right of management: the right of the state or relevant organization to manage a specific cultural heritage site in the public interest, including the right to share benefits and dispose of the resource.

-Right of cultural property: the right to receive benefits based on the cultural heritage owned or created by the owner.

-Right of cultural development: the right of the creators (individual or group) of a certain intangible cultural heritage to develop and create product content and type through transmission, promotion, absorption, and innovation.

b. Price of managerial authority

The price of managerial authority refers to the right of a natural or legal person to build, manage, and operate cultural heritage resources under specific conditions, such as the right to operate a tourist attraction acquired through government authorization or a contract. The price of the management right of a cultural heritage resource is the external embodiment of its value. In reality, the management rights of resources are entrusted to administrative departments or local governments, which in turn transfer the rights to tourism operators through a bidding process.

(3) The perspective from the resource markets

a. Economic value

The economic value of a cultural heritage resource is based on its historical, artistic, and scientific research value. In terms of economic benefits, the value assessment indexes of culture heritage resources include ticket income and the income from the sale of souvenirs and leisure and recreational activity products. For example, the ticket price of the large-scale song-dance performance "The Show of Songcheng"(《宋城千古情》)in Hangzhou(杭州)Songcheng scenic area(宋城景区)is between 200 and 880 yuan RMB.

b. Aggregate value

The aggregate value of cultural heritage resources emphasises the negative effect, cost effect, and environmental value that are missed in the assessment of their market value. In traditional economic evaluation, only the value created by labour is assessed, while the natural value of the environment tends to be ignored. Therefore, the calculation of the aggregate value of cultural heritage resources requires the deduction of these costs in order to obtain the true net value of the cultural heritage resources in the market.

3.2.2 Current cultural heritage tourism resources in China

After years of effort, the management system of cultural heritage in China has been established, and the management mode has matured. A series of laws, regulations, and policies have been enacted and announced, and the level of protection and utilization of cultural heritage resources has been improved. At the same time, public attention and awareness of protection and inheritance of heritage resources has significantly increased. The role of cultural heritage in improving social civilization and promoting economic and social development as well as cultural exchanges between China and other countries has become important.

(1) Tangible cultural heritage

Since the founding of the People's Republic of China, the country has conducted three times of national survey of cultural relics and one time of national survey of movable cultural relics. The third national survey of cultural relics that ended in 2011, registered nearly 767,000 immovable cultural relics, while the results of the first national survey of movable cultural relics, released in April 2017, gave the number of movable cultural relics collected and kept by state-owned units nationwide as above 108 million. At the end of 2019, there were 5,058 key national cultural relic protection units, 135 national historic and cultural cities, 312 historical and cultural towns, 487 famous villages, and 4,153 traditional villages. China has 55 World Cultural and Natural Heritage sites (tied with Italy for first place) including 37 cultural heritage sites, 14 natural heritage sites, and 4 dual cultural and natural heritage sites.

Cultural heritage resources provide opportunities for local tourism development, and

Case Study

Fujian Tulou

the tourism industry provides impetus for cultural heritage preservation. Many world heritage sites have been developed into tourist attractions; for example, the Huangshan Mountain(黄山)and the Daming Palace Heritage Park(大明宫遗址公园)have found a good balance between heritage conservation and tourism development. Some famous historical and cultural cities and villages approved by the National Cultural Heritage Administration and the Ministry of Housing and Urban-Rural Development of the People's Republic of China have also created their own tourism brands. The rich cultural heritage resources in China attract many tourists from home and abroad, and cultural heritage sites have become important tourist attractions with unique features.

(2) Intangible cultural heritage

To standardise the protection of intangible cultural heritage in China, the country established a four‑level protection system (national, provincial, municipal, and county levels) based on the principles of "protection first, rescue first, rational use, and inheritance development". Since 2002, the State Council of China has released five batches of intangible cultural heritage lists at national level(Table 3.2).

Table 3.2　Five batches of national intangible cultural heritage lists

Batch	Number of items	Time of release
1st	518 items	May 20, 2006
2nd	510 items	June 14, 2008
3rd	191 items	June 10, 2011
4th	153 items	July 16, 2014
5th	185 items	June 10, 2021

(Source: Self-made table based on information from https://www.ihchina.cn)

As with tangible cultural heritage, intangible cultural heritage also has important historical, artistic, and scientific value, and plays a vital role in passing on the cultural lineage of the nation. Therefore, many intangible cultural heritage resources (e.g., Beijing Opera (京剧), ethnic minority songs and dances) have the potential to become tourist attractions that enrich tourists' experience and prolong their length of stay. Additionally, intangible cultural heritage (e.g., paper‑cutting, clay sculpture, carving) is the basis of tourism souvenir design and innovation and can enrich the cultural connotations of tourism commodities.

Further Reading

Creating Magic from behind the Curtain: Shadow Puppetry

3.3 Tourism development of tangible cultural heritage

3.3.1 Relationship between protection and tourism development

The protection of tangible cultural heritage and the tourism development of heritage resources are complementary to each other. The practice should be to extend the lifespan of tangible cultural heritage while realizing a benign integration of its development with tourism. As relics of the dynamic development of human society, tangible cultural heritage resources are valuable cultural assets, most of which are unique and irreplaceable, providing a resource base for tourism products and supporting the sustainability of the tourism industry. Additionally, income generated from tourism development can provide support for the protection of tangible cultural heritage. Tourism brings economic benefits and stimulates the development of related industries such as hospitality and transportation. The income generated can be used for the protection and restoration of tangible cultural heritage resources. At the same time, tourists' pursuit of high-quality and experiential products forces tourism destinations and enterprises to adopt advanced technologies in tourism product development. The application of new technologies can promote the renewal and transformation of methods for protecting tangible cultural heritage. Therefore, tourism development of tangible cultural heritage and its conservation can be a win-win solution.

3.3.2 Problems in tourism development of tangible cultural heritage

(1) Lack of overall development planning

China has rich tangible cultural heritage resources, and there are numerous tourist attractions developed with these resources throughout the country. However, existing tangible cultural heritage attractions (tourism sites) are fragmented and without an effective connectivity across the map of the country. No inter-regional tourism development linkage has been formed. In addition, key heritage tourist sites play little role in driving the growth of surrounding small heritage attractions, many of which have low visibility and find it difficult to survive. There is no drive to combine the advantages of tangible cultural heritage sites within a region. Therefore, tourism development in tangible cultural heritage should consider a long-term plan to achieve a complementarity of resources and products within and outside a region, aiming to promote sustainable development of tangible cultural heritage tourism.

(2) Lack of in-depth understanding of the cultural core

Tangible cultural heritage resources are highly malleable and have inherent advantages for tourism use. However, most developed tourism products are sightseeing-oriented and lack vividness and fun, focusing only on the external image display and ignoring tourists' desire to explore the cultural core of the heritage. For example, in some ethnic villages, there are only a few old houses and roadside stalls, without the opportunity for tourists to have an in-depth experience of the history and culture of the villages, and a lack of artworks and traditional handicrafts with commemorative collection value reflecting the unique characteristics of the ancient villages.

(3) Excessive pursuit of economic interests

The Chinese government attaches great importance to tangible cultural heritage and promotes effective use and protection of scarce resources through initiatives such as the establishment of national historical relics and cultural cities. However, the practice of neglecting the protection and inheritance of culture itself through the excessive pursuit of economic interests still exists. For example, some tourism development agencies have built commercial and entertainment facilities around heritage tourism attractions to maximise economic benefits without considering whether the facilities are in harmony with the local environment. This can damage the initial appearance of tangible cultural heritage. In addition, the lack of management and protection of tangible cultural heritage resources has led to the theft of some cultural relics and the destruction of cultural sites, resulting in irreparable loss of the country's heritage assets.

3.3.3 Paths for the tourism development of tangible cultural heritage

(1) Planning as the forerunner of development

Conflicts between tourism development and tangible cultural heritage protection are unavoidable and therefore the scientific management of cultural heritage is crucial in avoiding such problems. The following aspects need to be considered. The most important thing is a master plan for the tourism development of heritage resources, to enable a standardised and orderly development of heritage tourism. The second is to improve the infrastructure within and surrounding heritage tourism sites, while introducing preferential policies for tourism product prices and financing. The third is to strengthen the protection of the ecological system in the development of tangible cultural heritage resources. Formulation of relevant laws and regulations will curb the destruction of cultural heritage resources. In addition to building and improving tourism infrastructure, attention should be paid to controlling the number of visitors to heritage sites to reduce pollution and damage to the cultural environment.

(2) Resource and market-oriented approaches work in parallel

Tourism product development involves both supply - side and demand - side perspectives. Tangible cultural heritage resources are the premise and basis of tourism development, and therefore the quantity and quality of such resources will affect the level of tourism development of the area where these resources reside. Additionally, the type of heritage resources determines the direction of the tourism product development. However, the needs and preferences of tourists will determine whether a tourism product will be accepted by the market. If there are clear resource advantages of the tangible cultural heritage that cultural tourism relies on, the ability to turn the resource advantage into a market advantage is key to the success of an area's tourism development, and requires the adoption of a combination of both resource and market oriented approaches.

(3) Highlighting distinctive heritage features

The tourism development model of tangible cultural heritage involves two categories of resources: heritage resources as the core, and other supplementary resources (e.g., natural landscapes, cultural landscapes, folklore landscapes, and souvenirs) forming a tourism product group. At present, there is little difference in China's development models, resulting in product duplicates and a decrease in product attractiveness. In this regard, it is important to identify and make good use of the distinctive features of heritage resources in the product development. This can be done by tapping into the connotations of heritage itself and promoting the formation of the personality of heritage tourist attractions.

(4) Emphasising community participation

The tourism development of tangible cultural heritage in China is largely government-led and commercially developed, with the role of the local community often ignored. This sometimes triggers conflicts among government, developers, and the local community.

Community residents are the inheritors and users of traditional culture and an important part of cultural heritage sites, reflecting the cultural changes in history; therefore, community residents have rights to participate in the planning and management of heritage sites. The inclusion of community residents in tourism development will not only effectively increase their income, but also help to mobilise their consciousness and initiative for the protection of the tangible cultural heritage.

Further Reading

Social groups encouraged to help preserve, use heritage buildings

3.4 Tourism development of intangible cultural heritage

3.4.1 Relationship between preservation and tourism development

The most controversial issue in the tourism development of intangible cultural heritage is whether to preserve the originality of intangible cultural heritage or carry out commercial development. The concern around commercial development is that it could destroy the originality of intangible cultural heritage resources. However, in the context of historical development, cultural traditions do not continue with their original meanings and functions unchanged, but rather have been in flux over time. Tourism development provides a way of presenting intangible cultural heritage, gives new meaning to the original heritage culture, and salvages dying cultural heritage by tapping resources, restoring, reviving, and innovating traditional culture. In this regard, commercialization does not necessarily bring negative effects to the original culture but adds new cultural connotations to intangible cultural heritage.

3.4.2 Problems in the development of intangible cultural heritage tourism

(1) Destruction of the original environment of intangible cultural heritage

Although tourism development of intangible cultural heritage brings opportunities for local economic development, it has also caused damage to the local ecological and social environment, particularly in some traditional villages. Tourism development requires infrastructure, and the massive construction of modern tourism infrastructure such as hotels and restaurants will inevitably replace local traditional or native architecture, causing damage to the original local ecological environment. In addition, some tourism products that rely on intangible cultural heritage such as traditional sports and folklore can bring many tourists to the heritage sites within a short period of time. An influx of tourists will not only lead to shortage of local resources (e.g., traffic congestion) and intensify damage to the environment, but will also impact cultural values and damage the local cultural ecology. This may affect the rules of the development of intangible cultural heritage.

(2) Ignorance of the cultural connotations of intangible cultural heritage

The involvement of tourism activities will certainly impact the natural evolution process of intangible cultural heritage resources. In the process of the tourism development of intangible cultural heritage, profit-oriented enterprises may ignore the connotation of heritage by focusing largely on economic benefits. This is manifested in the way that the selection and certification of heritage is determined by an authoritative discourse composed of elites and expert assessments. This may adversely affect the social development of heritage sites and can easily cause irreversible damage to intangible cultural heritage.

(3) Alienation of the cultural inheritance of intangible cultural heritage

Tourism development enables cultural inheritors to preserve features of intangible cultural heritage. However, some heritage sites are inevitably influenced by modern industrial products and western cultures, leading to a decline and alienation of their cultural meanings. Some tourism development models are a simple and crude aggregation of different intangible cultural heritages, namely cross-cultural integration, that do not consider the development rules of the heritage itself. These commercialised and vulgarised tourism developments may lead to the destruction of the connotation and the living environment of some heritage resources, and the permanent disappearance of cultural memories and cultural resources of heritage sites.

3.4.3 Paths for tourism development of intangible cultural heritage

Facing the negative impact that tourism development may bring to intangible cultural heritage, the focus of any development should aim to be mutually beneficial. With this in mind, tourism development should consider the following aspects.

(1) Emphasising live transmission

The core of intangible cultural heritage resources lies in the cultural traditions that have gradually formed over long history and vast geographical space. Tourists hope to learn about these cultural traditions when participating in intangible cultural heritage tourism. More importantly, tourists want to experience a "live" culture and feel the charm of the historical traditions, not only because intangible cultural heritage is important and needs to be inherited. Only when intangible cultural heritage resources feel alive can they be preserved and transmitted. Therefore, tourism development of intangible cultural heritage needs careful thought on how to bring an intangible cultural heritage alive.

(2) Innovation as a driver force

For an intangible cultural heritage to survive in a certain era, some of its characteristics must coincide with the needs of that era. In the present era, people's need for cultural products is booming, and their requirements for product quality are also increasing. If intangible cultural heritage is to survive in the current era, innovative attempts need to be made to meet the needs of contemporary people. Therefore, tourism development should not only follow the rule of development regarding intangible cultural heritage in respecting the cultural needs of local community in heritage sites but should also focus on the cultural connotations of intangible cultural heritage for innovative development. Any development should find the positioning of intangible cultural heritage in contemporary society and respond to the cultural taste and needs of tourists with innovation and change, thereby enabling intangible cultural heritage to bloom in the current era.

(3) A people-centred approach

The traditional practice of safeguarding intangible cultural heritage was mainly to protect representative material carriers, while the role of humans in the preservation and transmission of intangible cultural heritage was largely neglected. It should be noted that the principle of safeguarding intangible cultural heritage is to protect heritage in daily life and use. Therefore, to coordinate tourism development and intangible cultural heritage, a people-centred approach should be adopted. The people are those inheritors and local residents who participate in the inheritance of intangible cultural heritage. A people-oriented approach means that inheritors and local residents can actively participate in initiatives protecting and disseminating intangible cultural heritage, and play an irreplaceable role in the inheritance and development of intangible cultural heritage tourism. Those people who have witnessed and created their intangible cultural heritage can fully understand the connotation and significance of the heritage. People-centered tourism development promotes the pride of people in heritage sites to participate in tourism development activities and is conducive to the protection of intangible cultural heritage.

(4) Selecting appropriate development models

Tourism development of intangible cultural heritage should ensure that suitable tourism development models coincide with local conditions to keep the heritage alive in the long term. Existing developmental models are listed below.

a. Leisure tourism model

In contemporary society, leisure is an integral part of tourism, and leisure activity design has become an important aspect of tourism product design. Leisure tourism model refers to product development of charming and distinctive cultural leisure tourism projects with the help of heritage festival activities. Through a design of interaction and experience, tourists can "touch" intangible cultural heritage and interact with local inheritors. This model integrates the tourism development of intangible cultural heritage with sightseeing, leisure, and vacations, attracting tourists by highlighting the cultural connotation of intangible cultural heritage with its human characteristics.

b. Industrial tourism model

The industrial tourism model refers to tourism activities in relevant production enterprises such as tools, objects, and manufacturing processes related to skills so that tourists can learn production procedures and experience the fun of do-it-oneself. The integration of productive conservation and tourism activities is characteristic of the industrial tourism model. This model is currently used in the tourism development of Cloisonne handicraft production (e.g., the Beijing Enamel Factory Co., LTD) and the production of traditional Chinese medicine (e.g., the Beijing Tong Ren Tang Group). This model can also be used to showcase outstanding intangible cultural heritage resources by organizing lectures, forums, and training activities to explore the cultural value behind the production process.

c. Cultural creation development model

Innovation is the root of the vitality of intangible cultural heritage. Therefore, tourism development of intangible cultural heritage should encourage creative development. Heritage protection and innovation bases can be established to promote the development of creative tourism products related to intangible cultural heritage. The combination of tourism and cultural creativity can improve the dissemination of intangible cultural heritage and broaden the path of inheritance, and can also be a living form of protection for intangible cultural heritage.

(5) Emphasis on inheritor training

Intangible cultural heritage is the crystallization of people's collective wisdom. Based on the principle of live transmission, the emphasis of tourism development should be placed on the cultivation of inheritors. Training programs and courses need to be provided to train local successors. Professionals should be introduced to the local community of the intangible cultural heritage, and residents should be encouraged to participate in heritage promotion and product design. This is conducive to the preservation and transmission of intangible cultural heritage and a move towards sustainable tourism development.

Chapter Summary

Cultural heritage resources are valuable assets passed down across generations. These resources are alluring in their own right and are of critical importance to local tourism industries. In practice, the tourism development of tangible cultural heritage resources should focus particularly on the protection of the heritage itself as well as the involvement of the community. The tourism development of intangible cultural heritage should emphasise especially the activation of heritage resources and product innovation. In general, the tourism use of cultural heritage resources pursues a harmony of protection, inheritance, and development, so as to achieve the goal of sustainability with regard to both heritage protection and tourism development.

Issues for Review and Discussion

1. How should ICH tourism product innovation be carried out? Please give an example.
2. How should the preservation and development of ICH resources be balanced?
3. Compare the difficulties of the protection of tangible cultural heritage and the preservation of intangible cultural heritage.

Further Reading

Kunshan's opera preservation

China Story

Identifying the connection point between intangible cultural heritage resources and their market

Exercises

Recommended Reading

Chapter 4
Architecture

Learning Objectives

After reading this chapter, you should have a good understanding of
1. The evolution of ancient architectures in China;
2. The cultural connotations of ancient architectures in China;
3. Some historical architecture attractions in China;
4. The functions of altar, memorial temple and screen wall.

Technical Words

English Words	中文翻译
Palaeolithic Period	旧石器时代
Neolithic Period	新石器时代
stilt-style architecture	干栏式建筑
rammed earth	夯土
timberwork	木结构
bracket set	斗栱
grotto	石窟
mural	壁画
layout	布局
architectural complex	建筑群
masonry structure	砖石结构
Standardization in Architecture Rules	《营造法式》
Tibetan Buddhism	藏传佛教
glazed tile	琉璃瓦
central axis	中轴线
harmony between man and nature	天人合一
the Forbidden City	紫禁城

续表

English Words	中文翻译
The Book of Changes	《易经》
Hall of Supreme Harmony	太和殿
Hall of Preserving Harmony	保和殿
Palace of Earthly Tranquillity	坤宁宫
Palace of Heavenly Purity	乾清宫
Confucianism	儒家思想、儒学
double-eave hip roof	重檐庑殿顶
double-eave gable and hip roof	重檐歇山顶
single-eave hip roof	单檐庑殿顶
single-eave gable and hip roof	单檐歇山顶
overhanging gable roof	悬山式顶
hard gable roof	硬山式顶
paraboloid roof	卷棚顶
pyramidal roof	攒尖顶
auspicious animal	瑞兽
nine bays in width	面阔九间
five bays in depth	进深五间
dragon pattern	和玺彩画
tangent circle pattern	旋子彩画
Suzhou style pattern	苏式彩画
moat	护城河
turret	角楼
outer court	外廷
inner court	内廷
winter solstice	冬至
sacred road	神道
terra cotta warriors	兵马俑
fengshui	风水
sacrificial altar	祭坛
memorial temple	祠庙
Hall of Great Achievements	大成殿
Hall of Heavenly Blessing	天贶殿

续表

English Words	中文翻译
screen wall	影壁、照壁
beam bridge	梁桥
suspension bridge	吊桥
arch bridge	拱桥
zigzag bridge	曲桥
memorial archway	牌坊

Knowledge Graph

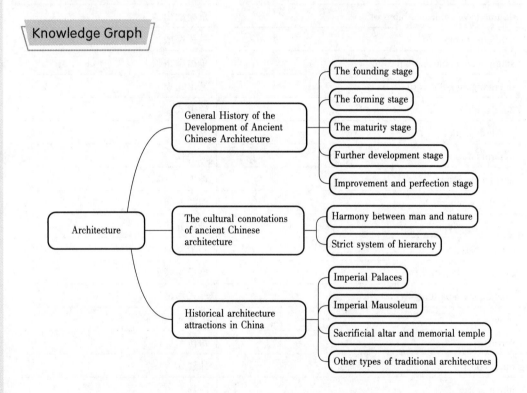

4.1 General History of the Development of Ancient Chinese Architecture

The development of architecture, to some extent, is the development of culture. The customs and cultural traditions of different nations have endowed architecture with different national characteristics. Architecture is the representation of social life;

meanwhile, it can also arouse people's emotional resonance. Among all the civilizations in the world, the Chinese civilization is one of the oldest and the only one that existed uninterruptedly. Therefore, the same is true of Chinese architecture. Throughout history, architectures in different historical periods inherited features from previous ones and also possessed distinct characteristics.

4.1.1 The founding stage

As early as the Palaeolithic Period (about three million years ago), primitive man took use of caves as shelters. In the Neolithic Period (about 5,000-2,000 years ago), semi-caves appeared in the northern part of the Yellow River drainage areas, followed by buildings that were totally above ground. Meanwhile, in the drainage areas of the Changjiang River, due to the humid and rainy climate, stilt-style architecture was created in order to avoid floods and wild beasts.

The establishment of the Xia Dynasty (about 2070 BC - 1600 BC) marked the beginning of the Slavery Society. During this period, skills of rammed earth were widely used in the construction of walls and terraces. In addition, the skills related to the building of wood structures also improved considerably. In the Warring States Period (770 BC-476 BC), the ducal states established their own capital cities surrounded by moats and with palaces built on rammed terraces at their centres. The wood structures, the towering city gates, the use of clay tiles and coloured paintings for decoration became the foundations of ancient architecture for successive dynasties.

4.1.2 The forming stage

The period from the Qin (221 BC-207 BC) and Han (202 BC- AD 220) Dynasties to the Southern and Northern Dynasties (AD 420- AD 589) was the forming stage of the ancient Chinese architectures. In 221 BC, after conquering the other six principalities, Emperor Qin Shi Huangdi established the first centralized feudal empire in Chinese history. The Qin and Han Dynasties lasted over 400 years, as a result of unification and mighty national power, and China's ancient architecture reached its first climax, which manifested as follows: the increasingly mature timberwork, the wide adoption of bracket set, the formation of various kinds of roofs and the new development of brick structure.

The span of 361 years from the Three Kingdoms Period (AD 220- AD 280) to the establishment of the Sui Dynasty (AD 581 - AD 618) was a time of turbulence and division. During this period, social and economic development declined. As a result, there was less architectural creation and innovation compared with the Han Dynasty period.

However, with the introduction and spread of Buddhism, a large number of Buddhist temples and grottoes emerged. The art of carvings and sculptures not only promoted the development of grottoes, Buddha statues, and murals, but also greatly influenced China's architecture. During this period, China's ancient architectural systems were formed and became the major pattern for later generations, lasting about 2,000 years.

4.1.3 The maturity stage

The Sui and Tang Dynasties (AD 618 - AD 907) witnessed the climax of China's feudal economy and culture, with great achievements in both art and architecture. On the basis of the architectural styles inherited from previous dynasties, as well as the influence from foreign cultures, the architecture during this period formed an individual and complete system. The architectural art has developed from individual buildings to the overall layout of architectural complexes and whole cities, which not only reached a stage of maturity, but also influenced architecture in neighbouring countries such as Japan and Korea. There were large-scale palaces, gardens, and official buildings both in Chang'an and Luoyang. In the Tang Dynasty, Chang'an was the largest city in the world. The Daming Palace was extremely magnificent, and its area was 4.5 times larger than the Forbidden City in Beijing.

There was frequent communication and exchange with foreign countries during the Sui and Tang Dynasties. Foreign trade reached as far as Afghanistan and what is today's Iran and Arabian region. Various aspects of exotic cultures, including religion, paintings, sculptures, music, dance, and customs, together with architectures, were introduced to China. However, the Chinese architectural system during this period had already become mature and closely related with social etiquette. Therefore, foreign architectures did not shake the status of local architecture; on the contrary, the decoration designs, carving skills and the use of colours, etc. helped to enrich the buildings in China. Besides wooden structures, masonry structures were mainly adopted in the building of Buddhist pagodas, bridges, and underground tombs. Simply speaking, the architectural styles and characteristics were majestic and solemn, simple but vigorous, which perfectly represented the spirit of the epoch.

4.1.4 Further development stage

During the period from the Song (AD 960 - AD 1276), Liao (AD 916 - AD 1125) and Jin (AD 1115 - AD 1234), the ancient Chinese architectures got further development. Thanks to the development of the urban economy, the manufacturing industry, as well as science and technology during the Song Dynasty, architects, carpenters, and craftsmen reached a relatively high level of skill, producing bracket set systems, architectural structures, and designs of a high calibre. However, partly influenced by literati politics and partly due to the pursuit of the combinations between natural landscapes and artificial buildings, the architecture in the Song Dynasty was quite elegant and exquisite, less magnificent and imposing than those in the Tang Dynasty. The architectural structures changed greatly, mainly characterised by the reduction of the load-bearing of bracket sets. Various kinds of sophisticated halls, terraces, towers, and pavilions came into being. More importantly, the architectural components, methods, and the estimate of labour and materials became more standardized than they were previously. The book *Standardization in Architecture Rules* (《营造法式》) written by Li Jie(李诫) in 1103 AD summarized the former architectural designs and construction experience. The book was regarded as the most comprehensive and scientific masterpiece on the subject of architectures in ancient China and was also the earliest and most complete in the world.

The architectures of the Liao Dynasty maintained the styles of the Five Dynasties and the Tang Dynasty. Due to the unconstrained spirit of nomadic ethnic groups, the buildings seemed to be dignified and solemn. In addition, some of the palaces and halls were built on the east-west axis, because of their living customs and religious belief that regarded the East as supreme. The architectures in the Jin Dynasty possessed the features of both the Song and Liao Dynasties, but adhered more to the former.

4.1.5 Improvement and perfection stage

The Yuan (AD 1271- AD 1368), Ming (AD 1368- AD 1644), and Qing (AD 1644- AD 1912) Dynasties witnessed the last climax of ancient Chinese architecture. During the Yuan Dynasty, the development of economy and culture slowed down, and, coupled with the less advanced architectural technologies of the Mongolian ruling class, most of the buildings were simple and unrefined. Because the Mongolians were fond of the colour white, they made extensive use of white tiles, which could be regarded as a kind of epoch character. In addition, because the Mongolian emperors believed in religion especially Tibetan Buddhism, religious buildings were significantly developed. For example, the White Pagoda in Miaoying Temple was an important historical relic in the Yuan Capital (Photograph 4.1). It is the earliest and largest lama pagoda existent in China; meanwhile, it is also regarded as the oldest landmark in Beijing. The design and construction of the pagoda involved Nepali craftsmanship; therefore, the pagoda also served as a testimony to the friendship between China and Nepal.

China in the Ming Dynasty was a powerful, unified, and multi-ethnic country. At the beginning of the Ming Dynasty, a series of measures in terms of officials, agriculture, water projects, etc., helped to promote economic development. Consequently, the recovery and development of the economy stimulated architectural prosperity. The architectural designs and patterns of the Ming Dynasty inherited the traditions of the Song Dynasty and also inspired the official styles of the Qing Dynasty. At first, the architectural style was unsophisticated and vigorous, similar to that of the Song and Yuan Dynasties; in the middle part of the Ming Dynasty, it was rigorous, becoming fussy in the late stages. Generally speaking, it is characterised

Photograph 4.1　The White Pagoda in Miaoying Temple, Beijing
(Source: https://unsplash.com/photos/plFCZkflmp0)

by majesty, magnificence, and large scale. Many large-scale architectural complexes were built in the Ming Dynasty, for example: the Baoen Temple in Nanjing; the imperial palace, mausoleums and the Temple of Heaven in Beijing; and the Taoist buildings on Wudang Mountain. Besides, the Confucius Temple in Qufu was enlarged and rebuilt many times. The Qufu complex of monuments has retained its outstanding artistic and historic character due to the devotion of successive Chinese emperors over more than 2,000 years.

Also, several military projects were undertaken, such as the Great Wall, and the fortification systems in the north and in the south-eastern coastal cities to defend against Japanese pirates. Architectural technology made some progress during the Ming Dynasty, for instance: the output and skills of brick production increased and the skills of glazed tiles also improved. Pagodas, gates, archways, and screen walls with glazed tiles were further developed. Another interesting point is that the concept of fengshui (风水) was quite popular in the Ming Dynasty, influencing building construction, from site selection and layout, through to the surrounding environment.

The Qing Dynasty was the last feudal dynasty in China. The architectures during this period inherited the traditions of the Ming Dynasty by and large, and included certain developments and innovations, mainly manifested in the importation of glass and the improvement of brick and stone buildings. The large imperial gardens were the architectural highlight of the Qing Dynasty, among which the Old Summer Palace (Yuanming Garden) and the Summer Palace (Yihe Garden) are reputed as paragons. Moreover, Tibetan Buddhism architectures with unique styles prevailed, represented by the Yonghe Lama Temple in Beijing and a group of Tibetan Buddhist temples in Chengde, Hebei Province (Photograph 4.2). At the end of the Qing Dynasty, new buildings combined with Chinese structures and western features appeared.

Photograph 4.2 The Mountain Summer Resort, Chengde
(Original picture form Bai Wei)

The symmetrical beauty of ancient Chinese architecture

4.2 The cultural connotations of ancient Chinese architecture

Ancient architecture is the carrier of traditional Chinese culture. The connotations and extensions of the excellent traditional culture can be fully expressed by a large variety of pillars and bay, terraces and halls, roofs and eaves, the philosophic concepts, hierarchical standards, and aesthetic trends are invariably reflected in ancient architectures.

4.2.1 Harmony between man and nature

Harmony between man and nature is the key component of China's ancient philosophy. "Man" refers to people and the subjective world while "nature" refers to the objective universe and the natural world. From the point of view of traditional Chinese culture, these two aspects depend on, influence, and promote each other. Chinese people have long pursued the perfect combination of the two, and conversely this theory has a far-reaching impact on the design and layout of ancient architectures. Whether a single building, a compound, a classical garden, or the overall layout of a city, all represented this idea without exception, showing perfect examples of the spirit of harmony between man and nature.

Let us take the Imperial Palace in Beijing as an example. Also known as the Forbidden City, the Imperial Palace is the largest and best-preserved timber palatial building complex in the world. Through its name, layout, design, space, etc., this ancient architectural complex built in 1420 clearly represented the idea that man is an integral part of nature.

The name "Forbidden City" first appeared in the historical records during the reign of Emperor Wanli of the Ming Dynasty. Its origin is mainly concerned with ancient astrology. Because ancient Chinese people believed that Polaris (Ziwei Star) lay in the centre of the celestial palace where the Jade Emperor (the Supreme Deity of Taoism) dwelled, Ziwei (紫薇) and Ziyuan (紫垣) became synonyms of the imperial palace. Feudal emperors called themselves the son of heaven, and, correspondingly, the place where they lived and handled state affairs was also the centre. The imperial palace was the forbidden area where the highest hierarchy dwelled and conducted their affairs, hence its name.

Furthermore, many individual buildings in the Forbidden City got their names from *The Book of Changes* (《易经》), which is also closely related with the theory of "harmony between man and nature". For example, the name of the Hall of Supreme Harmony (太和殿) means harmonious co-existence of all beings in heaven and on earth. Besides, the Palace of Earthly Tranquillity (坤宁宫) and the Palace of Heavenly Purity (乾清宫) implied that heaven was characterised by lofty wisdom while earth was represented by rich breadth and lenience.

4.2.2 Strict system of hierarchy

Confucianism, represented by "benevolence" and "etiquette" was the authoritative thought of the era and has a far-reaching impact on feudal society for more than 2,000 years. The laws and regulations in terms of clothing, food, housing, transportation, etc., were to be strictly obeyed. Therefore, they laid down a series of laws and regulations in order to consolidate their power and maintain a perfect social moral system. The architectural patterns and scales that were allowed to be used depended strictly on the owners' political status. This system appeared in the Zhou Dynasty at the latest and lasted until the end of the Qing Dynasty, and was one of the most important set of laws and regulations in ancient China.

(1) Roofs

The roofs of ancient architectures in China were mainly composed of surfaces and

Recommended Video
▼
故宫博物院研究员周乾主讲《紫禁城古建筑的营建思想与文化》见于故宫博物院官网。

ridges whose designs and patterns were rich and colourful. The roofs were not only practical but also clearly symbolized the distinct social status of different owners. The roofs commonly seen in ancient China could be divided into the following seven ranks:

a. Double-eave hip roof: the highest rank adopted by the main hall in the imperial palaces and mausoleums as well as the chief Buddhist hall in the temple (Photograph 4.3).

Photograph 4.3　The Hall of Supreme Harmony, double-eave hip roof
(Source: https://pixabay.com/zh/photos/beijing-forbidden-city-ancient-6506295/)

b. Double-eave gable and hip roof: mainly used in palaces, gardens, altars and temples. Buildings with this type of roof look magnificent and imposing (Photograph 4.4).

Photograph 4.4　The Tian'anmen Gate Tower, double-eave gable and hip roof
(Original picture from Bai Wei)

In addition, there was single-eave hip roof and single-eave gable and hip roof correspondingly. After the Ming Dynasty, the hip roof, and gable and hip roofs could only be used in the imperial palaces, mausoleums, and the main halls of the temples in order to demonstrate the supreme power of emperors.

Overhanging gable roof was the most common roof and was only used in folk buildings. While the hard gable roof was the lowest rank of the double‑slope roofs. According to the regulations in the Qing Dynasty, officials below the sixth grade, and ordinary people could only use the hard gable roof. However, the Chongzheng Hall in Shenyang Imperial Palace also adopted this type of roof (Photograph 4.5). This was mainly because it was built during the earlier stage of the Manchurian regime which was not influenced much by Han culture.

Photograph 4.5　Chongzheng Hall, hard gable roof
(Source: http://zgfsy.net/templ/comm/news_detailed.html?categoryId=47&articleId=618)

c. Paraboloid roof: the main difference between paraboloid roof and the overhanging and hard gable roof was that the former does not have a clear main ridge, possessing a kind of feminine beauty (Photograph 4.6).

Photograph 4.6　Exhibition Hall of Cultural Prosperity (文昌院), paraboloid roof
(Source:https://www.sohu.com/a/403819399_216077?_trans_=000014_bdss_dkwhfy)

In addition, there were several other types of roofs without grading, such as the pyramidal roof mainly used in pavilions and towers (Photograph 4.7 and 4.8).

Photograph 4.7　Hall of Prayer for Good Harvest (祈年殿), circular pyramidal roof
(Source:https://pixabay.com/zh/photos/temple-of-heaven-beijing-tiantan-park-7513135/)

Photograph 4.8　Hall of Grand Administrator (大政殿), octagonal pyramidal roof
(Original picture from Bai Wei)

(2) Room bays

Most ancient buildings in China were rectangular in shape. A rectangular building has two dimensions on a flat surface, i.e., width and depth. The former refers to the longer side, while the latter refers to the shorter side. The space between two pillars was called a "bay" and the ancient timber architectures usually took "bay" as the basic unit. The larger of the number of bays, and the higher the level of the building. In traditional Chinese culture, odd numbers were considered masculine while even numbers were feminine. Certain numbers had specific connotations, among which nine was the largest masculine number. Generally speaking, buildings with number nine or multiples of nine were those at the highest level. e.g., nine bays in width, doorsteps with nine layers, nine lines of doornails and nine auspicious animals on the roof ridges, etc. Besides the number nine, five was also an auspicious number. According to the *Book of Changes*, the combination of nine and five means a dragon flying in the sky. Therefore, they were the most auspicious numbers and thus became exclusive to emperors; for example, the Hall of Preserving Harmony in the Forbidden City is nine bays in width and five bays in depth.

However, there is an exception. As the most important hall in the Imperial Palace, the Hall of Supreme Harmony is eleven bays in width and five bays in depth just to emphasise its supreme status. But building with nine bays was still the highest level in theory and could only be adopted in imperial buildings. Other palaces, halls, and temples could adopt five or seven bays in width according to different ranks. Three or five bays in width could often be seen in folk buildings.

(3) Decorations

Besides the timberwork roofs and bays, there were also very strict restrictions in terms of decoration. One of the major decorations were the animals on roof ridges. There were ten of them altogether: dragon (symbol of emperors), phoenix (symbol of empresses), lion (symbol of bravery and solemnity), celestial horse and sea horse (incarnations of good fortune in ancient myth), Xiayu (a bizarre sea animal that can put out fire), Suanni (a fierce animal similar to a lion), Xiezhi (symbol of bravery and honesty), Douniu (an auspicious animal that can get rid of disasters), and Hangshi (a man with a monkey's face and wings that served as a lightning device), listed here in order of importance (Photograph 4.9).

Photograph 4.9 Ten ridge animals on the Hall of Supreme Harmony
(Original picture from Bai Wei)

Actually, the ridge animals are always displayed in odd numbers, with only one exception: the Hall of Supreme Harmony. The ten auspicious animals on its ridges not only fully represented the Hall's unique and paramount status, but also had an implied meaning of total perfection. There are nine and seven on the ridges of the Palace of Heavenly Purity and the Palace of Earthly Tranquillity respectively. Palaces lived in by concubines usually had five, although three or a single ridge animal were also commonly seen.

Besides the magnificent outlook of palaces and halls, the coloured drawings inside and outside the eaves could also draw people's attention. Thanks to these drawings, ancient architectures could still look resplendent and magnificent after hundreds of years of exposure to wind and rain. The coloured drawing is a popular and important way of decorating ancient buildings in China. Undoubtedly, the best example that could represent the highest drawing level is the Imperial Palace in Beijing. The coloured drawings in Qing style can be seen everywhere. Tangent circle patterns were adopted in ordinary palaces while dragon patterns were primarily used in main halls. The dragon patterns could be categorized according to ranking as dragon, phoenix, dragon and phoenix, dragon and auspicious grass, as well as the Suzhou style pattern.

As for colours, different dynasties used different colours. During the pre-Qin period, red was the most exalted colour. Recorded in the *Book of Rites* (《礼记》), the pillar colours for the Son of Heaven, feudal princes, senior officials and feudal scholars were red, black, cyan and yellow respectively. After the Sui Dynasty, the colour gold, red, and yellow became the most exalted. Cyan and green were lower, while black and grey were the lowest.

In ancient times, glazed tiles were the superior construction material and were used on buildings of higher rank. The same is true with their colours, among which yellow was the highest in rank. In the Ming and Qing Dynasties, yellow glazed tiles could only be used in palaces, mausoleums, and gardens of royal families followed by blue and green glazed tiles, which could be used by princes and aristocrats. Black glazed tiles were the lowest ranking and were commonly used in ancient libraries. Besides, as one of the Five Elements, water that subjugates fire corresponds to black. Therefore, the roofs of the Pavilion of Literacy Ripple (文澜阁) in Hangzhou and the Pavilion of Literacy Profundity (文渊阁) in the Imperial Palace were covered in black glazed tiles. In addition, altars and temples built with imperial edict were also allowed to use yellow glazed tiles, such as in the Confucius Temple and Guan Yu Temple. As Confucianism was the dominant ideology and Confucius was regarded as the sage, Confucius Temples enjoyed the same status as imperial buildings, so they were allowed to adopt red walls and yellow tiles.

Besides the roofs, number of bays in width and depth, dragon patterns, and colours mentioned above, several other factors such as the terraces, balusters, bracket sets, and pillars could all represent the level of ancient architecture.

4.3 Historical architecture attractions in China

A lot of historical architectures have now become landmarks of the area, attracting tourists from China and around the world. This section will introduce some famous architecture attractions in China.

4.3.1 Imperial Palaces

As early as 2000 BC, written language, bronze ware, palaces and altars appeared in China, symbolizing the Chinese nation had stepped into the stage of civilization. The imperial palace was an important token for measuring social civilization. As the most important and quintessential part of traditional Chinese architectures, the Chinese palace was a large-scale architectural complex in which ancient emperors dwelled. The emperors had these large and magnificent palaces built in order to consolidate their reign, demonstrate supreme power, as well as satisfy their spiritual and secular life. Throughout the long history of feudal society in China, the policy of imperial centralism was fully developed. As a result, the palace was the best-concentrated reflection of feudal thoughts and social etiquette. It represented the highest standard of traditional architectures.

During the long history of feudal dynasties, there were several famous imperial palaces, representing the apogee of their respectively dynasties. Some have disappeared because of fire, war, or some other reason; but fortunately, some have survived to the present day, demonstrating to the whole world the splendid civilization they represented.

(1) E Pang Palace

According to the descriptions of some historical records, the E Pang Palace was an extremely grand and glorious architectural complex ordered to be built by Emperor Qin Shi Huangdi in 212 BC. It was estimated that the front hall alone of the Palace covered an area of about 80,000 square meters. It measures about 690 meters from west to east and 115 meters from south to north. Legend has it that Xiang Yu set E Pang Palace on fire after overthrowing Qin and ending his cruel reign. However, after many years of laborious research, archaeologists concluded in 2007 that actually E Pang Palace was never completed and it was the Xianyang Palace that was destroyed by Xiang Yu. Nevertheless, the E Pang Palace was still regarded as one of the four major projects during the reign of Emperor Qin Shi Huangdi, together with the Great Wall, the imperial mausoleum and the highways for the emperor, which were a testimony to the unified Qin Empire.

In 1991, the planned E Pang Palace (never finished, but uncovered by archaeologists) were identified by the United Nations as the world's largest palace base and an ancient wonder. In 2012, the core archaeological site was established as a protected zone, covering an area of 2.3 square kilometres.

(2) The Potala Palace

According to historical records, Sontzen Gampo—the 33rd btsan po (king of the Tubo regime) moved the capital to Lhasa and began to construct the Potala Palace in the 7th century. The Potala Palace used to be quite splendid and large in scale until the 9th century when it began to decline with the disintegration of the Tubo Regime. In 1642, the 5th Dalai Lama established the integrated regime of religion and politics. Thus, Lhasa served as the political, religious, cultural, and economic centre again. The Potala Palace was rebuilt in 1645 and from then on became an important site for the Dalai Lama to live in and deal with political and religious affairs.

The complex, comprising the White and Red Palaces, with their ancillary buildings, was built on the Red Mountain, at an altitude of 3,700 meters. Inside the Potala Palace, there are more than 1000 rooms, chanting halls, a seminary, temples, diverse chambers for worshipping Buddha, and chambers housing the stupa tombs of eight Dalai Lamas. In addition, the palace is just like a huge treasure house, containing 698 murals, almost 10,000 painted scrolls, numerous sculptures, carpets, canopies, curtains, porcelain, jade, and fine objects of gold and silver, as well as a large collection of sutras and important historical documents.

The Potala Palace is the landmark of Tibet and is reputed as a shining pearl inlaid on the roof of the world, symbolizing Tibetan Buddhism and its central role in the traditional administration of Tibet(Photograph 4.10).

Photograph 4.10　The Potala Palace, Lhasa
(Source: https://pixabay.com/zh/photos/tibet-potala-palace-buildings-97006/)

Further Reading

Outstanding universal value of the Potala Palace

(3) The Imperial Palace in Beijing (The Forbidden City)

Throughout past dynasties, one of the important ways to manifest the supreme power and authority of emperors was to construct majestic and imposing palaces. As the symbol and carrier of traditional etiquette, there were strict restrictions on such details as colours, windows, doors, terraces, balusters, tiles, decorations etc. The best example is the Imperial Palace in Beijing.

It was first built in the 4th year (1406) and completed in the 18th year (1420) of Emperor Yongle of the Ming Dynasty. Located at the central axis in Beijing, the Imperial Palace is 961 meters from south to north and 753 meters from west to east, covers an area of about 720,000 square meters with a total of 9,999 bays of rooms. It's surrounded by 10-meter-high walls and a 52-meter-wide moat. There are four turrets on each of the corners, and each turret has nine beams, 18 pillars and 72 ridges, one can imagine how intricate the structure is (Photograph 4.11).

Photograph 4.11　The turret and moat of the Forbidden City
(Original picture from Bai Wei)

Rectangular in shape, the whole palace is divided into the outer court and the inner court. At the centre of the outer court are the Hall of Supreme Harmony, the Hall of Central Harmony (中和殿) and the Hall of Preserving Harmony (保和殿). They are flanked by the Hall of Literary Brilliance (文华殿) and the Hall of Martial Valour (武英殿). The Hall of Supreme Harmony was the site of grand ceremonies during the Ming and Qing Dynasties. Important occasions including the three major annual events (the lunar New Year's Day, the winter solstice and the emperor's birthday), enthronement ceremonies, imperial weddings, the coronation of empresses, the announcement of the Palace Examination results, and the launch of major military expeditions were all celebrated here.

At the centre of the inner court are the Palace of Heavenly Purity, the Hall of Union (交泰殿), and the Palace of Earthly Tranquillity. In the Ming Dynasty, the Palace of Heavenly Purity served as the emperor's residence. This role was maintained during the reign of Emperors Shunzhi and Kangxi in the early Qing Dynasty until Emperor Yongzheng moved his sleeping quarter to the rear chamber of the Hall of Mental Cultivation (养心殿). From then on, the Palace of Heavenly Purity continued to function as an important venue for emperors to meet courtiers, review memorials, handle daily government affairs, receive envoys, accept congratulations, and hold banquets. In addition, in the Ming and Qing Dynasties, the Palace was the place where the coffin of a deceased emperor was placed, in accordance with the belief that one should end his days in his bedchamber. The Palace of Earthly Tranquillity served as the residence of the empress in the Ming Dynasty. In traditional thought it formed a pair with the Palace of Heavenly Purity, with heaven characterised by lofty wisdom while the earth was represented by rich breadth and lenience. The Palace of Earthly Tranquillity that people see today was rebuilt in the 12th year of Emperor Shunzhi (1655) in the Qing Dynasty, imitating the Palace of Pure Tranquillity in Shenyang. The entrance is located on the east end of the building's façade, rather than in the middle, giving the palace a "pocket house" style with distinctive Manchu features. During Emperor Kangxi's reign, the two bays on the east end were used as the emperor's bridal chamber. The five bays on the west side were used as a shrine for Shamanistic sacrifices, housing a U-shaped *kang* on which the idols and a throne were placed, together with cauldrons for cooking sacrificial meat. Furthermore, there is also an imperial garden and some halls for worshipping Buddha in the Imperial Palace.

It is no exaggeration to say that the Imperial Palace in Beijing is the supreme model in the development of ancient Chinese palatial buildings. It provides insight into the social development of China's late feudal dynasty, especially the ritual and court culture. The layout and spatial design inherit and embody the traditional features of urban planning and palace construction in ancient China, featuring a central axis, symmetrical design and layout of front outer court and rear inner court. In addition, landscaped courtyards deriving from the Yuan dynasty is also indispensable. As the prominent paragon of ancient architectural hierarchy, construction techniques and architectural art, it influenced official buildings of the subsequent Qing Dynasty over a span of 300 years. The religious buildings, particularly a series of royal Buddhist chambers within the Palace, adopting abundant features of ethnic cultures, are a testimony to the architectural fusion and exchange among the Manchu, Han, Mongolian, and Tibetan culture since the 14th century. Furthermore, over a million valuable royal collections, articles used by the royal family, and a large number of archival materials on ancient engineering techniques, including written records, drawings, and models, are evidence of the court culture and law and regulations of the Ming and Qing Dynasties.

Besides its imposing buildings and precious cultural relics, the cats of the Forbidden City have also become internet celebrities, attracting more and more visitors (Photograph 4.12). The cats have their names and fans, and some of them have even been promoted as honorary ambassadors. The history of the palace cats can be traced back to the Ming Dynasty, when there was a special department in charge of looking after cats. The cats were raised not only for killing rats, but also for dispelling the loneliness of the imperial concubines. Emperor Jiajing of the Ming Dynasty and Empress Dowager Cixi were both cat lovers.

Photograph 4.12　the Forbidden City cat
(Original picture from Bai Wei)

4.3.2 Imperial Mausoleum

The tomb is an indispensable part of ancient Chinese architectures. This is mainly because the ancient Chinese believed that souls could live on after one's death; therefore, the dead should be treated equally with the living. Even ordinary people wanted to have their tombs finely built, let alone the emperors. Actually, many emperors had their mausoleums built as soon as they accessed to the throne. Just like the palace, the imperial mausoleum was also a kind of important political architecture with clear hierarchy. The layers of coffins, the shape of the mounds, the number of stone animals, and the length of the sacred way all depended on the owners' political status. Such factors had strong influence on the construction of imperial mausoleums, obviously manifested through the patterns, layout, furnishings and decorations, etc.

Throughout feudal society, since Confucianism had advocated filial piety, elaborate and generous funerals became an important way of expressing loyalty and obedience to the dead. Although several emperors, such as Liu Heng (Emperor Wen of the Western Han

Recommended Video

推荐观看由故宫博物院高级工程师曹振伟主讲的《紫禁城里的五色瑞光——建筑祥云彩画》，以及由周乾主讲的《紫禁城古建筑的营建思想与文化》。以上视频见于故宫博物馆官网。

Dynasty), Yang Jian (Emperor Wen of the Sui Dynasty), and Li Shimin (Emperor Taizong of the Tang Dynasty) ever proposed thrifty funerals, yet generous funerals prevailed during almost the whole of ancient society. The underground palace was the main body of the imperial mausoleum and no effort was spared to imitate the palaces of the emperor before his death, with buildings for dealing with state affairs in the front and residential buildings at the rear. For example, there were Buddha images and Buddhism scriptures on the stone gates and arches in the underground palace of Emperor Qianlong, truly reflecting his belief in Buddhism.

Generally speaking, there were three major types of mausoleums throughout history, namely, mausoleums covered by rammed earth, hills or mountains as well as circular brick castles. Graves covered by rammed earth as the mound were major structures in the Qin and Han Dynasties. They looked like a pyramid with the top cut off, just like an upended *Dou* (A kind of container for measuring grain), hence the name *fudou* (覆斗). Because the top was flat and spacious, it is also called *fangshang* (方上). The paragon of this type of mausoleum is the Mausoleum of Emperor Qin Shi Huangdi, which took about 700,000 laborers about 40 years to build. Graves covered by rammed earth were not only time‐and‐labour‐consuming, but were also easily eroded. Therefore, during the Tang Dynasty, imperial mausoleums topographically built on mountains prevailed. The magnificent mountain could manifest the supreme power of the emperors and prevent the mausoleums from being robbed. Imperial mausoleums adopted in the Ming and Qing Dynasties were called "treasure wall" (宝城) and "treasure dome" (宝顶). Lofty circular or oval brick wall, which was called "treasure wall", was constructed above the underground palace; rammed loess inside the treasure wall with a dome higher than the wall was called "treasure dome". Circular domes were commonly adopted in the Ming Dynasty, while oval ones were commonly found in Qing mausoleums.

During historic evolution, Chinese mausoleum architectures, especially the imperial mausoleums, gradually blended with painting, calligraphy, sculpture, as well as other varieties of art. As a kind of unique human resource, the Chinese mausoleum also enjoys very important status in the history of world civilization.

During the approximately 3,000 years from the first slavery dynasty (Xia) to the last feudal dynasty (Qing), there were about 500 emperors in all and more than 100 imperial mausoleums whose traces can be found, distributed in half the provinces of China. These imperial mausoleums were not only large in number, but also famous for their strict layout, exquisite design and large scale.

(1) Mausoleum of the First Qin Emperor

Located at the northern foot of Lishan Mountain, 35 kilometres northeast of Xi'an,

Shanxi Province, Qin Shi Huangdi Mausoleum is the tomb of the founder of the first unified empire in Chinese history. However, the tomb was built in 246 BC long before he established the Qin Dynasty in 221 BC. As the King of Qin State, he still wanted to have the same military power and status in the afterlife as he had enjoyed during his earthly lifetime. Originally, the grave mound was 115 meters high. After over 2,000 years of weathering, it still remains more than 70 meters in height. Approximately 500 satellite tombs and pits containing thousands of life-size terra cotta warriors, horses, bronze chariots, and weapons have been discovered in the vicinity of the mausoleum, among which the terracotta army was regarded as one of the eight wonders of the world and one of the greatest archaeological discoveries of the 20th century.

The burial pits of the terracotta warriors and horses are located about 1.5 kilometres east of Emperor Qin Shi Huangdi's Mausoleum (Photograph 4.13). It is believed that they were created to safeguard and serve the emperor in the afterlife. The terracotta warriors and horses are all life-sized, orderly arrayed in rows and lines. These figures of warriors and horses make up a great underground army consisting of war chariots, infantrymen, cavalrymen, and other armed servicemen. A more amazing fact is that all these warriors and horses were made by hand and no two figures are exactly alike. Each warrior has unique facial features, clothing, and hairstyle. Hollow torso, solid head, arms, and legs were created separately and then assembled. Each warrior was stamped with the name of the foreman responsible for its creation in order to track any mistakes.

Photograph 4.13 The Terracotta Warriors
(Source: https://pixabay.com/zh/photos/terracotta-army-warrior-volume-177475/)

As mentioned earlier, the tomb of the first emperor who unified the country, took over 700,000 laborers nearly 40 years to build. This underground tomb had a unique standard and layout, and a large number of exquisite funeral objects. It is testimony to the founding of the first unified empire, which wielded unprecedented political, military, and economic power and advanced the social, cultural, and artistic level of the empire.

(2) The Imperial Tombs of the Ming and Qing Dynasties

The Imperial Tombs of the Ming and Qing Dynasties were built between AD 1368 and AD 1915, scattered in Beijing Municipality, Hebei, Hubei, Jiangsu and Liaoning Province. These imperial tombs are located in topographical settings carefully chosen according to Fengshui and comprise numerous buildings of traditional architectural design and decoration. The tombs and buildings are laid out according to Chinese hierarchical rules and incorporate sacred ways lined with stone monuments and sculptures designed to accommodate ongoing royal ceremonies as well as the passage of the spirits of the dead. They illustrate the great importance attached by the Ming and Qing rulers over five centuries to the building of imposing mausoleum, reflecting not only the general belief in an afterlife but also an affirmation of authority.

High Ranking Officer

The Qian Mausoleum

The Imperial Tombs of the Ming and Qing Dynasties are masterpieces of human creative genius by way of their organic integration into nature, and a unique testimony to the cultural and architectural traditions of the last two feudal dynasties in the history of China between the 14th and 20th centuries. They are fine works combining the architectural arts of the Han and Manchu civilizations. Their siting, planning and design reflect both the philosophical idea of "harmony between man and nature" according to fengshui principles and the rules of social hierarchy, and illustrate the conception of the world and power prevalent in the later period of ancient Chinese society.

4.3.3 Sacrificial altar and memorial temple

(1) Sacrificial altar

China is a country with a long history; it was the saints who created splendid civilizations and the ancestors who gave birth to later generations. China is also a country of agriculture, so ancient civilizations worshipped heaven and earth to be granted favourable weather and good harvests. Therefore, offering sacrifice in ancient China was not a religious behaviour, but originated from the awe and gratitude to nature, deities, and ancestors. Offering sacrifice during certain events and occasions had been a tradition since ancient times. Simply speaking, altars and temples were sacrificial buildings and their appearance was the result of the strict patriarchal clan system and the feelings of awe and gratitude of ancient civilizations.

Offering sacrifice in China can be classified into two categories. One was to natural deities such as heaven, the earth, the sun, and the moon. This kind of sacrifice reflected the relationship between man and nature, among which offering sacrifice to heaven was the most supreme and could be done only by emperors, since emperors called themselves sons of heaven. Altars, also known as sacrificial altars, are lofty terraces piled with soil on flat ground. Sacrifices to the natural deities mentioned above were mainly held on altars. Influenced by the Chinese *Yin*(阴) and *Yang*(阳) concept, sacrifices to heaven, the earth, the sun, and the moon were offered in the south, north, east, and west respectively. Ancient civilizations believed that only in this way could harmony be achieved under heaven. Besides these four altars, there is another altar in Beijing, namely the altars for the God of agriculture.

(2) Memorial temple

The other kind of sacrifice was to ancestors, men of virtue, as well as the gods of mountains and rivers; these were generally offered at memorial temples. Without doubt, the highest ranking was the imperial ancestral temple, where emperors offered sacrifices and veneration to their ancestors. The main hall was built on the central axis with a double-eave hip roof, which proved that offering sacrifice to ancestors was a very important political ceremony in feudal society. Moreover, there are also many ancestral temples for ordinary persons in China. For example, the Chen Clan Ancestral Temple in Guangzhou and the Hu Clan Ancestral Temple in Anhui are paragons of this type of building.

During China's long history, a galaxy of outstanding persons appeared, just like countless shining stars. People built memorial temples in order to remember their achievements and express admiration. Examples of these are, the Memorial Temple to Military Marquise Zhuge Liang (武侯祠) in Chengdu, the Memorial Temple to Qu Yuan in Miluo, and the Memorial Hall to Li Qingzhao in Ji'nan. Among so many memorial temples, the highest ranking was the Confucius Temple in Qufu, Shandong Province. The sacrifices offered in memorial temples reflected the social relationship among people.

In addition, mountain culture is an integral part of traditional Chinese culture and the legends about mountain gods can be traced back to ancient times. Both the emperors and ordinary people preferred mountains as their pilgrimage destinations. For example, the Dai Temple in Tai'an, Shandong Province was the site where emperors offered sacrifice to heaven and the God of Mount Taishan. The Heavenly Blessing Hall in the Dai Temple is one of the three palatial buildings in China together with the Supreme Harmony Hall in the Forbidden City and the Great Achievement Hall in Confucius Temple (Photograph 4.14).

Case Study

Confucius Temple in Qufu

Photograph 4.14 The Hall of Great Achievements
(Original picture from Bai Wei)

4.3.4 Other types of traditional architectures

(1) Screen wall

The screen wall, was a wall used as a barrier facing the entrance. Originating from China, it was a special type of architecture that could be found in palaces, temples, yamen (衙门, government offices in feudal China), and private mansions. According to archaeological research, the screen wall appeared as early as the Western Zhou Dynasty. At an architectural site in Shanxi Province, ruins of a 240-centimeter-long and 20-centimeter-high screen wall were excavated; this might be the earliest screen wall in China. The screen wall was not only practical, but also a symbol of the owner's social status. Because of its important location, much attention was correspondingly paid to its designs and decorations. The pattern of its roofs could be hip roof, gable-and-hip roof, overhanging gable roof, and hard gable roof depending on different rankings, similar to the roofs of halls.

Of all the existing screen walls in China, the Nine-dragon Screen (九龙壁) in Beijing Imperial Palace is the most luxuriantly decorated. The cultural connotations of number nine and five were fully displayed in it. There are nine dragons distributed in five parts; there are 45 cushion boards with dragon patterns under the eave; there are 270 panels on the screen. All the numbers are multiples of number nine and five, symbolizing the supreme power and status of emperors. The Nine-dragon Screen in Beijing Imperial Palace, the Nine-dragon Screen in Beihai Park (Beijing), and the one in Datong, Shanxi Province, reputed as the three most famous nine-dragon screens in China (Photograph 4.15).

Photograph 4.15　The Nine-dragon screen in the Imperial Palace, Beijing
(Original picture from Bai Wei)

As a key component in traditional architectures, the screen wall, houses, and courtyard are supplementary to each other, emerging as an organic whole. The screen walls not only possessed significance of architecture and humanity, but also had high aesthetic value.

(2) Bridge

China enjoyed a reputation as the "hometown of bridges". Bridges appeared in the Shang Dynasty at the latest, and were popularized in the Han Dynasty. People could find bridges on the stone reliefs of the Han Dynasty. Bridge construction technologies developed greatly in the Sui Dynasty and remained at the forefront worldwide during the Tang and Song Dynasties. In the world-famous painting—*Riverside Scene at the Qing Ming Festival*, there is a wooden arch bridge.

Generally speaking, ancient bridges in China can be classified into three categories, namely beam bridge, suspension bridge, and arch bridge. Besides, there is a certain kind of bridge specific to classical gardens—the zigzag bridge. Similar to the pavement and corridor, the bridge was also an indispensable part of Chinese gardens. Not only could it divide bodies of water, but also slow down visitors' pace so that they may leisurely enjoy the scenery. The zigzag bridge could also enable visitors to see a different view when they make a turn, as if representing an endless view within a limited space(Photograph 4.16).

Among a large number of bridges in China, the four most famous and representative are Guangji Bridge in Chaozhou, Guangdong Province, Zhaozhou Bridge in Shijiazhuang, Hebei Province, Luoyang Bridge in Quanzhou, Fujian Province and Lugou Bridge in Beijing. The Zhaozhou Bridge built in the Sui Dynasty was 64.4 meters long with a span length of 37.02 meters; it was the longest in span length and earliest built open-shoulder single arch stone bridge in the world. Over 1,400 years, the Zhaozhou Bridge has withstood many floods, wars, and earthquakes, and still stands firmly.

Photograph 4.16 The nine-zigzag bridge of the Yuyuan Garden, Shanghai
(Original picture from Bai Wei)

During their long evolution, bridges in ancient China not only provided convenience, but also symbolized the aesthetic value of the Chinese people. Ancient Chinese were fond of bridge, and thus bridges could be often found in legendary stories, historical records and literary works. Bridges are the crystallization of the wisdom and hard work of the ancient Chinese. Many construction technologies used in bridge-building were pioneering technologies worldwide and many designs even influenced modern bridge construction. Meanwhile, bridges are just like living historical books, recording the splendid Chinese civilization, and fully demonstrating the wisdom and talents of the ancient Chinese.

(3) Huabiao (Ornamental column)

Huabiao is one of the traditional Chinese architectures, enjoying a long history. It is a huge decorative column erected in front of palaces and mausoleums. Legend has it that Huabiao was a totem sign in the tribal age. It is said that Emperor Shun ever erected wood pillars on road for common people to write expostulatory words on, which was believed to be the embryonic form of the Ornamental Column.

The most well-known Huabiao in China are the two standing in front of Tian'anmen Gate Tower. They were built during the reign of Emperor Yongle of the Ming Dynasty, thus having a history of more than 500 years. They were made of white marble, were 9.57 meters high with a diameter of 98 centimetres and weighed about 20,000 kg each. On top of each column, there is an auspicious animal called Hou. One is facing toward the palace, signifying the emperor should not indulge in family life but go outside to experience the people's life; the other is facing away from the palace, signifying the emperors should go back inside for state affairs. Nowadays, the functions of the ornamental column have gone out of fashion, yet the spirit, and glamor it embodied still exist, and will so for a long time (Photograph 4.17).

Photograph 4.17 The ornamental column in front of the Tian'anmen Gate Tower
(Original picture from Bai Wei)

Chapter Summary

Architecture is an important and integral part of human civilization. In general, a prominent building may embody a particular artistic and cultural feature as well as the technical skill of its time. The designs of ancient Chinese architecture were also influenced by traditional philosophy, religion, art and aesthetics. Over thousands of years, ancient Chinese architecture gradually formed its own style and a complete system of design, and thus enjoys an important status in the history of world architecture. Numerous ancient buildings have been well preserved up to the present day, manifesting their glorious achievements to the whole world.

Issues for Review and Discussion

1. Why is the number of bays usually in odd number?
2. Why did Emperor Qin Shi Huangdi have so many terracotta warriors and horses made?
3. What do you understand by the integration of man and nature?
4. What do you think of *Fengshui* principle?

Chapter 5
Literature

Learning Objectives

After reading this chapter, you should have a good understanding of
1. The brief history of ancient Chinese literature;
2. The relationship between tourism literature and tourism;
3. The major styles of poetry in the Tang Dynasty;
4. Some famous scenic spots in China and their relevant literary works.

Technical Words

English Words	中文翻译
The Book of Poetry	《诗经》
Elegies of the South	《楚辞》
The Grand Scribe's Records	《史记》
The History of the Former Han Dynasty	《汉书》
landscape pastoral poetry	山水田园诗
frontier fortress poetry	边塞诗
romantic poetry	浪漫主义诗歌
realism poetry	现实主义诗歌
The Tang Legend	《唐传奇》
lyric	词
Dream in Peony Pavilion	《牡丹亭》
The Peach Blossom Fan	《桃花扇》
The Three Kindoms	《三国演义》
Outlaws of the Marsh	《水浒传》
Journey to the West	《西游记》
The Golden Lotus	《金瓶梅》
A Dream of Red Mansions	《红楼梦》

续表

English Words	中文翻译
The Classic of Mountains and Seas	《山海经》
men of letters	文人墨客
Yellow Crane Tower	黄鹤楼
Wuhou Shrine	武侯祠
Charm of a Maiden Singer	念奴娇
Gathering Mulberry Leaves	采桑子
The River All Red	满江红
Fragrance of Laura Branch	桂枝香
Phoenix Hairpin	钗头凤
Literary Anthology by Prince Zhao Ming	《昭明文选》
Compendium of Materia Medica	《本草纲目》
Great Canon of the Yongle Reign	《永乐大典》
The Travels of Xu Xiake	《徐霞客游记》
antithetical couplet	对联
Heavenly Kings Hall	天王殿
Maitreya Buddha	弥勒佛

Knowledge Graph

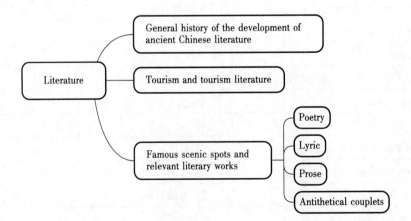

Chinese literature is one of the brightest stars in the sky of world literature. This is not only because of its long history and profound connotations, but is also owing to its distinct national characters and countless literary works in various styles.

5.1 General History of the Development of Ancient Chinese Literature

The history of Chinese literature can be traced back to the Pre-Qin Period which originated from primitive ballads and legendary myths. *The Book of Poetry* and *Elegies of the South*(《楚辞》) laid the foundations of realism and romanticism for Chinese literature. Historical proses and proses written by philosophers of different schools during this period added splendour to each other, and not only recorded historical evolution, but also presented the artistic skills of describing figures and events, forging the direction for later historical works.

In the Han Dynasty, fu (赋, a literary form characterised by sentimental or descriptive composition, often rhymed), poetry, and prose were in a situation of tripartite confrontation. *Fu*, represented by Sima Xiangru, featured the extolling of emperors' achievements and virtues. Poetry during this period was represented by Yuefu(乐府) Poetry and the Nineteen Poems of Ancient Styles, while proses was mainly composed of two styles of political commentary and historical records. *The Grand Scribe's Records of China* written by Sima Qian and *The History of the Former Han Dynasty* by Ban Gu can be regarded as the most outstanding masterpieces of this kind.

During the 369 years of the Wei, Jin, Southern and Northern Dynasties, society underwent continuous upheaval and assimilation. On the one hand, previous literary forms matured and were perfected; on the other hand, the appearance of mystery novels along with novels recording people's sayings and anecdotes symbolized the embryonic forms of the novels. However, among various literary forms of this period, the development of poetry was the most splendid. From Cao Cao, Cao Pi, and Cao Zhi's poems expressing their own minds, to Tao Yuanming and Xie Lingyun's landscape pastoral poetry, all contributed significantly to later generations.

The Tang and Song Dynasties were the golden age of poems and lyrics. The puissant national power and the relatively clear political environment helped to promote the development of Tang poetry. Many famous poets and various styles of poetry symbolized its apogee. For example: Landscape Pastoral Poetry was represented by Wang Wei and Meng Haoran. Many of its themes are mountains and waters, clouds and hermits with a quiet and peaceful character. The preeminent representatives of Frontier Fortress Poetry are Gao Shi, Cen Shen, and Wang Changling. This kind of style focused on describing the magnificent frontier scenery, exotic customs, the brutality of war, and the hardships of the battlefield, or extoling the heroic spirit of defending the homeland. The two most eminent poets of the Tang Dynasty, Li Bai and Du Fu, collectively known as "Li Du", were acknowledged as the paragons of Romantic Poetry and Realism Poetry.

Ci (词, lyric), as a sort of musical literature, reached its apogee in the Song Dynasty. Due to economic development, social stability as well as the imperial advocacy of the management of state affairs by civilians, Song lyrics enjoyed a rapid and flourishing development. Prominent composers from various schools came forth one after another. The works created by composers such as Su Shi, Yan Jidao, Li Qingzhao, Xin Qiji, and Lu You remain influential up to this day. One can still experience the glamor of both composers and their works today thanks to the preservation of over 20,000 Song lyrics by more than 300 composers.

Besides poetry and lyrics, other literary forms were also flourishing. The Ancient-prose Movement represented by the eight great masters in both the Tang and Song Dynasties broke the shackles of Pianwen (骈文, rhythmical prose characterised by parallelism and ornateness). As for novels, the change from *The Tang Legend* written in classical style Chinese to the Song's Script of Story-telling written in vernacular Chinese showed that novels were increasingly maturing.

The rise of Sanqu (散曲, a type of verse popular in the Yuan, Ming, and Qing Dynasties, with tonal patterns modelled on tunes drawn from folk music), opera, and the long novel brought vigorous vitality to the literature of these dynasties. The Zaju (杂剧, drama of the Yuan Dynasty) was like a shining pearl in the opera history of China due to its unique style and techniques of expression. By the time of the Ming and Qing Dynasties, great works such as *Dream in Peony Pavilion*(《牡丹亭》) and *The Peach Blossom Fan*(《桃花扇》) were born. As for long novels, The *Three Kingdoms*(《三国演义》) written by Luo Guanzhong was reputed as being the blueprint for later works. *Outlaws of the Marsh*(《水浒传》), *Journey to the West*(《西游记》), and *The Golden Lotus*(《金瓶梅》) sprung up in the middle of the Ming Dynasty. In the middle of the Qing Dynasty, the emergence of *"A Dream of Red Mansions"*(《红楼梦》) symbolized the climax of Chinese classical novels.

China's ancient literature is no doubt a priceless cultural legacy, enjoying a very important status globally for its incomparable achievements and unique features.

5.2 Tourism and Tourism Literature

Ancient Chinese literature is an important part of traditional Chinese culture. Simply speaking, tourism literature is a kind of literature that can reflect tourism activities. The thoughts, emotions and aesthetic interests of tourists can be expressed or displayed by describing or recording natural landscapes, buildings and folk customs, etc. Therefore, tourism literature possesses certain features such as informativeness, sentiment, and aesthetic; meanwhile, it also reflects the social life of those times. To some extent, tourism literature itself is a certain kind of emotional tourism resource.

As for the cradle of tourism literature, opinions are widely divided. Some scholars think that the travelogue originated from *The Classic of Mountains and Seas* (《山海经》); some think that it can be traced back to *Elegies of the South*; some believe that the article written by Ma Dibo in the Eastern Han Dynasty recording Emperor Guangwu's offering sacrifice to Mount Taishan is the earliest travelogue; and some scholars also propose that *The Sea* (《观沧海》), written by Cao Cao, is the earliest travelling poem. In any case, it can be concluded that tourism literature in China has a rather long history.

There are several reasons that can account for the vitality of Chinese tourism literature. In ancient China, travelling was mainly necessitated by political, economic, religious and cultural factors. For example, the imperial examination system promoted travel among ancient scholars. Meanwhile, some local officials themselves were famous poets; an example of this is Bai Juyi, who served as inspector in Hangzhou. Besides many beautiful poems, he was also associated with a picturesque scenery—Bai Causeway—that was named after him and is still popular with contemporary tourists. In addition, the tradition of worshipping ancestors and men of virtue helped to arouse journeys of searching for one's roots or pondering the past. Furthermore, as a civilized multi-ethnic and multi-cultural country with a long history and vast territory, various kinds of natural landscapes, places of cultural interests, traditional festivals and folk customs in China have always been sources of inspiration for Chinese artists and scholars. Men of letters in different dynasties created countless poems, lyrics, proses and antithetical couplets whenever and wherever they travelled.

Tourism and tourism literature are closely related. On the one hand, tourism provides abundant resources and inspiration for literary creation; on the other hand,

Case Study

Tang Poetry Road in Eastern Zhejiang Province

tourism literature can bring enjoyment of beauty and emotional experience, thus influencing people's subconsciousness and cultivating their temperament. With the help of various literary forms and their artistic glamor, tourism resources and classical literary works emerged as an organic whole. And finally, tourism literature can increase people's motives and desire for travelling just like an invisible hand.

5.3 Famous Scenic Spots and Relevant Literary Works

Ancient Chinese tourism literature comes in various forms and styles, mainly poetry, lyric, prose, and antithetical couplets. Each has its unique features and attractions. Both the beautiful natural scenes and places of historical interest become more connotative with the help of these famous literary works.

5.3.1 Poetry

Poetry is the earliest literary form in China. Even the poems recorded in *The Book of Poetry* were already a true reflection of the social life and people's wishes in concise and vivid expression. No doubt, Tang poetry is a most precious cultural heritage in the treasure house of Chinese poetry. It is varied in style and abundant in quantity. However, numerous natural scenes or places of cultural interests appeared in poems regardless of style or time of creation.

(1) The Yellow Crane Tower

A must-see in Wuhan is the Yellow Crane Tower (黄鹤楼)(Photograph 5.1). Regarded as one of the Four Great Towers in China, it stands on the banks of the Yangtze River at the top of Snake Hill. With yellow upturned eaves, each floor seems to have been designed to resemble a yellow crane spreading its wings to fly. The tower was first built in AD 223 as a watchtower during the Three Kingdoms Period. After hundreds of years, its military function gradually disappeared. Throughout history, many poets and artists travelled there for inspiration and created many famous works about the tower, among which Cui Hao's poem is said to be one of the greatest works in the Chinese poetic canon.

The Yellow Crane Tower

The Yellow Crane Tower [1] (《黄鹤楼》)

Cui Hao

The sage on yellow crane was gone amid clouds white,
To what avail is Yellow Crane Tower left here.
Once gone, the yellow crane will ne'er on earth alight,
Only white clouds still float in vain from year to year.
By sunlit river trees can be counted one by one,
On Parrot Islet sweet green grass grows fast and thick.
Where is my native land beyond the setting sun,
The mist-veiled waves of River Han make me homesick.

It was said that even the great Poet Li Bai had to admit that it was hard to write a poem better than Cui's when he was standing on the tower. After writing "*It's impossible to write a poem describing such a wonderful view before your eyes because Cui's poem already exists*", and then departed. Although it was just an interesting anecdote, nobody can deny that it was Cui Hao's poem that made the Yellow Crane Tower's reputation more widespread. Besides its magnificent appearance and beautiful legend, its cultural significance might be the most attractive highlight of the Yellow Crane Tower.

Photograph 5.1 The Yellow Crane Tower, Wuhan City
(Original picture from Bai Wei)

(2) The West Lake in Hangzhou

The West Lake is the famous fresh water lake located in the historic city of Hangzhou. Its basic layout is "one hill, two causeways, three islands, and five lakes". Its beauty has been celebrated by writers and artists since the Tang Dynasty. From Bai Juyi's "*I love best the east of the lake under the sky*[2]; *The bank paved with white sand is shaded by willows green*" and "*Who opens a southwest lane to the temple scene? It slants like a silk girdle around a skirt green*"[3], people can experience the graceful spring scene of the Bai Causeway. From Yang Wanli's "*Green lotus leaves outspread as far as boundless sky; Pink lotus blossoms take from sunshine a new dye*"[4], one can imagine the grand view of

---

[1] Xu Yuanchong, Ma Hongjun: *300 Tang Poems: An Annotated Edition with Commentaries*
[2] Xu Yuanchong, Ma Hongjun: *300 Tang Poems: An Annotated Edition with Commentaries*
[3] Xu Yuanchong, Ma Hongjun: *300 Tang Poems: An Annotated Edition with Commentaries*
[4] https://www.ximalaya.com/waiyu/38136128/308353122

the blooming lotus in summer. In any case, to most tourists, the poem written by Su Shi might be the most memorable.

View West Lake over Drinking^① (《饮湖上初晴后雨》)
Su Shi
The brimming waves delight the eyes on sunny days,
The dimming hills present rare view in rainy haze.
West Lake may be compared to Lady of the West,
Whether she is richly adorned or plainly dressed.

Su Shi wrote many poems describing the West Lake from 1071 to 1074 when he acted as Tongpan (通判, an official under the magistrate who administers lawsuits etc.) This poem was written on a sunny and then rainy day in 1073. The poet was intoxicated by both the wine and the beautiful scenery. From the comparison with Xi Shi—one of the Four Beauties of ancient China, one can easily imagine the poetic and picturesque sentiment of the West Lake. As a result, the West Lake is also called Xi Zi Lake (Photograph 5.2). The West Lake is not only famous for its picturesque natural landscape, but was also associated with many scholars, national heroes and revolutionary martyrs. Therefore, it plays an important role in many aspects of Chinese culture.

Photograph 5.2 The West Lake, Hangzhou
(Original picture from Bai Wei)

(3) Mount Lushan

Mount Lushan is located in Jiujiang City, Jiangxi Province. Bordered on the north by

---

①https://new.qq.com/rain/a/20210617A0BPAF00

the Changjiang River and on the south by Poyang Lake, Mount Lushan presents an integral scene of river, hills, and lake, the beauty of which has attracted spiritual leaders, scholars, artists, and writers for over 2,000 years. The mountain boasts mighty peaks, roaring waterfalls, a mysterious sea of cloud, philosophical religions, ancient academy, numerous remains from the ice age, and many western-styled villas. Two poems about Mount Lushan written by Li Bai and Su Shi, clearly represent the romantic and philosophical features of poems of the Tang and Song dynasties, respectively.

*The Waterfall in Mount. Lu Viewed from Afar*① 《望庐山瀑布》
Li Bai
The sunlit Censer Peak exhales incense-like cloud,
Like an upended stream the cataract sounds loud.
Its torrent dashes down three thousand feet from high,
As if the Silver River fell from the blue sky.

The Waterfall in Mount. Lu Viewed from Afar

*Written on the Wall at West Forest Temple*② 《题西林壁》
Su Shi
It's a range viewed in face and peaks viewed from the side.
Assuming different shapes viewed from far and wide.
Of Mountain Lu we cannot make out the true face,
For we are lost in the heart of the very place.

Written on the Wall at West Forest Temple

Since ancient times, thousands of poets and literary men came to Mount Lushan and wrote about 4,000 poems, adding rich cultural ambience to the mountain. The natural beauty of Mount Lushan is perfectly integrated with its historic buildings and natural features, creating a unique cultural landscape that embodies the outstanding aesthetic value powerfully associated with Chinese spiritual and cultural life.

(4) Chengdu Wuhou Shrine

The Wuhou Shrine in Chengdu was constructed as a temple to commemorate Liu Bei, Zhuge Liang and other eminent Shu Han figures. Occupying 150,000 square meters, the shrine complex is made up of three main sections: the Three Kingdoms Cultural Relics Preservation Zone, the Three Kingdoms Culture Experience Zone, and the Jinli Folk

---

① Xu Yuanchong, Ma Hongjun: *300 Tang Poems: An Annotated Edition with Commentaries*
② https://www.ximalaya.com/sound/298772397

Customs Zone. The Wuhou Shrine is known as the "mecca of the Three Kingdoms" because it is the only shrine in China where emperor and ministers are enshrined together. Since the magnificence of Zhuge Liang overshadows that of Liu Bei in the hearts of many common folk, in general the complex is referred to as "Wuhou Shrine". One will naturally think of Zhuge Liang's heroic stories described in *Three Kingdoms* written by Luo Guanzhong. Besides, Du Fu's *Temple of the Premier of Shu* also comes to mind.

Temple of the Premier of Shu

Temple of the Premier of Shu [1] (《蜀相》)

Du Fu

Where is the famous premier's temple to be found?
Outside the Town of Brocade with cypresses around.
In vain before the steps spring grass grows green and long,
And amid the leaves golden orioles sing their song.
Thrice the king visited him for the State's gains and pains,
He served heart and soul the kingdom during two reigns.
But he died before he accomplished his career,
How could heroes not wet their sleeves with tear on tear!

(5) Yangzhou

Yangzhou, also known as Guangling, Jiangdu, and Weiyang in ancient times, has a history as a city that can be traced back to 486 BC. Yangzhou's glorious past reached its climax in the Tang and Qing Dynasties. Especially during the Tang Dynasty, its economic status even surpassed that of Chang'an and Luoyang, and thus enjoyed the reputation that "Yangzhou ranks first and Yizhou ranks second". Yangzhou has long been a place favored by men of letters, among whom Tang poet Du Mu might be the best exponent. From his *"Twenty-four fairies on the bridge steeped in moonbeams, are they still playing on the flute now as before?"* [2], one can experience the charming sight of the Slim West Lake, while in his other two poems, Yangzhou seemed to be a most sentimental place.

At Parting (I) [3] (《赠别》)

Du Mu

Not yet fourteen, she's fair and slender,
Like early budding flower tender.

---

① Xu Yuanchong, Ma Hongjun: *300 Tang Poems: An Annotated Edition with Commentaries*
② Xu Yuanchong, Ma Hongjun: *300 Tang Poems: An Annotated Edition with Commentaries*
③ Xu Yuanchong, Ma Hongjun: *300 Tang Poems: An Annotated Edition with Commentaries*

Though Yangzhou Road's beyond compare,
Pearly screen up rolled, none's so fair.

At Parting [①] *(II)*

Deep, deep our love, too deep to show,
Deep, deep we drink, silent we grow.
The candle grieves to see us part,
It melts in tears with burnt-out heart.

At Parting

Besides Du Mu, Li Bai expressed his reluctance to part with Meng Haoran by *"My friend has left the west where the Yellow Crane towers, for River Town green with willows and red with flowers"*[②] and Xu Ning's *"Of all the moonlit nights on earth when people part, two-thirds shed sad light on Yangzhou with broken heart"*[③] vividly expressed his lovesickness. Emotions of happiness or sorrow, excitement or loneliness were all involved in the poems concerning Yangzhou.

5.3.2 Lyric

Relevant News

Lyric originated in Liang of the Southern Dynasty, rose in the Sui and Tang Dynasties and finally reached its heyday in the Song Dynasty. After 300 years of decline during the Yuan and Ming Dynasties, it rose again during the Qing Dynasty. It was composed with banquet music. Compared with poetry, lyrics were greatly favoured because of their musical cadence, changeable rhythm, irregular sentences and strong emotions. When chanting the excellent lyrics, people feel an irresistible impulse to travel to those sites they describe.

The Fifth Session of International Poetry and Lyric Contest

(1) Chibi

There is a martial Chibi(武赤壁) and a literary Chibi(文赤壁) in Hubei Province. Located in Chibi City, the martial Chibi, also known as General Zhou Chibi, is the historical site of the famous Chibi Battle. The literary Chibi is located in Huangzhou, because one of the most excellent lyrics—*Charm of a Maiden Singer* by Su Shi was written here, hence the name literary Chibi or Dongpo Chibi.

Recommended Video

推荐中央电视台纪录片《跟着书本去旅行》：金秋月明下扬州——湖光月色。可于中央电视台网站检索收看。

---

① Xu Yuanchong, Ma Hongjun: *300 Tang Poems: An Annotated Edition with Commentaries*
② Xu Yuanchong, Ma Hongjun: *300 Tang Poems: An Annotated Edition with Commentaries*
③ Xu Yuanchong, Ma Hongjun: *300 Tang Poems: An Annotated Edition with Commentaries*

Charm of a Maiden Singer [1] (《念奴娇·赤壁怀古》)

Su Shi

The endless river eastward flows;
With its huge waves are gone all those
Gallant heroes of bygone years.
West of the ancient fortress appears
Red cliff where General Zhou won his early fame
When the Three Kingdoms were in flame.
Rocks tower in the air and waves beat on the shore,
Rolling up a thousand heaps of snow.
To match the land so fair, how many heroes of yore
Had made great show!
I fancy General Zhou at the height
Of his success, with a plume fan in hand,
In a silk hood, so brae and bright,
Laughing and jesting with his bride so fair,
While enemy ships were destroyed as planned
Like castles in the air.
Should their souls revisit this land,
Sentimental, his bride would laugh to say:
Younger than they, I have my hair turned grey.
Life is but like a dream.
O moon, I drink to you who have seen them on the stream.

Although a thousand years have passed, yet *"to match the land so fair, how many heroes of yore had made great show"* will to this day still stimulate people to travel to both places of historical interest to experience the ancient fierce battlefield and literary appeal.

(2) Yingzhou West Lake

Su Shi said that the West Lake in Hangzhou was the most beautiful among the 36 west lakes under heaven. However, the West Lake in Yingzhou was the one Ouyang Xiu loved most. He showed special preference for the West Lake when he acted as magistrate in Yingzhou, since he wrote ten sets of lyrics with the same tune of "Gathering Mulberry Leaves".

---

① Xu Yuanchong: *Song Lyrics in Paintings*

Gathering Mulberry Leaves [1] (《采桑子》)

Ouyang Xiu

All flowers have passed away, West Lake is quiet;
The fallen blooms run riot.
Catkins from willow trees
Beyond the railings fly all day, fluffy in breeze.
Flute songs no longer sung and sightseers gone,
I begin to feel spring alone.
Lowering the blinds in vain,
I see a pair of swallows come back in the rain.

Gathering Mulberry Leaves

Thanks to Ouyang Xiu's works, the West Lake in Yingzhou District, Fuyang City is reputed as one of the three most famous West Lakes in China together with the other two in Hangzhou and Huizhou.

(3) Yue Fei Memorial Temple

General Yue Fei is the well-known hero in the war against Jin invaders during the Southern Song Dynasty. Although he and his army had won many great battles, he was wrongly accused of seriously defying military orders and was subsequently put to death at the age of 39. It was until 21 years later that Yue Fei was rehabilitated by Emperor Xiaozong. Before entering the temple, a pair of antithetical couplets extracted from his *The River All Red* will first draw people's attention.

The River All Red [2] 《满江红》

Yue Fei

Wrath sets on end my hair;
I lean on railings where
I see the drizzling rain has ceased.
Raising my eyes
Towards the skies,
I heave long sighs,
My wrath not yet appeased.
To dust is gone the fame achieved in thirty years;
Like cloud-veiled moon the thousand-mile plain disappears.
Should youthful heads in vain turn grey,

The Rriver All Red

---

①Xu Yuanchong: *Song Lyrics in Paintings*
②Xu Yuanchong: *Song Lyrics in Paintings*

We would regret for aye.
Lost our capitals,
What a burning shame!
How can we generals
Quench our vengeful flame!
Driving our chariots of war, we'd go
To break through our relentless foe.
Valiantly we'd cut off each head;
Laughing, we'd drink the blood they shed.
When we've re-conquered our lost land,
In triumph would return our army grand.

In this day and age, one can still be touched by the indignant lines and feel an eagerness to personally admire such a patriot at the memorial temple (Photograph 5.3).

Photograph 5.3　Yue Fei Memorial Temple, Hangzhou
(Original picture from Bai Wei)

(4) Nanjing

Nanjing is the capital city of Jiangsu Province, and was also known as Jinling, Jiangkang, and Yingtianfu in ancient times. As the ancient capital of six dynasties and one of the important birthplaces of Chinese civilization, it has long been a city in which education and literature were valued. The first book on poetry theory and criticism—*Grade of Poetry* (《诗品》), the first book on literary theory and criticism—*Carving a Dragon at the Core of Literature*(《文心雕龙》), the first enlightened book for children—*Thousand Character Classic* (《千字文》) and the earliest existent literary anthology—

Literary Anthology by Prince Zhaoming(《昭明文选》) were all created in Nanjing. More than 10,000 literary works had a close relationship with Nanjing, including the eminent works— "*A Dream of Red Mansions*", *Compendium of Materia Medica* and *Great Canon of the Yongle Reign*. In addition, Nanjing also enjoyed an unmatchable reputation as the literary centre of China (《天下文书》) due to the Confucius Temple constructed during the Wanli Reign of the Ming Dynasty. Nanjing was also designated as the "Capital of Literature" in 2019 by UNESCO.

Throughout literary history, Jinling or Jiankang frequently appeared in classic poems and lyrics. For example:

The Terrace Wall[①] *(《台城》)*

He Zhu

Gallant the Southern land far and wide,
Six Dynasties in opulence vied.
Wine, woman and song on Terrace Wall,
Eight beauties wrote verse in palace hall.
In summer clear they mounted the cloud-scraping height,
Under the jadelike moon they loitered in long night,
They drank and crooned the years away.
Leaving the lovebirds tiles pell-mell
They tried to hide like frogs in a well.
On street of mansions overgrown with grass
No cabs could pass.
The swallows in the mansions of bygone days,
In whose hall now do they stay?
Over the tower the Silver River bars the sky,
The Plough hangs high.
The tide runs up and down on frosty River Huai.
The shadow of town walls on cold sand falls.
Through the window gap of the bower
I see the songstress sing the Backyard Flower.

The Terrace Wall

---

① Xu Yuanchong: Song *Lyrics in Paintings*

(5) Shen's Garden

Shen's Garden is located in Shaoxing, Zhejiang Province. It used to be the private garden of a wealthy businessman in the Southern Song Dynasty with the family name Shen. When mentioning this garden nowadays, one cannot help thinking of the disconsolate love story between Lu You and his wife Tang Wan. The couple's happy marriage life lasted only three years, ending when they were forced to divorce by Lu's mother. Eleven years after their divorce, they met again in Shen's Garden. Deeply moved by their past love, Lu You wrote the famous *Phoenix Hairpin* on the wall (Photograph 5.4).

*Phoenix Hairpin*① 《钗头凤》
Lu You

Phoenix Hairpin

Pink hands so fine,
Gold-branded wine,
Spring paints the willows green palace walls can't confine.
East wind unfair,
Happy times rare.
In my heart sad thoughts throng;
We've severed for years long.
Wrong, wrong, wrong!
Spring is as green,
In vain she's lean.
Her kerchief soaked with tears and red with stains unclean.
Peach blossoms fall
Near deserted hall.
Our oath is still there. Lo!
No words to her can go.
No, no, no!

Lu You and Tang Wan's love story is very moving and the lyric expressing sincere affection are more heart-breaking.

---

①Xu Yuanchong: *Song Lyrics in Paintings*

Photograph 5.4 Lu You's *Phoenix Hairpin* in Shen's Garden
(Original picture from Zheng Yijiao)

5.3.3 Prose

There are various styles of ancient prose, mainly Ji (记, articles of describing landscapes or expressing one's emotions), Shuo (说, a literary form of narration, comment, or explanation), Biao (表, articles written by ministers to emperors), Zengxu (赠序, articles or encouragement given to a friend at parting), and travelogue.

When talking about travelogues, one cannot fail to mention the great works created by Xu Xiake, who was a famous traveller, geographer, and writer in the Ming Dynasty. During 34 years of travelling around China, he wrote 17 articles about Mount Tiantai, Mount Yandang, Mount Huang, Mount Lu and other famous mountains in China, as well as travelogues in Guangxi, Guizhou, Yunnan, etc. Xu Xiake made detailed records of geography, geology, hydrology, and botanical resources. In addition, his talented linguistic expression made his work a masterpiece both in geography and literature. Xu Xiake is also significant for China's tourism industry. China's Tourism Day is on May 19 because the first article in *The Travels of Xu Xiake* was written on May 19, 1613. After over 400 years, the natural landscapes depicted in his travelogue still attract tourists both locally and from abroad. For instance, he had been to Mount Huangshan twice and left a very high appraisal that is summarized by contemporary Chinese people as "one needn't go to the Five Sacred Mountains after visiting Mount Huangshan".

Compared with poems, lyrics, and antithetical couplets, prose and travelogues are not confined in terms of length. Therefore, writers can describe scenes vividly and express their feelings freely.

(1) Wulingyuan scenic area

There are several places named The Peach Colony in China, such as Changde in Hunan Province, Youyang in Chongqing Municipality, and Nanyang in Henan Province. However, the prototype of such a perfect place is not ascertained. Most scholars believe that it was a utopia yearned for by Tao Yuanming and the people of that time, reflecting their discontentment with their social reality.

*The Peach Colony*① *《桃花源记》*

Tao Yuanming

During the reign of Taiyuan of Chin, there was a fisherman of Wuling. One day he was walking along a bank. After having gone a certain distance, he suddenly came up on peach grove which extended along the bank for about a hundred yards. He noticed with surprise that the grove had a magic effect, so singularly free from the usual mingling of brushwood, while the beautifully grassy ground was covered with its rose petals. He went further to explore, and when he came to the end of the grove, he saw a spring which came from a cave in the hill. Having noticed that there seemed to be a weak light in the cave, he tied up his boat and decided to go in and explore. At first the opening was very narrow, barely wide enough for one person to go in. After a Aozen steps, it opened into a flood of light. He saw before his eyes a wide, level valley, with houses and fields and farms. There were bamboos and mulberries; farmers were working and dogs and chickens were running about.

The Peach Colony

(2) Yueyang Tower

The Yueyang Tower was first built in 215 during China's Three Kingdoms Period, when Lu Su, commander in chief of the forces of Wu, was sent to the area to fortify it and make it into a military training base for his fleet of ships. Standing at a height of 19.42 meters, the tower is a three-layer building made of pure wood and its unique architectural structure vividly shows the delicate designs and skills of ancient workers.

Standing on the tower, visitors can enjoy a panoramic view of the Dongting Lake. As one of the three famous towers of Jiangnan, the Yueyang Tower has long enjoyed a good reputation, ever since the Tang Dynasty. Literary works about Yueyang Tower and Dongting Lake are countless. Liu Yuxi's *"The autumn moon dissolves in soft light of the*

---

① 英文译文参考《林语堂英文作品集：古文小品译英》

lake, unruffled surface like an unpolished mirror bright" [1] displayed a grand and beautiful view for readers, while Du Fu expressed his feeling of sadness: *"No word from friends or kinsfolk dear, a boat bears my declining years. War's raging on the northern frontier, leaning on rails, I shed sad tears."* [2] However, it was Fan Zhongyan's *Yueyang Tower* that made Yueyang Tower's fame even more widespread.

Yue Yang Tower [3] (《岳阳楼记》)

Fan Zhongyan

In the spring of the fourth year of the reign of Qingli, Teng Zijing was banished from the capital to be the governor of Bailing Prefecture...

Now I have found that the finest sights of Bailing are concentrated in the region of Lake Dongting, nibbling the distant hills and gulping down the Yangtze River...

...

But again when I consider the men of old who possessed true humanity, they seem to have responded quite differently. The reason, perhaps, may be this: natural beauty was not enough to make them happy, nor their own situation enough to make them sad. When such men are high in the government or at court, their first concern is for people; when they retire to distant streams and lakes, their first concern is for sovereign...

(Excerpt)

Yue Yang Tower

Fan Zhongyan not only described the strategic position and spectacular view of the Dongting Lake, but also expressed his devotion to the country. His article has been deeply rooted in Chinese people's minds generation after generation.

(3) Prince Teng's Pavilion

The Prince Teng's Pavilion is located in Nanchang, Jiangxi Province and is regarded as the landmark of Nanchang city (Photograph 5.5). The Pavilion was initially built in the fourth year of the Yonghui Period in the Tang Dynasty by Prince Teng, the younger brother of Emperor Li Shimin, when he ruled as the Military Governor of Hongzhou Prefecture. It was in the year 675, on his way to visit his father who was exiled in the country of Jiaozhi (today's Vietnam), that Wang Bo, who was reputed as one of the four talented poets during the early Tang Dynasty, happened to come across with a grand banquet celebrating the reconstruction of the Pavilion. It was at this banquet that Wang Bo

---

①Xu Yuanchong, Ma Hongjun: *300 Tang Poems: An Annotated Edition with Commentaries*
②Xu Yuanchong, Ma Hongjun: *300 Tang Poems: An Annotated Edition with Commentaries*
③Luo Jingguo: *A Selection of Classical Chinese Essays*

wrote a long article handed down through the ages. And it was also this article that made the Prince Teng's Pavilion famous in China; meanwhile, it established Wang Bo's important status in Chinese literature.

Preface to Prince Teng's Pavilion [①] *(《滕王阁序》)*

Wang Bo

It is September, the third month of autumn. The puddles on the ground have dried up and the water in the pond is cool and translucent. At the dusk the rays of the setting sun, condensed in the evening haze, turn the mountains purple...

The rain has just let up and the rainbow has vanished. The sunlight shoots through the rosy clouds, and the autumn water is merged with the boundless sky into one hue. The fishermen can be heard singing the evening songs, their voices drifting as far as the banks of the Poyang Lake...

(Excerpt)

Unfortunately, on his way back from the country of Jiaozhi, Wangbo drowned and palpitated to death at the age of only 27. But fortunately, his article had already become immortal and the *"The rainbow clouds with lonely bird together fly. The autumn water blends with the endless blue sky"* is the best testimony to the grand view.

Photograph 5.5 Prince Teng's Pavilion, Nanchang
(Original picture from Bai Wei)

(4) Mount Taishan

A large and impressive rock mass covering 25,000 hectares and rising to 1,545 meters above the surrounding plateau, Mount Taishan is China's most famous sacred mountain, with exceptional historic, cultural, aesthetic, and scientific value. It was also an important cradle of oriental East Asian culture since the earliest times. Mount Taishan was an important destination for cult worship even before 219 BC, when Emperor Qin Shi Huangdi paid tribute to the mountain to inform heaven of his success in unifying all of China. On the mountain there are 12 historically recorded imperial ceremonies in homage to heaven and earth, about 1,800 stone tablets and inscriptions, and 22 temples, which together make Mount Taishan the most important monument in China, a world-renowned

---

① Luo Jingguo: *A Selection of Classical Chinese Essays*

treasure house of history and culture.

Confucius ever said that the Lu State seemed to be smaller when he was on top of the East Hill and the world was even smaller when he was on top of Mount Taishan. Du Fu's *"I will ascend the mountain's crest; it dwarfs all peaks under my feet"*[①] also eulogized the mountain's magnificence. Besides this, there is a travelogue written by Yao Nai, who was a famous scholar of the Qing Dynasty. In his *Ascend to Mount Taishan*, Yao vividly depicted the splendid view of Mount Taishan and his experience of watching the sunrise in the snow(Photograph 5.6).

Ascend to Mount Tai[②] *(《登泰山记》)*
Yao Nai

In the twelfth month of the thirty ninth year of the Qianlong period, I set out from the capital in a snowstorm, passing by the counties of Qihe and Changjing, then took my way through the northwest valleys of Mount Tai and crossed the Great Wall, arrived at Tai'an.

...

It was in the main a rocky mountain with little earth. The rocks, greenish black, were for the most part square, and round stones were quite scarce. Bushes were few and pines, grown out of the stone crevices, were many, having all levelled tops.

...

But the moment we made the summit, we saw that the dark green mountain was laden with snow, and the sky in the south was suffused with its dazzling light. With the town bathed in the twilight of sunset, the River Wen and Culai Hills were picturesque, and the mountain was girded with a belt of fog.

(Excerpt)

Ascend to Mount Tai

As one of the four wonders of Mount Taishan, the sunrise came alive in the picture Yao described. Something to be proud of is that Mount Taishan was the first cultural and natural heritage site in the world. It was inscribed on the World Heritage List in 1987 by UNESCO, with the comment that "The sacred Mount Taishan was the object of an imperial cult for nearly 2,000 years, and the artistic masterpieces found there are in perfect harmony with the natural landscape. It has always been a source of inspiration for Chinese artists and scholars and symbolizes ancient Chinese civilizations and beliefs."

---

① Xu Yuanchong, Ma Hongjun: *300 Tang Poems: An Annotated Edition with Commentaries*
② Xie Baikui: *A Collection of Chinese Ancient Prose Writings*

Photograph 5.6　The sunrise on Mount Tai
(Original picture from Bai Wei)

(5) Old Drunkard Pavilion

The Old Drunkard Pavilion is located in Chuzhou City, Anhui Province. In 1045, Ouyang Xiu was banished from the court to Chuzhou and soon became bosom friends with a monk in Langya Temple named Zhi Xian. Zhi Xian built a pavilion at the foot of Langya Hill especially for him in the 6th year of Emperor Qingli in the Northern Song Dynasty (1046), and in return, Ouyang Xiu created the now famous prose to mark this event and called it Old Drunkard Pavilion. The prose displayed the surrounding elegant natural beauty and brought fame to the pavilion.

The Roadside Hut of the Old Drunkard [1] 《醉翁亭记》
Ouyang Xiu

The District of Chu is enclosed all around by hills, of which those in the southwest boast the loveliest forests and dales. In the distance, densely wooded and possessed of a rugged beauty, is Mount. Langya. When you penetrate a mile or two into this mountain you begin to hear the gurgling of a stream, and presently the stream—the Brewer's Spring—comes into sight cascading between two peaks. Rounding a bend you see a hut with a spreading roof by the stream, and this is the Roadside Hut of the Old Drunkard. This hut was built by the monk Zhixian. It was given its name by the governor, referring to himself. The governor, coming here with his friends, often gets tipsy after a little drinking; and since he is the most advanced in years, he calls himself the Old Drunkard. He delights less in drinking than in the hills and streams, taking pleasure in them and

The Roadside Hut of the Old Drunkard

---

[1] Luo Jingguo: *A Selection of Classical Chinese Essays*

expressing the feeling in his heart through drinking.

…

Then the sun sinks towards the hills, men's shadows begin to flit about and scatter; and now the governor leaves, followed by his guests. In the shade of the woods birds chirp above and below, showing that the men have gone and the birds are at peace. But although the birds enjoy the hills and forests, they cannot understand the men's pleasure in them; and although men enjoy accompanying the governor there, they cannot understand his pleasure either. The governor is able to share his enjoyment with others when he is in his cups, and sober again can write an essay about it. Who is this governor? Ouyang Xiu of Luling.

(Excerpt)

The Old Drunkard Pavilion takes first place in China's Four Famous Pavilions, together with Taoran Pavilion in Beijing, Aiwan Pavilion in Changsha, and Mid-Lake Pavilion in Hangzhou. It is also the most representative symbol of Chuzhou City. This is mainly because of its unique cultural connotations and profound humanistic spirit. Reading through the whole passage, it seems that one can really experience the pleasure of hill and spring, the pleasure of birds in the forest, and the guests at the banquet with the author. Nowadays, travellers are still attracted to the Old Drunkard Pavilion. In fact, what attracts them is the upright, sincere and optimistic moral quality of Ouyang Xiu as well as his love for his people. The so-called "Old Drunkard Spirit" centered around the Pavilion and Ouyang Xiu's prose has become the most vigorous and distinct image of Chuzhou.

5.3.4 Antithetical couplets

Antithetical couplet refers to the antithetical lines written on paper, cloth, or carved on bamboo and wood. Originating from the tradition of hanging Taofu (桃符, peach wood charms to ward away evil, hung on gates on the Lunar New Year's Eve in ancient times), the antithetical couplet is a unique artistic form of the Chinese language and a treasure of traditional Chinese culture. Influenced by rhythmical proses and poems, during its evolution, antithetical couplets absorbed the features of old-style poems (a form of pre-Tang poetry, usually having five or seven characters to each line, without strict tonal patterns or rhyme schemes), proses, and lyrics. The antithetical feature of couplets actually interlinked with the ancient philosophical concept of *Yin* and *Yang*, displaying the wisdom of the Chinese people.

Antithetical couplets can often be seen in scenic spots in China. The Grand View

Tower in Kunming is renowned for having the longest couplets (180 Chinese characters in all) in China:

五百里滇池奔来眼底,披襟岸帻,喜茫茫空阔无边。看:东骧神骏,西翥灵仪,北走蜿蜒,南翔缟素。高人韵士何妨选胜登临。趁蟹屿螺洲,梳裹就风鬟雾鬓;更苹天苇地,点缀些翠羽丹霞,莫辜负:四围香稻,万顷晴沙,九夏芙蓉,三春杨柳。

数千年往事注到心头,把酒凌虚,叹滚滚英雄谁在?想:汉习楼船,唐标铁柱,宋挥玉斧,元跨革囊。伟烈丰功费尽移山心力。尽珠帘画栋,卷不及暮雨朝云;便断碣残碑,都付与苍烟落照。只赢得:几杵疏钟,半江渔火,两行秋雁,一枕清霜。

The couplets hung on the front hall of Meng Jiangnv Temple in Qinhuangdao City are quite fascinating because of different pauses in reading and the various pronunciations of the same Chinese character:

海水朝朝朝朝朝朝朝落
浮云长长长长长长长消

Compared with other classic literary forms, antithetical couplets are more readable, thus more suitable for ordinary people.

(1) Tanzhe Temple

Located in the Western suburbs of Beijing, Tanzhe Temple was first built in the first year of the Yongjia Reign of the Western Jin Dynasty. It was the first Buddhist temple in Beijing after Buddhism was introduced there. The temple has undergone various cycles of rise and fall throughout its history. In the Heavenly Kings Hall, a statue of Maitreya Buddha is enshrined. Chinese people are quite familiar with the image of the Maitreya Buddha, whose bare breast and smiling face make people feel comfortable and welcomed. There are different antithetical couplets about the Maitreya Buddha in many Chinese temples, but the one in Tanzhe Temple might be the most memorable.

His belly is big enough to contain all intolerable things on earth
His mouth is ever ready to laugh at all snobbish persons under heaven[①]
(大肚能容,容天下难容之事;开口便笑,笑世间可笑之人)

This pair of couplets not only truly depict the portrait of the Maitreya Buddha, but also imply profound wisdom. Whether one believes in Buddhism or not, it is sure to be enlightening, spurring one on to try to be generous and optimistic.

---

①陈刚. 旅游翻译与涉外导游[M]. 北京:中国对外翻译出版社,2004.

(2) Yue Fei Memorial Temple

Besides the main hall and the tombs of Yue Fei and his son Yue Yun, there are also four kneeling statues cast out of white iron in Yue Fei Memorial Temple in Hangzhou (Photograph 5.7). In the eighth year of Emperor Zhengde of the Ming Dynasty, a commander named Li Long cast three kneeling copper statues of Qin Hui, Qin's wife and Moqi Xie in front of Yue Fei's tomb. And in the 22nd year of Emperor Wanli (1594), the vice surveillance commissioner Fan Lai recast the kneeling statues in iron and added a statue of Zhang Jun. The four statues have been damaged and recast for several times. The current four statues were cast in 1979. Beside the kneeling statues, one can also see a pair of antithetical couplets.

The green hill is fortunate to be the burial ground of a loyal general
The white iron was innocent to be cast into statues of traitors[1]
（青山有幸埋忠骨，白铁无辜铸佞臣）

Photograph 5.7   Yue Fei Memorial Temple
(Original picture from Bai Wei)

The sharp contrast between the brave and dignified statue of Yue Fei and the kneeling statues of the four traitors as well this pair of couplets, prove that Chinese people have long admired heroes and adhered to the unified nation.

(3) Pavilion of the Surging Wave

As the oldest classic garden in Suzhou, the Surging Wave Pavilion was first built during the Qingli Reign during the Northern Song Dynasty (Photograph 5.8). It is one of

---

[1]陈刚. 旅游翻译与涉外导游[M].北京：中国对外翻译出版社，2004.

the four famous gardens in Suzhou, together with the Humble Administrator's Garden, the Lion Forest Garden, and the Lingering Garden. The classical gardens in Suzhou can definitely reflect the profound metaphysical importance of natural beauty in Chinese culture through their meticulous design. Words inscribed on plaques, tablets, or pillars all have the purpose of expressing the owner's temperaments, deep emotions, and noble thoughts. There is a stone pavilion named Surging Wave Pavilion on an earthen hill. On the pillars of the pavilion are carved a pair of antithetical couplets compiled by Liang Zhangju, who was a scholar of the Qing Dynasty.

Refreshing breeze and bright moon are of priceless treasures
Nearby water and the distant hill all have tender sentiments[①]

Photograph 5.8　The Pavilion of Surging Waves
(Original picture from Yang Zhaoyu)

Actually, the two lines are quotations from poems written by Ouyang Xiu and Su Shunqin, respectively, both of whom were famous poets in the Northern Song Dynasty. The method of creating poems or antithetical couplets by extracting lines from various poets was called Jiju (cento), and was quite popular during the Song Dynasty. Besides the one in the Surging Wave Pavilion, there are still several other couplets of this kind in China. For example:

Empress Wu Zetian Temple in Lvliang, Shanxi Province.

---

①冯玮.新编导游英语[M].武汉:武汉大学出版社,2003.

She outshone in six palaces the fairest face (Bai Juyi)
She received ministers of ten thousand countries (Wang Wei)
（六宫粉黛无颜色，万国衣冠拜冕旒）
Mochou Lake in Nanjing, Jiangsu Province
The water is emerald like, the hill is dark (Han Yu)
Her robe is made of cloud, her face of flower made (Li Bai)
（水如碧玉山如黛，云想衣裳花想容）
Jiaoshan Hill in Zhenjiang, Jiangsu Province
The setting sun seems so sublime (Li Shangyin)
The tower is too high and cold for me (Su Shi)
（夕阳无限好，高处不胜寒）

The above antithetical couplets were all quoted from poems written by the eminent poets of the Tang and Song Dynasties. As a kind of recreation of poems, Jiju did not lose the connotations of the original poems; on the contrary, they could also produce a brand-new artistic conception, thus having a high artistic and appreciative value. In addition, Jiju could vividly manifest the linguistic attractions of Chinese and the wisdom of the Chinese people.

China Story

Do you want free access?

Exercise

Recommended Reading

Chapter Summary

Ancient Chinese literature has witnessed the long history of China in the form of *Chinese characters*. The appearance of each literary style was the reflection of the social norms of its time and provides precious data for us to study the past. In *A Dream of Red Mansions*, known as an encyclopaedia of China's feudal society, people can find a lot of information about the Qing Dynasty's officialdom, family structure, ethics, architecture, ceremony of weddings and funerals, cuisine, clothing, medicine, poetry, festivals and so on.

Ancient Chinese literature, especially tourism literature, has played an important role in the development of tourism. Nowadays, with the increase in cultural self-confidence and the popularity of some cultural TV programs, the promotion effect of tourism literature has become even more prominent. To some extent, tourism literature helps to popularize scenic spots as an advertisement commentary. Beyond this, the scenic spots' cultural connotations and aesthetic value are also promoted.

Issues for Review and Discussion

1. What are the major styles of poetry of the Tang Dynasty?
2. Do you know of other antithetical couplets concerning famous places of interests in China?
3. What do you think is the importance of literature to tourism development?
4. Do you want to get a free access to the scenic spots by reciting relative literary works?

Chapter 6
Chinese Calligraphy and Painting

Learning Objectives

After reading this chapter, you should have
1. An understanding of the characteristics of Chinese painting and calligraphy;
2. An understanding of the development of Chinese painting and calligraphy in China;
3. An appreciation of Chinese painting and calligraphy as tourist attractions.

Technical Words

English Words	中文翻译
calligraphy	书法
Chinese brush	毛笔
inkstone	砚台
rice paper	宣纸
conception	构想,意境
stroke	笔画
rhythm	节奏感
oracle bone inscription	甲骨文
calligraphy scroll	书法条幅
model	字帖
plaques	匾额
cliff inscription	摩崖
Forest of Steles	碑林
figure painting	人物画
fresco/mural	壁画

Knowledge Graph

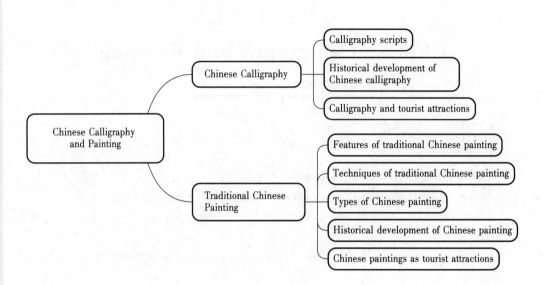

Chinese calligraphy is the stylized artistic writing of Chinese characters. The earliest Chinese characters can be traced back to the script engraved on animal bones and tortoise shells over 3,000 years ago. During its development, Chinese calligraphy has evolved from pictographs into five major categories, seal script (篆书), clerical script (隶书), regular script (楷书), semi-cursive script (行书), and cursive script (草书), each of which has its own different stylistic characteristics. Chinese calligraphy is usually produced using an animal-hair brush, ink, inkstone, and rice paper or silk. An art form closely related to Chinese calligraphy is Chinese painting, which involves the use of similar tools. The main themes of traditional Chinese painting include portraits, landscapes, flowers, birds, animals, insects, and fish.

Chinese calligraphy and painting are treasures of Chinese culture and serve as tourist attractions. The Beilin Museum, with its collection of over 4,000 inscribed tablets dating back to as early as 745 CE, is the must-see place for Chinese calligraphy of diverse styles. On the first day of its exhibition at the Palace Museum, the Qingming Shanghe Tu Scroll[①] attracted 8,500 visitors. This chapter will introduce the features of traditional Chinese painting and calligraphy and their historical development and also some attractions associated with Chinese painting and calligraphy.

---

① The title means "Along the River during the Qingming Festival". It is a scroll (528.7 centimeters long, 24.8 centimeters wide) depicting life and people in Bianjing, the capital of the Northern Song dynasty, painted by Zeduan Zhang over 800 years ago.

Chapter 6 Chinese Calligraphy and Painting

6.1 Chinese Calligraphy

Chinese calligraphy is a symbolic art based on Chinese characters. The beauty of Chinese calligraphy is the beauty of its strokes and styles. A work of calligraphy is made up of a certain number of Chinese characters, seal script (篆书), clerical script (隶书), regular script (楷书), semi-cursive script (行书), and cursive script (草书), each of which is made up of a combination of dots and lines of different forms. The power, rhythm, and strength of the strokes are the aesthetic characteristics of the calligraphic art. The art reflects the spirit, personality, taste, and style of the calligrapher. Many ancient scripts by established calligraphers are still used as models for practice for students and those interested in calligraphy.

Writing brush, inkstick, paper, and inkstone are called the 'Four Treasures of the Study' (Photograph 6.1) and are the common tools used to produce calligraphic works. The brush is made from animal hair shaped with a tapering end and attached to a wooden or bamboo handle. The inkstick is rubbed on the inkstone with water to make liquid ink. Although rice paper is the most commonly used material for practicing calligraphy today, calligraphy work was produced on wood, bamboo, and silk during different historical periods. Chinese calligraphy is used as a classic decorative art and can be found on screens, wall scrolls, and fans and as inscriptions on steles, the plaques of temples or residences, the pillars of pavilions, and rocks on mountains.

Photograph 6.1 Four Treasures of the Study: Writing brush, inkstick, paper, and inkstone

Cangjie is known as the inventor of Chinese characters. Legend has it that he created Chinese characters on the basis of his observations of the footprints of birds and animals. The first characters to be created were nouns based on simplified images of the objects they signify. Then, words with more abstract meaning, such as emotions, behaviors, and judgements, followed. The shape and form of Chinese characters changed gradually throughout the development process.

6.1.1 Calligraphy scripts

Chinese calligraphy can mainly be presented in five scripts, namely seal script (zhuan shu), clerical script (li shu), regular script (kai shu), semi-cursive script (xing shu), and cursive script (cao shu), each of which has its own distinct style.

Seal script

Seal script is a formal style used for seals and other official documents. Each character is presented in an imaginary square of the same size with lines of even thickness (see Photograph 6.2). Curves and circles are commonly seen in this style. This style was created by Li Si, the first prime minister of the Qin dynasty and is still in use for seal carvings and occasional inscriptions, providing an antique flavor.

Photograph 6.2 *Wen Ming* (meaning "civilization") in seal script
Source: Shi Dai

Clerical script

Clerical script, as its name indicates, is used for keeping official records and documents. The style is characterised by its flat and square structure (see Photograph 6.3). Different from the circular strokes of seal script, clerical script has angular and regulated strokes. The beginning of horizontal lines resembles the head of a silkworm, and the end looks like the tail of a wild goose. In the Han dynasty, clerical script was used for writing all official documents and stele inscriptions.

Photograph 6.3 *Wen Ming* (meaning "civilization") in clerical script
Source: Shi Dai

Regular script

Evolving from clerical script in the late Han dynasty, regular script turned from flat form into an upright and regular structure (Photograph 6.4). It was the standard form for printing and is the script most widely used today. Learners usually begin with regular script to study the placement and balance of calligraphy art and then progress to other scripts after mastering the skill of controlling the brush.

Photograph 6.4　*Wen Ming* (meaning "civilization") in regular script
Source: Shi Dai

Semi-cursive script

Semi-cursive script was developed from regular script in the late Han dynasty and can be written faster and smoother than the latter due to its fluid structure. There are fewer angular lines than in regular script. The characters are rounded in shape (Photograph 6.5). There is more flexibility for calligraphers to create their own style with this script. Learners usually practice regular script before semi-cursive script and then move on to cursive script.

Photograph 6.5　*Wen Ming* (meaning "civilization") in semi-cursive script
Source: Shi Dai

Cursive script

Cursive script is also called running script as the strokes are much simplified and quick to produce. The characters can be finished with a single, continuous movement of the brush, taking a rounded and angle-less form (Photograph 6.6). This script evolved from clerical script in the Han dynasty and developed until the middle of the Tang dynasty. It is the "wildest" among the five main scripts. Calligraphers have considerable freedom to express their feelings via this script, and the characters can be difficult to recognise immediately. It is worth noting that there are still rules for the production of this script, despite the merging and linkage of strokes.

Photograph 6.6   *Wen Ming* (meaning "civilization") in cursive script
Source: Shi Dai

6.1.2 Historical development of Chinese calligraphy

The beginning stage

Chinese characters can be traced back to the script written on tortoise shells and animal bones, known as *Jiaguwe*. That script was widely used in the Shang dynasty for divinations, sacrifices, and other sacred rituals, and so it is also called oracle bone script. It represents the beginning of Chinese calligraphy.

Later, Chinese characters were used on bronze vessels which were used to hold wine or food in ancestor worshipping ceremonies in the late Shang dynasty. As they were cast on the inside of bronze vessels, these characters were called metal script, or *Jinwen*. While their general structure was similar to that of oracle bone script characters, metal script characters were more elaborate and expressive.

During the Warring States period, writing was used on stone drums. The writing of this period shows a balanced and graceful structure with smooth lines and no trace of pictographic characters. Stone drum script has an important position in the history of calligraphy as it served as the foundation for the formation of seal script.

The development stage

Ying Zheng, the first emperor of the Qin dynasty, united China under one government. He ordered his prime minister, Li Si, to standardize Chinese characters. Li Si unified the different styles and created the seal script. The font of seal script is quite standard. Its structural characteristics directly inherit the characteristics of stone drum script. One of the most celebrated calligraphy works by Li Si is the Mount Taishan Inscription, which was initially carved on Mount Tai in 219 BC and is now located in the Dai Temple in Tai'an City.

It is time-consuming to write in seal script due to its complex rules. Clerical script was created to facilitate writing. It is said that Cheng Miao of the Qin dynasty created clerical script when he was in prison. The emperor Ying Zheng was pleased with the new script and set him free. Clerical script was then in use during the Qin dynasty and thrived during the Han dynasty, when it was used for official records and documents.

The cursive script that evolved from seal script is faster to write and was one of the most popular scripts in the Han dynasty. The first book on Chinese calligraphy, titled *Cao Shu Shi*(《草书势》), was written by Cui Yuan during the Eastern Han dynasty and covered the skills of cursive script.

The prosperity stage

During the Wei, Jin, Southern, and Northern dynasties, calligraphy entered an unprecedented period of prosperity. Regular script developed from clerical script during the era of the Three Kingdoms and matured during the Eastern Jin dynasty. Semi-cursive script was created during the Jin dynasty. Wang Xizhi, the Saint of Calligraphy, produced the work *Lan Ting Xu*(《兰亭序》, literally *Preface to Orchid Pavilion*), known as the best semi-cursive script in China's history. However, the original version has not been found. Photograph 6.7 shows a model by Feng Chengsu, a calligrapher during the Tang dynasty. This version is recognised as the best extant model of Wang Xizhi's *Lan Ting Xu*.

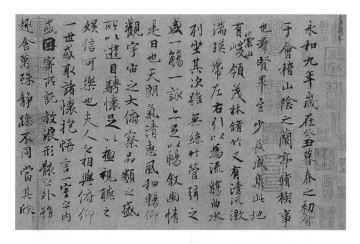

Photograph 6.7 Feng Chengsu's model of Wang Xizhi's *Lan Ting Xu*
Source: https://www.shumobaijia.com/beitie/1899.html

The development of calligraphy art in the Sui, Tang, and Five dynasties was unparalleled. The unification of the country and the emphasis on cultural undertakings led to great progress in calligraphy art. A large number of established calligraphers emerged, such as Ouyang Xun, Yan Zhenqing, Zhang Xu, and Liu Gongquan.

The uneven stage

Chinese calligraphy faced a challenging period during the Song, Yuan, Ming, and Qing dynasties due to the complicated internal and external environment. During the Song dynasty, calligraphy art focused on uniqueness instead of skills. One of the most influential calligraphers of the Yuan dynasty was Zhao Mengfu, whose style is regarded as one of the top four examples of Chinese calligraphy, the others being the styles of Ouyang

Xun, Yan Zhenqing, and Liu Gongquan. The Ming dynasty saw more liberated and diverse styles of calligraphy. The calligraphers in the Qing dynasty took more interest in seal and clerical inscriptions and developed a Stelae School in opposition to the Model Book School.

6.1.3 Calligraphy and tourist attractions

Chinese calligraphy and tourism are closely linked, and calligraphy can be found at many tourist attractions in China in the form of couplets, plaques, and stone inscriptions. The calligraphy is often highly skillful and exceptionally exquisite. This section briefly examines couplets, plaques, and cliff inscriptions.

Couplets

A couplet is a pair of consecutive verses characterised by rhythmic correspondence. Originating in the period of the Five dynasties, Chinese couplets are not only a classic literary style but also a popular decorative element of natural and man-made attractions that highlight the charm of a place. The number of words in a couplet is not fixed, but a couplet requires neat pairs and harmonious pings and tones. Generally, couplets do not have punctuation marks. For some long couplets, it can be difficult to accurately break a sentence down. One can try to break a sentence on the basis of the content and antithesis rules.

After being written, couplets are usually pasted, engraved, or hung on walls and columns. A couplet is divided into an upper line, which is put on the right, and a lower line, which is put on the left. The upper line and the lower line should have inverse (or identical) tone patterns, although usually this rule is not closely followed. Corresponding characters should have the same word category (noun-noun, verb-verb, etc.). The last character of the upper line should be of an oblique tone, and its counterpart in the lower line should be of a level tone.

A selection of couplets from tourist destinations is provided below.

Photograph 6.8 shows the couplet inscribed into the Nantian Gate, located close to the top of Mount Taishan, which describes the amazing view from that location. "门辟九霄,仰步三天胜迹;阶崇万级,俯临千嶂奇观" means the gate is located in the sky, leading to the magnificent view after a long climb; the thousand steps arise, overlooking the wonder of the countless peaks of the mountain.

Photograph 6.8 Couplet on Nantian Gate on Mount Taishan
Source: https://www.163.com/dy/article/GOGD40VF05488C2U.html

Photograph 6.9 shows the couplet on the Surging Wave Pavilion in Cang Lang Garden in Suzhou (苏州). "清风明月本无价；近水远山皆有情" means the breeze and moon are priceless, and rivers and mountains are affectionate. The upper line was taken from the poem *Surging Wave Pavilion* by Ouyang Xiu, who was a friend of the owner of the garden, Su Shunqin. The lower line was taken from the poem *Passing Suzhou* written by Su Shunqin himself. However, the two lines were not put into a couplet until 800 years later by Liang Zhangju, who wrote a book on couplets. Liang repaired Surging Wave Pavilion and wanted to put the couplet on it. However, he was not happy with the calligraphy work after trying many times. After a few decades, the couplet was written by the scholar Yu Yue and carved into the pillars of the pavilion.

Photograph 6.9 Couplet on Cang Lang Pavilion
Source: https://dp.pconline.com.cn/dphoto/list_3198107.html

Plaques

A plaque is a flat tablet hung above a gate or door or below an eave for decoration, and it is used to indicate the name or nature of a building or to express feelings or ideas. The plaque "正大光明", meaning "just and honorable", above the imperial throne in Palace of Heavenly Purity in the Forbidden City was written by the Emperor Shunzhi (Photograph 6.10). Photograph 6.11 shows the plaque "万世师表", meaning "an exemplary teacher for all ages", written by the Emperor Kangxi when he paid respect to Confucius at the Confucius Temple in Qufu (曲阜) in 1684.

Photograph 6.10　The plaque "just and honorable" above the imperial throne in Palace of Heavenly Purity
Source: https://baijiahao.baidu.com/s?id=1686668930814941826&wfr=spider&for=pc

Photograph 6.11　The plaque "an exemplary teacher for all ages" at the Confucius Temple
Source: https://baike.so.com/gallery/list?ghid=first&pic_idx=1&eid=7138828&sid=7362317

Cliff inscriptions

Cliff inscriptions date back to the Qin dynasty. They have been widely used through all dynasties to record history, praise merits and achievements, and express views and affection. In some cases, images are carved along with the texts. Photograph 6.12 shows the cliff inscription "五岳独尊" (meaning "Top of the Five Sacred Mountains") written in regular script at Mount Taishan by Yu Gou in 1907 during the Qing dynasty. Photograph 6.13 shows an inscription by one of the most established calligraphers of the Song dynasty, Mi Fu (1051 – 1107). 南明山 is the name of the mountain and means "Southern Bright Mountain".

Photograph 6.12 Cliff inscription 五岳独尊 ("Top of the Five Sacred Mountains") on Mount Taishan.
Source: https://baike. so. com/gallery/list? ghid=first&pic_idx=1&eid=6585927&sid=6799698

Photograph 6.13 Cliff inscription on Southern Bright Mountain.
Source: http://lsrb. lsxw. net. cn/Article/index? aid=1675711

Case Study

Forest of Steles

6.2 Traditional Chinese Painting

Chinese painting is one of the world's oldest artistic traditions, with 6,000 years of history. It is closely associated with Chinese calligraphy. Both art forms involve the use of a brush, ink, and paper or silk. Like calligraphy, traditional paintings produced on paper and silk can be mounted on scrolls and hung on the wall as decoration. Paintings can also be produced on album sheets, walls, lacquerware, folding screens, and other media. It is common for Chinese paintings to have calligraphy elements in them.

6.2.1 Features of traditional Chinese painting

The pursuit of resemblance is an important feature of Chinese painting. While Western painting emphasises 'likeness of form', Chinese painting seeks 'resemblance of spirit'. For example, Chinese painting aims to show the spirit and personality of a person in a portrait; in the case of animals and plants, the focus is their morphological characteristics and liveliness. One of the main features of Chinese painting is the use of lines and strokes. The variations in the density, complexity, straightness, rigidity, and softness of the lines and strokes create a rich rhythm. The standards for evaluating a Chinese painting are the vitality of the brushstrokes and the harmonious rhythm of the composition.

Another feature of Chinese painting is its emphasis on symbolism. For example, the blossom of the Chinese plum symbolizes the spirit of bravery and endurance, fighting against the cold and unfavorable environment. Chinese painters tend to select painting subjects to express their aspirations, principles, and feelings. Therefore, when we appreciate Chinese painting, we need to study the context of the painting when it was produced to fully understand its artistic conception.

The third feature of Chinese painting is that it is usually accompanied with poetry, calligraphy, and a seal impression. Before the Tang period, painters either did not leave their names on their paintings or put them in a discreet corner to avoid disrupting the composition of the art work. Starting in the Song dynasty, painters began to use tikuan(题款), words that indicated when and where the painting was completed and the name of the painter, usually completed with a seal. During the Yuan dynasty, it became more common to have a tiba(题跋), or preface and postscript, on the painting. A tiba can take the form of a poem or a short essay to note down the painter's feelings or thoughts associated with the painting. The style of the tiba should be compatible

Photograph 6.14 "Bamboo and Rocks"(《竹石图》)by Zheng Banqiao

with that of the painting. For example, regular script and cleric script are usually used for meticulous-style paintings, while semi-cursive and cursive script are usually used for freehand-style paintings.

Photograph 6.14 shows the masterpiece "Bamboo and Rocks" by Zheng Banqiao, one of most outstanding artists of the Qing dynasty. He was renowned for his talent in painting, calligraphy, and poetry. The poem in the painting means "Between broken rocks striking my root deep, I bite the mountain green and won't let go. From whichever direction the winds leap, I remain strong, though dealt many a blow"[①] (咬定青山不放松,立根原在破岩中。千磨万击还坚劲,任尔东西南北风)". Bamboo is strong and resilient, symbolizing a proud and unyielding spirit. The poem helps to point out the theme of the painting, through which Zheng praised the bamboo for its virtues.

In addition, Chinese painting may transcend time and space. Scenes of different moments in time and space can be put in the same picture. Chinese painting is not limited by time and space. For example, the "Hundred Flowers Scroll"《百花图卷》(Photograph 6.15) painted by Zhou Zhimian in the Ming dynasty intricately organizes the flowers of the four seasons in one painting. The painting "This Land so Rich in Beauty"《江山如此多娇》by Fu Baoshi and Guan Shanyue depicts stunning views from different places, including a snowcapped mountain, the Great Wall, and the Yellow River under the rising sun.

Photograph 6.15 "Hundred Flowers Scroll" by Zhou Zhimian

6.2.2 Techniques of traditional Chinese painting

There are two major painting techniques in traditional Chinese painting: gongbi style and xieyi (写意) style. Gongbi (工笔), or the meticulous style, meaning "working pen", is a realist technique which pays close attention to details and fine brushwork. It is usually highly coloured and used for portraits or narrative subjects.

---

① Translated by Xing Quanchen (邢全臣)

In contrast, xieyi, or freehand style, generalizes shapes and employs ink techniques frequently. It emphasises flexibility in brushwork, unrestricted by insignificant details and discarding the realistic effects valued by the meticulous style. The painting process is at the will of the artist's mood and subjective state. Although this style appears whimsical and the subject is shown in exaggerated forms, it demands close observation of the painting subject and a high level of technical proficiency.

6.2.3 Types of Chinese painting

Chinese painting can be classified into three categories by theme: figures, landscapes, and birds and flowers. Figure painting is a generic term for paintings with people, including emperors, court ladies, common people, and religious figures, as the main subject. In figure painting, the artist strives to portray characters in a realistic way through depictions of the environment and atmosphere and people's manner and posture. Wu Daozi, known as the Saint of Chinese painting, was especially good at painting religious figures and people. One of his masterpieces depicts the King holding his newborn son Sakyamuni to thank the Buddhist gods after the birth of the baby (Photograph 6.16).

Photograph 6.16 "Heavenly King Sending the Son"《天王送子图》by Wu Daozi
Source: https://www.juhaohua.com/art/48529.html

Landscape painting depicts the natural scenery of mountains, rivers, buildings, transportation vehicles, bridges, weathers, and seasons. It gradually developed during the Wei, Jin, and Northern and Southern dynasties but was mostly used as background for figure painting. It became an independent theme during the Sui and Tang dynasties and flourished during the Five dynasties and the Song dynasty. Landscape painting can take different modes, including the blue-green mode, which use the mineral colours blue and green for decoration, and the gold-blue-green mode, which adds gold to obtain a rich decorative effect.

Landscape painting stresses the importance of structure and artistic conception. *Spring Outing* (《游春图》) (Photograph 6.17), which displays a delightful spring scene with mountains, trees, a lake, a bridge, a waterfall, and people riding horses, boating, and enjoying the views, is a great example of early landscape painting by Zhan Ziqian in the Sui dynasty.

Photograph 6.17 *Spring Outing* by Zhan Ziqian

Source: https://www.comuseum.com/painting/masters/zhan-ziqian/spring-excursion/#Spring%20Excursion

Flower-and-bird painting is a traditional Chinese painting discipline and refers to paintings in which plants and animals are the main objects of depiction. Although called flower-and-bird painting, this category of painting actually covers a wider range of themes, such as fruit, vegetables, grass, insects, fish, and beasts, in addition to flowers and birds. These objects mainly appear as ornamental patterns on daily utensils or in the background of early figure paintings. It was not until the Wei, Jin, Southern, and Northern dynasties that flower-and-bird painting became an independent art form. Many of the subjects of flower-and-bird paintings have been given symbolic meaning. Typical examples of flower-and-bird paintings are "Four Gentlemen" and "Three Friends of Winter". The Four Gentlemen refer to the plum blossom, the orchid, the bamboo, and the chrysanthemum, which represent the traits of fortitude, nobleness, integrity and modesty. The Three Friends of Winter are the pine, the bamboo, and the plum blossom as they endure in unfavorable conditions. Photograph 6.18 shows *Butterflies Sketched from Life* painted by Zhao Chang in the Song dynasty.

Photograph 6.18 *Butterflies Sketched from Life* by Zhao Chang

6.2.4 Historical development of Chinese painting

The earliest paintings were found on Stone Age pottery and were ornamental patterns such as spirals, zigzags, and animals. It was not until the Warring States period that paintings became representational. Many of the early Chinese paintings were discovered at burial sites. Some were produced on silk, lacquered items, and tomb walls. Paintings from this era can be seen on an artistically elaborate lacquer coffin from the Baoshan Tomb. An early painting on silk from the Western Han dynasty was found along with exquisitely decorated funerary items in a tomb at Mawangdui, Changsha, Hunan (湖南长沙).

In the first century, Buddhism was introduced to China and religious murals became popular. Paintings were found on the walls of grottoes and temples. Many valuable Chinese paintings can be seen on the walls of the Dunhuang Grottoes in Dunhuang and the Maijishan Grottoes in Tianshui (天水).

The period of the Sui and Tang dynasties was a prosperous era for Chinese culture and art. During the Tang dynasty, figure painting featuring Buddhas, monks, emperors, and officials was highly developed, especially in Buddhist painting and court painting. Yan Liben was one of the most established painters of the Tang dynasty, and he was particularly good at figure painting. Examples of his great artwork include *Bu Nian Tu* (《步辇图》), depicting Emperor Tang Taizong meeting Tibetan emissaries, and *Emperors of Previous Dynasties* (《历代帝王图》). In this period, landscape and flower-and-bird painting also began to develop as independent disciplines. Landscape painting in particular developed into a variety of styles and schools, such as the "blue and green landscape" school represented by Li Sixun and his son Li Shaodao and the "ink landscape" school represented by Wang Wei, who was also an established poet. The ink landscapes do not depict real landscapes in a realist manner but rather seek to capture the spirit and rhythm of nature.

The Song dynasty was a period when landscape painting and flower-and-bird painting flourished. During the Song dynasty, painting was incorporated into the imperial examinations, and a style of court painting characterised by elegance and fine workmanship was formed. Landscape painting placed great emphasis on the spiritual qualities of the painting and on the ability of the artist to reveal the inner harmony of human and nature promoted by Daoist and Buddhist teachings. The subjects of figure painting extended beyond religious themes to include historical events and everyday life. The techniques of figure painting also became further refined. During the Southern Song period, court painters such as Ma Yuan and Xia Gui used strong black brushstrokes to sketch trees and rocks and pale washes to suggest misty space.

During the Yuan dynasty, landscape painting, flower-and-bird painting, and figure painting all developed significantly. Many famous painters emerged, the most influential of whom were Zhao Mengfu and the 'Four Masters of the Yuan Dynasty'—Huang Gongwan, Wu Zhen, Ni Zan, and Wang Meng. Huang Gongwang's famous painting *Dwelling in the Fuchun Mountains* (《富春山居图》) depicts the exquisite scenery of the Fuchun River with pale, clean brushwork and a beautiful mood. Wu Zhen specialized in painting landscapes, plum blossoms, bamboo, and rocks. One can tell his aspiration for solitude from the pale and tranquil scenery of the mountains and rivers in his paintings. Most of Ni Zan's works were characterised by desolate artistic conception and dry brushwork. He used ink monochrome only and left large areas of the paper empty. His paintings are usually composed of a rustic hut and some trees and mountains, with no indication of human presence. The extant works of Ni Zan include *Dwelling amidst Water and Bamboo* (《水竹居图》), *Riverside Pavilion and Mountain Hues* (《松林亭子图》), *Enjoying the Wilderness in an Autumn Grove* (《秋林山色图》), and *Six Gentlemen* (《六君子图》). Wang Mengduo depicted the life of seclusion in the deep mountains in his paintings, such as *Reading in Spring Mountain* and *Dwelling in Summer in the Mountains*. Painting in the Yuan dynasty attached great importance to the expression of subjective taste and the style of brush and ink. In addition, the integration of poetry, calligraphy, and painting was popular.

In the early Ming dynasty, painting followed the style from the previous dynasty. In the mid 15th century, Suzhou became the economic and cultural center of south China. The strong retro-cultural trend led to the rise of the Wu School of painting and the emergence of the four Wu School artists—Shen Zhou, Wen Zhengming, Tang Bohu, and Qiu Ying. Shen Zhou's style of painting is sophisticated. His works show his open-minded personality and his pursuit of spiritual freedom, as in the paintings *Poet on a Mountaintop* (《杖藜远眺图》) and *Landscape with Autumn Foliage* (《秋景山水图》). Tang Bohu was Shen Zhou's student. His paintings are rich in themes and fresh and natural in style. He was good at landscape painting, figure painting, and flower-and-bird painting, as can be seen from masterpieces such as *Companions in the Spring Mountains* (《春山伴侣图》), *Autumn Wind* (《秋风纨扇图》), and *Bamboos in the Rain* (《雨竹图》). Wen Zhengming was a friend of Tang Bohu. The subjects of his paintings were mainly landscapes, with light and soft colours. His masterpieces are *Spring in the South* (《江南春图》) and *Tall Trees in the Deep Spring* (《春深高树图》). Qiu Ying was an energetic and diligent painter. He produced many complicated and elaborate long scrolls. His painting style was rigorous but not dull, with smooth strokes and elegant charm. His masterpieces include *Sword Pavilion*(《剑阁图》), *Chibi* (《赤壁图》), and *Spring Morning in Han Palace* (《汉宫春晓图》).

After the Ming dynasty, landscape painting, flower-and-bird painting, and figure painting all made great strides, giving rise to numerous styles and schools of painting. In the early Qing dynasty, the Four Wangs School, represented by Wang Shimin, Wang Jian, Wang Hui, and Wang Yuanqi, attached much importance to ink techniques and harmonistic conceptions. They were the conventional school favored by the emperor. In contrast, the Four Monks (Shi Tao, Zhu Da, Shi Xi, and Hong Ren) and the Eight Jinling Families (Gong Xian, Fan Qi, Gao Cen, Zou Zhe, Wu Hong, Ye Xin, Hu Zao, and Xie Sun) were the unconventional schools, pursuing novelty, unquietness, and straightforwardness. In the mid Qing dynasty, the Eight Eccentrics of Yangzhou (扬州八怪) were influential artists, each with their own peculiar style. They were adept at using splash ink techniques and freehand style to express their thoughts and feelings. In the late Qing dynasty, two schools emerged, the Haishang School and the Lingnan School. The former promoted diversity, tolerance, and creative freedom and was especially good at flower-and-bird painting using the freehand style. The latter advocated introducing Western painting styles and integrating them with Chinese painting.

Modern Chinese painting has developed under the influence of traditional painting, folk art, and Western art. A number of schools centered around Shanghai, Beijing, and Guangzhou and exploring new styles have emerged. Shanghai had been the regional center for artists in Jiangsu and Zhejiang provinces from mid 19th century to the early 20th century. This cluster had the largest number of artists, including Liu Haisu, Feng Zikai, and Zhang Daqian. Chinese painting associations, such as Yi Guan, Shanghai Chinese Painting Association, and Baichuan Calligraphy and Painting Association, were set up in Shanghai, Hangzhou, and Nanjing. A number of colleges and universities began to offer Chinese painting programs.

Beijing was the center for artists living in Beijing and Tianjin from the early 20th century. Renowned artists in this region included Qi Baishi, Chen Shiceng, and Qin Zhongwen. In 1920, Jin Cheng and Zhou Zhaoxiang set up the Society for the Study of Chinese Painting, which specialized in teaching and researching traditional Chinese painting. They also organized four Sino-Japanese painting exhibitions.

During the first half of the 20th century Guangzhou had been the regional center for artists living in south China. Famous artists in this area included Gao Jianfu, He Xiangning, and Guan Shanyue, among others. They proposed the reform of Chinese painting and were very influential.

Art academies were established in the 1950s and 1960s in Beijing and Shanghai, respectively, with the mission of developing the Chinese art sector through research, teaching, creating artworks, and international communication. The National Art Museum of China was built for the purpose of the collection, exhibition, and restoration of artworks and research, education, and international exchange and was opened to the public in 1963.

6.2.5 Chinese paintings as tourist attractions

Chinese paintings are important elements of Chinese culture. Historical paintings found on the walls of palaces, caves, and tombs attract tourists from around the world because of their aesthetic, cultural, and educational value. Outstanding artworks by renowned artists have been exhibited in museums and galleries for visitors to appreciate their timeless charm. The following sections will introduce three attractions associated with Chinese painting.

Frescoes in the Mogao Grottoes

The Mogao Grottoes, also known as the Thousand Buddha Caves, are a massive group of caves that were carved into a cliff in the eastern foothills of the Mingsha Mountains in Dunhuang, Gansu Province between the 4th and 14th centuries. In AD 336, some Chinese Buddhist monks and believers began to dig caves on mountains near Dunhuang to house Buddhist statues and for meditation. Most cave owners or patrons had the inside walls and ceilings of their caves painted with religious images and stories.

The Mogao Grottoes were designated a UNESCO World Heritage site in 1987. The site is famous for its statues and wall paintings. The frescoes include Buddha images, Buddhism story paintings, sutra illustrations, human portraits, decorative paintings, and landscape paintings.

The Buddha images include figures of various gods and spirits worshipped by Buddhists, such as Buddha, bodhisattvas, and Buddha guards. A total of 12,208 Buddha figures with different postures have been found in Mogao Grottoes. The Buddhism story paintings are associated with the life story of Shakyamuni and how he helped people with their difficulties. The sutra illustrations use paintings to explain Buddhist sutras with pictures. The themes of some of the frescoes are traditional Chinese legends associated with Taoism. The appearance of Taoist thoughts in Buddhist grottoes reflects the mutual influence of the two religions in China.

The frescoes also show figures of almsgivers, that is, Buddhists who financed the building of grottoes. These figures range from emperors/empresses, royal family members, and government officials to common people and servants. Photograph 6.19

shows the image of Princess of Huihu in an almsgiver painting.

The decorative paintings include sunken panel, rafter, and edge decoration. The pattern changed with time, taking various forms, such as flowers, animals, fire, clouds, and flying apsaras, and revealing the outstanding painting skills and extraordinary imagination of the artists.

Yongle Palace murals

The Yongle Palace (Palace of Eternal Joy), one of the three biggest Taoist temples in China, is located in Ruicheng County, Shanxi Province. It was built to worship Lv Dongbin, the founder of the Quanzhen School of Taoism. It is famous for its Taoist murals, which cover more than 1,000 square meters in different halls of the palace. Construction of the palace started in 1247 during the Yuan dynasty. It took 111 years to complete the palace and the murals in it.

Photograph 6.19 Princess of Huihu in Mogao Grottoes
Source: https://www.sohu.com/a/375166537_120116137

The first building, Sanqing Hall, or the Hall of the Three Saints, is the largest hall of the temple. The walls of Sanqing Hall are covered with intricate murals depicting a grand congregation scene, with Taoist saints and more than 280 other figures, including serene goddesses, obedient attendants, and argumentative followers. The murals demonstrate the superb Taoist painting techniques passed down from the Tang dynasty and the Song dynasty. The meticulous details of the figure painting resemble the style of Wu Daozi. The painting can be seen in Photograph 6.20.

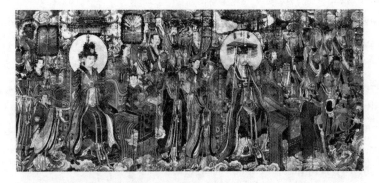

Photograph 6.20 Mural in Sanqing Hall of Yongle Palace

The Chunyang Hall, or the Hall of Pure Yang, is devoted to Lv Dongbin. The mural in this hall portrays scenes from the life of this Taoist master, who was worshipped as an immortal. In depicting the life story of Lv, the murals show ordinary people's daily activities, such as drinking tea, cooking, working in the fields, fishing, cutting firewood, teaching, chatting, and holding memorial or religious ceremonies. There is also a mural on the back of a wall showing a conversation between Lv Dongbin and Zhong Lihan about Taoism.

Chongyang Hall is dedicated to Wang Chongyang, another founder of the Taoist Quanzhen School, and his seven followers. The style of the murals in this hall is quite similar to that of the murals in the Hall of Pure Yang. The murals in Chongyang Hall are believed to have been painted by Zhu Haogu, a leading craftsman in Shanxi Province during the Yuan dynasty, and his students. The paintings are useful references to learn about the architecture, clothing, food, and dress of that time.

Baisha murals

The Baisha murals are religious murals created on the wall of temples in Baisha village during the Ming and Qing dynasties. Baisha village is located about 10km northwest of Lijiang Old Town in Yunnan and is part of the World Heritage Site. Different from other religious murals, the Baisha murals demonstrate a mixture of different religious cultures and artistic forms from Buddhism, Lamaism, Daoism, and the Naxi Dongba religion. According to *Lijiang Fuzhi* (《丽江府志》), the official annals of local history, the murals were painted by Ma Xiaoxian, a painter from the Han ethnic group; Guchang, a Tibetan painter; and other painters from the Naxi and Bai ethnic groups. Therefore, the Baisha murals are a representation of the communication and collaboration between different ethnic groups.

The murals are mainly preserved in Dabaoji Palace, Liuli Temple, Dading Pavilion, and Dajue Temple in Baisha village. Built in 1582, Dabaoji Palace preserves 12 pieces of murals with 167 portraits. The themes of the paintings are mainly religious stories of Taoism, Buddhism, and Lamaism. One of the most famous paintings depicts Sakyamuni explaining the sutra to his followers (Photograph 6.21). There are 16 pieces of murals in Liuli Temple with paintings of mainly Buddha figures. The Liuli Temple was established in 1416 by the chief of the Mu Clan to worship Rulai. The 16 murals show a simple and elegant style without complicated ornaments or diverse colours.

The Dading Pavilion, standing next to the Dabaoji Palace, was built in the Ming dynasty and repaired in 1743 during the Qing dynasty. The 17 well-preserved mural paintings in the Dading Pavilion were created in the Qing dynasty. The bodhisattvas are presented in a vivid state, with decorative birds, flowers, and mountains.

Dajue Temple was built during the Longqing period of the Ming dynasty. The six murals in Dajue Temple mainly follow the Han style. The expression and posture of the figures are lively and precise, reflecting high-level painting techniques. The Baisha murals are an important source for the study of the history of arts and religions in China.

Photograph 6.21 Mural depicting Sakyamuni explaining the sutra to his followers in Dabaoji Palace

Chapter Summary

Chinese calligraphy and painting are enduring art forms with unique Chinese characteristics. Both are produced using an animal hairbrush, ink, inkstone, and rice paper or silk. Traditional Chinese painting pursues 'resemblance of spirit' and emphasises symbolism. It is usually accompanied with Chinese calligraphy, poetry, and a seal impression. There are a lot of classic calligraphy and painting artworks by renowned Chinese artists inscribed into cliffs, painted in grottoes, exhibited at museums, attracting millions of art-lovers and tourists every year.

Issues for Review and Discussion

1. What are the major scripts of Chinese calligraphy and their respective characteristics?

2. What is the relationship between Chinese calligraphy and traditional Chinese paining?

3. What are the major techniques of traditional Chinese painting and their respective features?

4. Give examples of Chinese calligraphy and painting as tourists attractions and discuss their value in enhancing the attractiveness of a place.

China Story

"A Panorama of Mountains and Rivers"

Exercise

Recommended Reading

Chapter 7
Festivals and Events

Learning Objectives

After reading this chapter, you should have a good understanding of
1. The evolution of Chinese festivals and events;
2. The types of modern festivals and events;
3. Modern festivals and events as tourism resources;
4. The paths for tourism development of festivals and events.

Technical Words

English Words	中文翻译
festivals and events	节事
Double Ninth Festival	重阳节
Luner Calendar	农历
tomb-sweeping	扫墓
clan rituals	宗族仪式
put cornel on the head	头上插茱萸
hang wormwood on the door	门上挂苦艾
scented sachet	香袋
chrysanthemum wine	菊花酒
revolving a round the mountain	绕山灵
Water Splashing Festival	泼水节
Nadam Fair	那达慕大会

Knowledge Graph

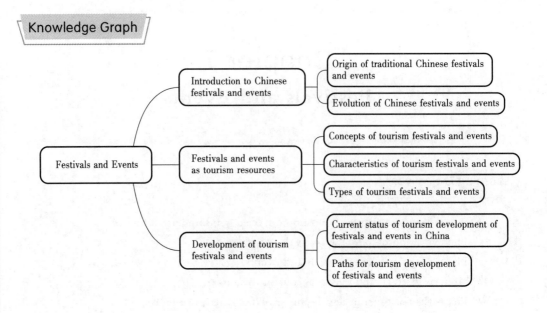

7.1 Introduction to Chinese festivals and events

7.1.1 Origin of traditional Chinese festivals and events

Festivals and events are celebration activities relating to the history, culture, art, sports, and customs of a region. In Western studies, festivals and special events are often discussed as a whole, abbreviated to FSE (Festival & Special Events).

The origin of Chinese festivals and events can be traced back to ancient times. The Spring Festival, Lantern Festival, Dragon Boat Festival, Mid-Autumn Festival, and Double Ninth Festival are the most popular ones continuing today. These festivals and events as well as the activities celebrating them contain unique Chinese cultural memories and are the products of social development associated with different time periods. Since ancient times, festivals and events have been intertwined with astronomy, the agricultural calendar, folk beliefs, and cultural psychology across the history of China, and are permeated with rich connotations of the philosophy, literature, and art of the country. The origin of traditional Chinese festivals and events includes the following aspects.

(1) Agricultural cultivation

Agriculture was the basis of peoples' survival and livelihoods in ancient China, and farming was of great importance to ancient people. The primitive root of the most important traditional Chinese festival, the Spring Festival, is farming. For farmers whose survival depends on the weather, the Spring Festival reflects the desire that "the harvest is abundant". The origins of this festival lie in the celebration of the harvest at the end of the year and indicate a good time to start a new year with a new agricultural production cycle. In the rural areas of China today, people start their spring festival preparation on the 23rd day of the last month of the year of the Chinese Lunar Calendar, and the celebration lasts until the Lantern festival, which is the 15th day of the first month of the year according to the Lunar Calendar.

(2) Ethics of filial piety

Chinese people have a deep affection for their ancestors, whom they worship as gods because ancestors represent their origin and are superior to them in blood relationships. This has been the spirit of Chinese culture for thousands of years, and Chinese people still attach great importance to the birthdays and death dates of their ancestors.

In the Qin and Han dynasties, the custom of tomb-sweeping was infused with etiquette and rituals. Tomb sweeping is a folk tradition in which descendants visit the tombs of their ancestors, clean the tombs and offer food and wine, expressing their memories of their ancestors. Tomb-sweeping is usually organised by a family, a village, or a clan. It is a family ritual of ancestor worship held to pay tribute to deceased ancestors (e.g., deceased grandparents, parents). In addition to family rituals, there were also village rituals and clan rituals, which were grand in scale. These rituals of ancestor worship have today evolved into the Tomb-sweeping Festival (also called the Qingming Festival), which has become the grandest festival of ancestor worship in China. The Tomb-sweeping Festival would not have become a festival of the people without the deep foundation of the traditional Chinese culture of respect for family relationships.

(3) Blessing

Ancient people believed that all things in nature had life and magical powers, so they expressed reverence for the mountains, rivers, lakes, and seas and sought their blessings. People believed that blessing could bring the capture of prey, the arrival of timely wind and rain, and even the harvest of crops. Some of these ancient religious rituals were illustrated on vessels and placed in tombs with the dead. On a bronze shell storage vessel excavated in Shizhai Mountain, Jinning, Yunnan(云南晋宁石寨山), there are pictures of ancient rituals, such as one showing people crowded in a square, singing, dancing, eating, and drinking, as in a festival scene. As time passed many of the religious rituals based on these primitive beliefs evolved into festivals of the people and are the embryonic form of modern festivals and events.

(4) Social entertainment

Festivals and events for social entertainment are parties by nature and their main contents are activities of entertainment, amusement, or competition. Although the entertainment activities of these festivals are not strictly distinguishable from those annual festivals celebrating the harvest and welcoming the new year, social entertainment festivals strengthen interpersonal relationships. The most representative festivals and events for social entertainment are those of festive songs, dances, and folk activities popular in minority areas in China. For example, the Dali(大理)Bai people's annual event "Revolving around the Mountain" from April 23rd to 25th (Chinese Lunar Calendar) is one such, when people dress in festive costumes, singing and dancing in the mountains and forests between the Cang Mountains and Erhai Lake (苍山洱海).

7.1.2 Evolution of Chinese festivals and events

Festivals and events emerged from ancient social life and have been passed down in cultural consciousness. With society's development and changes, festival culture has continued to change over time. From ancient ritual celebrations to today's revelry, the evolution of traditional festivals has seen great changes in the purpose of holding festivals and events, the ways they are held, the host institutions, and the scale of the festivals. Some festivals have ended as they did not adapt to the times, while others have changed their original purpose and manner to adapt to new circumstances and gain a new life. Some of the traditional festivals have been changed to a new form and have once again gained popularity among the public. Many of the changes in the evolution of traditional festivals and events involve the following aspects.

The first is a change in the purpose of festivals and events being held. These changes are manifested in the transformation from traditional festivals and events relating to religious sacrifice, agricultural production to modern festivals with an economic and entertainment aspect. However, the process of transformation has never been smooth, and only those festivals with a unique charm and those that relate closely to local cultural traditions have been able to make such a change. For example, the Xishuangbanna(西双版纳)Dai people's Water Splashing Festival had been a custom of splashing water to wash away the stains of the body and the fatigue of the year, and to pray for the elimination of disasters in the coming year. Nowadays, due to the economic development of tourism, this festival has become a tourist product that brings joy and experience to tourists.

The second is a change in the host organizations and institutions. Traditional festivals and events are usually organised by religious groups, clan groups or the public. These festivals and events are held for commemoration and blessing, containing good wishes for the future. Due to the decline of religious and clan organizations in modern society, many festivals are now organised by the government or enterprises. Some of the modern festivals are the reproduction of traditional ones, some are planned to meet the needs of modern tourists. For example, the Nadam Fair, held every August by the local government of Erdos(鄂尔多斯), has strong nomadic characteristics; in addition to the traditional sports competitions such as wrestling, archery and horse racing which are popular with the Mongolian people, modern commercial activities such as exhibitions, trade fairs and artistic performances are also included in the Nadam Fair.,

The third is a change in the scale of festivals and events. In the process of transformation from traditional festivals to modern ones, the scale of some becomes smaller or larger. There are also new festivals and events born out of thin air, while others are gradually disappearing. Traditional Chinese festivals have had a significant and far-reaching impact on Chinese people's values, moral standards, aesthetic characteristics, and even national spirit. However, with the advent of modernization and influence of Western culture, the precious folk culture created by Chinese ancestors for thousands of years once faded in people's hearts. Fortunately, Chinese traditional festivals have shown a revival trend from the call of scholars to promote Chinese traditional festival culture to the proposal of the deputies of the National People's Congress to increase the number of traditional festival holidays, it can be seen that Chinese traditional festivals are getting more and more attention of the public.

7.2 Festivals and events as tourism resources

7.2.1 Concepts of tourism festivals and events

Tourism festivals and events, as the name suggests, are a fusion of tourism with festivals and events. Festivals and events refer specifically to celebrations that take place at a specific time and for a long time were synonymous with traditional and national festivals and events - typically a large scale celebration held spontaneously and periodically in a certain region or city, based on its unique history, culture, art, customs, or geographical advantages. They are celebrations that are gradually agreed upon by people according to long-standing customs and tend to transform with changes in social customs and ideas. Through these festivals and events and their related activities, people can feel the history of a region and experience its customs and folklore. Therefore, festivals and events are the external expression of tourism festivals and the carrier of cultural succession. Furthermore, the development of the modern tourism industry has added a strong economic significance to festivals and events. More tourism festivals and events have come into being, and in some ways, the nature of tourism is the essence of tourism festivals and events.

China's traditional festivals and events have a long history and contain unique cultural memories of the Chinese people. Many popular festivals such as the Spring Festival and the Lantern Festival have been celebrated for a thousand years or more. Tourism festivals and events take place within the context of modern society where tourism economy brings benefits to places. Although tourism festivals and events are very different from the traditional ones in terms of their formation, many of them rely on the rich connotation of the traditional festivals and events.

Tourism festivals and events are special tourism products developed by the government or enterprises, based on the resources and cultural characteristics of the place where they are held, with tourism as the purpose and various types of events as the carrier. In order for a festival to become a tourism festival, it is important to have a tourism value (i.e., a tourism cultural value and a market value). The cultural value indicates that tourism festivals display regional cultural characteristics, so that the regional culture can be highlighted and inherited, while the economic value refers to the tourists that festivals can attract to the host region, thus bringing economic benefit to the region. In this regard, festivals and events with rich cultural connotations and strong market attraction have a high tourism value, while some traditional national festivals, although they have wide influence, cannot be developed into tourism festivals due to a lack of economic or cultural elements.

Tourism festivals and events not only share commonality with other festivals and events, but also have their own uniqueness. Their uniqueness is mainly reflected in the following aspects: ① purpose-they are held to promote the development of local tourism industry and drive the local economy; ② content-they consider both the needs of local residents and of tourists; ③ form-they are organised events by special organizations to pre-arrange and design the content and form of the festivals.

In summary, tourism festivals and events are dynamic tourism products, and their

Further Reading

International Beach Culture Festival opens in Dalian

most important feature is the pursuit of tourism development. This requires event planners to focus on the needs of consumers in the planning and development of the events, and to explore the highlights and selling points of the products from the market perspective.

7.2.2 Characteristics of tourism festivals and events

As special tourism products, tourism festivals and events have the following characteristics.

(1) Periodicity

Tourism festivals and events are held within a certain period of time, for example, once a year. It is the periodicity of events that breaks the normal order of people's lives and brings novelty and excitement to people. Additionally, the fixed time is conducive to event organization in marketing and tourist reception.

The time and periodicity of tourism festivals are typically determined by the nature, theme, and type of event, as well as the market preference and economic strength of the host region. Some tourism festivals and events use primitive agricultural time as the basis for scheduling event intervals, some depend on seasonal factors (e.g., the Ice and Snow Festival in Harbin), some are related to myths and legends and commemorative activities at specific times (e.g., the Dragon Boat Festival and Qu Yuan legend in Yueyang), and others are arranged at specific times (e.g., the winter swimming festival and rafting festival). No matter what determines the timing of the event, the most important thing is to give people the novelty of breaking the daily norm and to arouse interest and enthusiasm for participation.

(2) Comprehensiveness

The comprehensive nature of tourism festivals and events can be manifested in many ways. The first is its comprehensive content. Tourism festivals and events, especially large events, can comprehensively exhibit the characteristics of a region's folklore, culture, and history that represent the diverse culture of the place. The second is the comprehensive nature of the organization sector. The organization and management of large events involves many departments such as transportation, health, medical, security, urban management, culture, and tourism, requiring strong comprehensive organization and coordination. The third is its comprehensive function. Tourism festivals have a variety of functions including tourism, economy, culture, celebration, and regional image building. This inspires event planners to set up the event and also to plan the event environment and atmosphere to achieve multiple purposes in terms of regional development.

(3) Locality

Locality has long been considered the essence of tourism festivals and events. Locations that have natural, economic, cultural, and historical resources with unique local characteristics are more likely to create event products preferred by tourists and local residents, and are more competitive in the market. The locality provides the charm and life of many tourism festivals and events; if they leave the place of their birth, the personalised appeal of these events will disappear. Accordingly, the extent to which the uniqueness of the local spirit is shown is the key to the success of tourism festivals and events, and this is also the first consideration of festival and event planners.

(4) Participation

Festivals and events need many participants to create a festive atmosphere, otherwise activities will not take place and the event will be dull due to a lack of vitality. Therefore, participation is one of the reasons why tourism festivals and events attract tourists. People participate in events to satisfy their own interests, demonstrate their specialities, or learn new skills through event activities (e.g., wine tasting skills). Only tourism festivals and events with high participation will have a strong vitality.

(5) Entertainment

Tourism festivals and events should avoid being complicated and old-fashioned. Activities that make people feel relaxed and happy will arouse tourists' interest, while complex and bureaucratic rules will result in tourists staying away. An event becomes attractive when people affirm the beauty of their existence with joyous reactions. Sometimes organisers don't want to make the festivals and events easy and straightforward; however, tourists often enjoy events such as fireworks and tug-of-war. While festival planners focus on the purpose and effectiveness of a tourism event, it is important not to make the mistake of assuming that the focus of the organisers is also the focus of tourists who do not go to festivals for the revitalization of the festival site. Without understanding this, even the greatest effort and planning of the largest festivals may not be welcomed by tourists.

The abovementioned characteristics highlight the attributes of "new, novel and special" in tourism products and reflect the dynamic local culture. If tourism festivals and events emphasise these characteristics, they are likely to attract tourists.

7.2.3 Types of tourism festivals and events

China has many different types of tourism festivals and events. By making the characteristics of each type of tourism festival and event clear, the planning of event activities can meet the requirements of the target market. Tourism festivals and events can be classified using the following criteria.

(1) Classification based on event origin

Based on their origin, tourism festivals and events can be divided into those of traditional folklore or modern commercial tourism. Although these two types have different origins, they both aim to bring tourism benefits to the host region as tourist attractions.

a. Traditional folklore tourism festivals and events

This type of tourism festival and event originates from seasonal festivals or folk festivals with a long history. With the development of the tourism economy, these events have gradually developed into tourism products as their cultural connotations which have great potential for attracting tourists. By adding commercial and tourist activities, seasonal festivals or folk festivals are re-planned and packaged to showcase and spread the local spirit. Traditional folklore tourism festivals and events focus on the medium and long-term effects of the comprehensive development of the local economy and culture, and their roles are to enhance local pride and a sense of community belonging as well as to expand local cultural influence. Examples of this type of event include the Xishuangbanna Water Splashing Festival, the Qinghai June 6 Flower Festival, and the Inner Mongolia Naadam Fair.

b. Modern commercial tourism festivals and events

Modern commercial tourism festivals and events originated in the early 1980s and increased rapidly with the development of the tourism economy. Such events tend to be organised by governments or enterprises, who are also the planners of the events. The purpose of these events is to improve the local tourism structure, upgrade the quality of tourist products, strengthen local economic and trade exchanges with the outside world, and promote the accumulation of the stream of people, logistics, and cash flow to achieve both short and medium-term economic benefits for the host regions. This type of event includes food and cultural festivals, Kungfu arts festivals, eco-tourism festivals, carnivals, and mountain climbing festivals. Examples are the Qufu Confucius International Cultural Festival, the Tianshui Fuxi Cultural and Tourism Festival, and the Hohhot Zhaojun Tourism and Culture Festival.

(2) Classification based on operation models of tourism festivals and events

Based on their operation models, tourism festivals and events can be divided into three types: the government-run model, the fully market-oriented model, and the multi-party co-organised model.

a. Government-run model

The government-run model was once widely adopted by cities and small towns to hold tourism festivals and events. The characteristic of this model is that the government plays multiple roles in organizing the event, and is the decision maker in determining the content of festival activities, venue and time, participating units, and so forth. This model places a great financial burden on the government, and it has been found that many events do not lead to the desired economic, social, and cultural benefits. The government has become aware of the drawbacks of the model, and now often cooperates with enterprises and social groups in event planning to improve the quality and success rate of the events.

b. Fully market-oriented model

Tourism festivals and events are a type of economic activity, and the purpose of holding them is to obtain economic benefits and market effects. The fully market-oriented model indicates the tourism festivals and events that take the route of marketization. The advantages of this model include a) cost saving: under the fully market-oriented model, the choice of time, place, and advertising methods are in accordance with the needs of the market, saving costs and avoiding unnecessary waste caused by the intervention of administrative forces; b) maximizing revenue: the benefits are economic and social (e.g., improvement of the image of local government).

c. Multi-party co-organised model

The multi-party co-organised model can also be called the government coordination and guidance, social participation, and market operation model.

This model is more applicable to modern China's conditions and the superiority and benefits of this model are increasingly recognised by all parties. Under this model, the government is still an important organiser, and its coordination and guidance roles are reflected in the organization and deployment of forces, decision-making of the theme, name, and time of the festival, and event promotion. Social participation means the full mobilization of all forces of society to support the event, and the role of social power is reflected in the festival theme, creation of the festival atmosphere, and active participation in event activities. Market operation means that the tourism festivals and events are run using a market operation approach. For example, the naming rights of tourism festivals, sponsors, and advertising can be obtained through bidding, which can stimulate enterprises and institutions to participate. This can expand the visibility of enterprises and institutions, and generate income from the activities supporting the event.

Further Reading

Beer festival showcases brews to outside world

(3) Classification based on event themes

Successful tourism festivals and events have a clear theme that reflects the unique features of the place where the event is held. Tourism festivals and events can be divided into eight types of themes: ethnic cultural tourism, specialty tourism, unique landscape tourism, religious cultural tourism, historical and cultural tourism, folk culture tourism, entertainment and cultural tourism, and recreation and sports cultural tourism.

a. Ethnic cultural tourism festivals and events

Ethnic culture tourism festivals and events reflect the folk customs of the hosting region. These events are attractive to tourists because of their strong ethnic characteristics relating to the host region. In recent years, China's Yunnan, Guangxi, and Guizhou regions, and other areas with a high concentration of ethnic minority groups, have started to hold this type of event. Examples of such events include the Inner Mongolia Grassland Tourism Festival, the Miao People's "March 3", and the Naxi Dongba Cultural Festival.

Ethnic Tujia celebrate Sheba Day in Hunan

b. Specialty tourism festivals and events

Specialty tourism festivals and events refer to those that make use of rare local specialties as the event's selling point, to demonstrate the advantages of local resources, products, and the resulting economic and cultural effects. Investment negotiation, commercial transaction, displays of local speciality products, scientific and technological cooperation, and talent introduction are the main agenda for such festivals. Examples of this type of event include the Shaoxing Yellow Wine Festival, Turpan Grape Festival, Wuchang Fish International Cultural Tourism Festival, Jingdezhen Ceramic Festival, Dalian International Fashion Festival, and Suzhou China Silk Tourism Festival.

c. Unique landscape tourism festivals and events

Unique landscape tourism festivals and events are designed with the local natural and human landscape in mind, using plants and flowers as the carrier of the event. Activities of such events include natural sightseeing, accompanied by certain amusement projects. Examples of this type of event include the Harbin Ice and Snow Festival, China Shennongjia International Ecological Tourism Festival, Guizhou Huangguoshu Waterfall Festival, Luoyang Peony Flower Festival, Qiantang Tide Festival, and Nanjing International Plum Blossom Festival.

Luoyang balances traditions and modern industries

d. Religious cultural tourism festivals and events

Religious cultural tourism festivals and events are related to religious rituals or worship of gods and are held in places with a long history and a rich religious culture. Rural temple fairs and regular worship events at religious sites are the most common events of this type. Examples include the Putuo Mountain South Sea Guanyin Cultural

Festival and the Mount Wutai Buddhist Culture Festival.

Qixi-themed event kicks off in Jiading

e. Historical and cultural tourism festivals and events

Historical and cultural tourism festivals and events are designed using local historical figures, events, and culture as carriers of the event. Some of these festivals include memorable ceremonies and activities relating to decreased celebrities. For example, the China Qufu International Confucius Culture Festival holds sacrificial activities to express the descendants' respect and memory of the master Confucius. Other examples include the Anyang Yin Shang Tourism Festival, Qufu International Confucius Cultural Festival, Silk Road Cultural Festival, and Pingyao Ancient City Cultural Festival.

f. Folk culture tourism festivals and events

Folk culture tourism festivals and events make use of regional folklore to showcase and promote the essence of local folk culture, bringing economic and cultural benefits to the host region. The main purpose of these events is to show visitors the unique folk culture of the region, material or spiritual. Examples of this type of event include the Dragon Boat Festival, Ghost City Fengdu Folk Culture Festival, International Kite Flying Festival, and Longqingxia Ice Lantern Festival.

g. Entertainment and cultural tourism festivals and events

Entertainment and cultural tourism festivals and events do not rely on the local cultural and tourism resources of the host region. In fact, the host region does not typically have any valuable resources for use; however, the location usually has strong economic power, good infrastructure, advanced technology, and the ability to organise large-scale tourism events. In these areas, the local government or the commercial sector is prompted to organise various kinds of tourism festivals and events to satisfy the cultural needs of the residents. The main purpose of these festivals is to bring pleasure to the participants. Examples of this type of event include the Hainan Island Fun Festival, Hangzhou Carnival, and Shenzhen Overseas Chinese Town Fun Festival.

h. Recreation and sports cultural tourism festivals and events

Recreation and sports cultural tourism festivals and events are developed using martial arts, bathing programs, or fitness and recreational activities. The purpose is to let tourists experience spiritual enjoyment and improve their physical fitness at the same time, so this type of event has become very popular among young participants in recent years. Examples include the Yueyang International Dragon Boat Festival, Zhengzhou International Shaolin Festival, and Wuhan River Crossing Festival.

(4) Classification based on the major function of tourism festivals and events

Based on their major functions, tourism festivals and events can be divided into four types: sightseeing tourism, commercial and economic tourism, folk culture tourism, and multi-functional comprehensive tourism.

a. Sightseeing tourism festivals and events

Sightseeing tourism festivals and events showcase the beautiful natural scenery, man-made landscapes, and the historical and cultural sites of the host region as attractions, and sightseeing is an integral part of this type of event. The aims are aesthetic enjoyment as well as emotional and physical pleasure through event participation. Examples include the Shennongjia International Ecological Tourism Festival and the Hubei Dabie Mountain Ecological Tourism Festival.

b. Commercial and economic tourism festivals and events

This type of event provides a showcase of a variety of local specialities and business and trade opportunities, in which visitors are also direct or potential participants of the business activities relating to the event themes. The original purpose of commercial and economic tourism festivals and events is to promote inter-regional trade and commerce using the event as a vehicle. Examples include the Dalian Fashion Festival and the Jingdezhen Ceramic Tourism Festival.

c. Folk culture tourism festivals and events

Folk culture tourism festivals and events provide tourists with local folk culture. Tourists can gain cultural knowledge through participation in these events. Examples include the Ma'anshan International Poetry Festival and the Nanning International Folk Song Festival.

d. Multi-functional comprehensive tourism festivals and events

This type of event is comprehensive in both themes and contents, with multiple components, such as sightseeing exhibitions, commercial and trade conventions, and folk culture tourism activities. These festivals are generally held in large cities, and have a rich content, cultural diversity, and significant economic, social, and cultural benefits. Examples include the Beijing International Cultural Tourism Festival and the Wuhan International Tourism Festival.

7.3 Development of tourism festivals and events

7.3.1 Current status of tourism development of festivals and events in China

Tourism festivals and events differ from general tourism products in that they are not only a tourism project, but also a carrier of human, logistic, information, and capital flows. Because of these characteristics, tourism festivals and events have developed rapidly in a short time throughout the country since the 1980s, with the developmental trend described as "starting a prairie fire". In the past few decades, holding tourism festivals and events has been the choice of many regions to boost their local economy. The development of tourism festivals and events tends to have the following characteristics.

Firstly, the content and type of festival tourism activities are diverse. At present, tourism festivals and events are held all over the country. From first-tier cities to small counties and towns, tourism festivals and events are becoming more diverse in both their content and type; for example, festivals and events based on history and culture, exhibitions, sports and leisure, entertainment and leisure, and folk customs.

Secondly, tourism festivals and events are mostly organised by local governments of the host region in China. The development of tourism in China has long used a government-led strategy. Since the central government of China promoted tourism as a pillar industry of the country and supported its development and growth, most provincial and municipal governments of the country have positioned tourism as the development priority of their local economy. In this context, governments at different levels as promoter and facilitator of tourism destinations have naturally become the organisers of tourism festivals and events.

Thirdly, tourism marketing of festivals and events has begun to receive attention. With the development of the market economy in China, the marketing concept has been applied to the tourism industry, and marketing initiatives of tourism festivals and events have been emphasised. With the continuing expansion of tourism festivals in the country, this type of tourism is facing fierce market competition. Under such conditions, the role of marketing in event management will receive more attention.

7.3.2 Paths for tourism development of festivals and events

(1) Emphasising event planning and integration of festival tourism resources

Tourism development should focus on planning first. In view of the current problems in the development of tourism festivals and events, both the government and event organisers need to focus on the overall planning of festival tourism development within a particular region. For a specific event, the planning focus should clarify the purpose and the level of the event, and the resources available for planning. At the same time, a clear organizational management system should be established so the festival can be integrated into the area's regional development, thus reducing the negative impact of individual festivals. Furthermore, planning should focus on the scenic spots and festival requirements, so that tourism facilities and equipment can meet the requirements of the festival activities, especially those dependent on cultural resources.

(2) Emphasising the marketing efforts of the festival to expand tourism awareness

It is necessary to increase the use of new media forms to promote tourism festivals and events. Different marketing strategies should be used to enlarge the influence of publicity. For example, in the 16th Guangzhou Asian Games, a joint marketing strategy was adopted by the event organiser and JiaDuoBao Group, who conducted a series of joint marketing activities, including the attractive event title, designated products, an Asian Games cheerleading team selection, and Wanglaoji Asian Games Star selection. This had a win-win effect of creating the atmosphere of the event and raising corporate awareness. In addition, event organisers should also use the role of travel agencies as a bridge connecting tourism products and the source market, as their participation can help to promote tourism awareness and increase product sales. The current participation of travel agencies in festival tourism development is limited, due to the lack of direct connection with the event organisers. Therefore, it is necessary to establish and improve supporting measures for travel agencies to participate in tourism development to promote the development of tourism in the region more effectively.

(3) Establishing a management system

The development of festivals and events tourism should meet the demands of all parties and mobilise all interests in participation. It is also necessary to improve the organization and management system of event management. During the World Expo 1999, Kunming Tourism Bureau, through research and development, formulated the *Proposal for Tourism Festivals and Events in Kunming in 2000 and Beyond*. This proposed five major types of events in Kunming, of festivals, meetings, exhibitions, performances, and competitions, and set up a special Leading Group of Kunming Municipal People's Government for Exhibition Work. The Office of Large-scale Exhibition and Convention Activities of Kunming Municipal People's Government was set up to be responsible for the daily work of event management. In this way, a government-led and effectively coordinated model of festival tourism development was formed.

(4) Accentuating cultural soft power

Cultural soft power is part of national comprehensive power, and it differs from tangible power such as military, economy, science and technology. Its power is rooted in the inner spirit, thought and emotion, and cultural values, and its effectiveness is subtle, silent and attractive, with the characteristics of borderless communication, audience diversity, with a wide and diverse influence. To achieve the widest public participation and development purpose, event organisers should further explore and make good use of the cultural resources of the host region. This will eventually lead to the formation of regional cultural attractiveness and cultural soft power. Only when the cultural concepts and values of host regions are widely spread in China and extend to the international community, will culture have soft power.

Chapter Summary

Festivals and events are an inseparable part of human society. They evolved from primitive gatherings of ancient people for religious reasons into a wide variety of modern events. Festivals and events have significant impacts on the development of a place and are important motivators of tourism. In practice, the tourism development of festivals and events should focus particularly on systematic planning and the building of unique event brands. Only when the festivals and events are well defined can they be recognised in the market and obtain advantage over the competition, which in turn results in greater attractiveness to visitors and creates the possibility of repeat visits. At the same time, effective management is vital to promote a mutual development of the festivals/events and tourism industry of the host region.

China Story

Overseas Chinese Town: developing festival activities through inter-provincial linkages

Issues for Review and Discussion

1. What are the advantages of the government-led model?

2. What ways are there to promote an ethnic cultural tourism festival? Give an example.

3. How can the problem of a lack of featured souvenirs in the event industry be solved?

Exercises

Recommended Reading

Chapter 8
Chinese Crafts

Learning Objectives

After reading this chapter, you should have a good understanding of
1. The origin and development of Chinese crafts;
2. Features and categories of Chinese crafts;
3. The importance of Chinese crafts to tourism culture;
4. The well-known Chinese crafts (Chinese paper cutting, Chinese ceramics, and Chinese carving).

Technical Words

English Words	中文翻译
textile	纺织物
bronzeware	青铜器
lacquerware	漆器
ceramics	陶瓷
jadeware	玉器
dyeing and weaving	染织
gold and silverware	金银器
kiln	窑
cloisonne	景泰蓝
embroidery	织绣
jade carving	玉雕
Buddha sculpture	佛像雕塑
papier-mâché offerings	纸扎
Hungry Ghost Festival	中元节
The Butterfly Lovers	《梁祝》
Legend of the White Snake	《白蛇传》

续表

English Words	中文翻译
The Eight Immortals Crossing the Sea	《八仙过海》
pottery	陶
porcelain	瓷
silicate	硅酸盐
clay	黏土
synthetic raw material	人工合成原材料
glazed pottery	釉陶
celadon	青瓷
kaolin	高岭土
feldspar	长石
quartz	石英
blue-and-white porcelain	青花瓷
ceramic whiteware	白瓷
rice-pattern decorated porcelain	玲珑瓷
colour-glazed porcelain	颜色釉瓷
green body	生坯
underglaze coloured porcelain	釉下彩瓷
nanmu	楠木
red sandalwood	紫檀
camphor wood	樟木
cypress	柏木
ginkgo	银杏
agarwood	沉香
mahogany	红木
rafter	椽
door lintel	门楣
gold foil	金箔
pottery figurine	陶俑
wooden figurine	木俑
Qin Shi Huang Mausoleum	秦始皇陵
Buddhist statues	佛教造像
coloured glaze	琉璃

续表

English Words	中文翻译
round carving	圆雕
relief carving	浮雕
openwork carving	透雕

Knowledge Graph

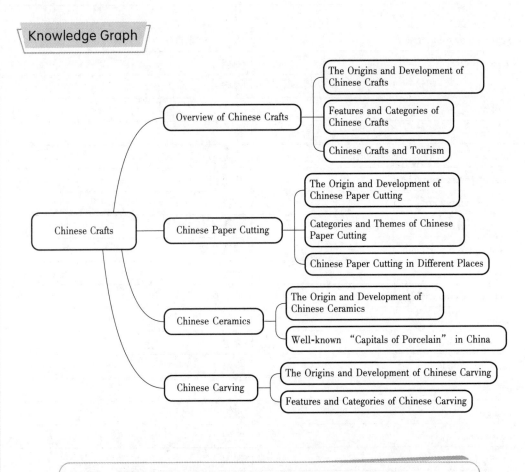

8.1 Overview of Chinese Crafts

  Chinese crafts, as one of the symbols of traditional Chinese culture, are an important part of Chinese tourism culture. These crafts are artforms created by working people of different regions and cultures, demonstrating the Chinese people's exceptional creativity. Chinese crafts typically take the form of expressing working people's real lives and directly expressing their simple and pure feelings. They hold an important place in Chinese history and culture, and have been cherished and loved by Chinese people and foreign tourists since ancient times.

Chinese crafts not only reflect the Chinese people's pursuit of refined aesthetics and a better life, but also are profound cultural repositories and have rich cultural connotations. With the rapid development of modern tourism, Chinese crafts and tourism have gradually integrated with each other and seen unprecedented development in the tourism market. Chinese crafts bring rich cultural resources and personalized experiences to tourism, making tourism more cultural and experiential. At the same time, the vast tourism market provides a platform for the cultural transmission, inheritance and development of Chinese crafts. Understanding the development, features and categories of Chinese crafts will help readers further their understanding of Chinese culture, and better think about the innovative development of tourism in the context of cultural and tourism integration.

8.1.1 The Origins and Development of Chinese Crafts

Chinese crafts are not only the remains of material culture, but also the remains of spiritual culture. They have played a huge role in people's social lives in different historical periods. The development of Chinese crafts can be roughly divided into four periods: emergence period, development period, maturing period, and flourishing period.

(1) Emergence Period (before 221 BC)

Chinese crafts started with the creation and application of labor tools. In ancient times, people used sticks, branches, and stones as tools to defend themselves against wild animals and obtain food. The early tools were made in a simple way without much processing. Later, people gradually mastered processing methods and made tools that could be used for scraping, hammering, chopping, and stabbing. When the Neolithic Age began, people's primary means of subsistence changed from primitive hunting and gathering to primitive agriculture, and the growth of primitive agriculture further encouraged the production of primitive crafts. Various shapes, functions, and sizes of pottery were successively produced, including utensils for transporting drinking water, storing grain, and cooking food, as well as pottery tools such as knives. In the late Neolithic Age, pottery-making skills were further improved and black and painted pottery appeared, which were practical as well as aesthetic.

(2) Development Period (221 BC – AD 581)

During the Qin and Han dynasties, the advancement of social productivity, science, and technology also promoted the rapid development of crafts. Both the variety and quantity of products, as well as the level of production, were greatly improved in comparison to the Emergence Period. Textile, bronze, lacquerware, ceramics, jade, and other crafts were all very developed during the Qin Dynasty, demonstrating a trend of all-around development. During the Western Han Dynasty, a special handicraft industry management agency was set up from the central to the local level to implement hierarchical management of traditional handicrafts, and effective steps were taken to encourage the growth of crafting activities in various regions. Textile-making was an important handicraft production sector at that time, and silk fabrics were rich and exquisitely woven. Bronzeware began to develop into daily utensils, such as plates, lamps, and bronze mirrors(Photograph 8.1). The use of lacquer gradually expanded, and the production technology of ceramics was also innovated. During the Three Kingdoms, the Jin, and Southern and Northern dynasties, various production tools were continuously improved. Crafts such as ceramics, lacquerware, and dyeing and weaving were generally developed.[①]

Photograph 8.1　Ancient Chinese bronzeware
(Source: https://pixabay.com/zh/photos/cultural-relics-natural-history-807102/)

(3) Maturing Period (581-1271 AD)

During the Sui and Tang dynasties, the production technology and artistic level of various crafts advanced greatly. The Tang court established special institutions to manage craft industries such as ceramics, dyeing and weaving, and goldand silverware, which effectively promoted the advancement of crafts. Various craft workshops gradually expanded. Folk workshops for crafts such as brocade, dyeing, and paper could be found throughout towns and cities, and a wide range of crafts made for daily necessities complemented a vibrant social life that reflected the times with the development of urban industry and commerce. The art of crafts developed rapidly during the Song Dynasty. At

---

①黄爱莲，陈红玲，李劲松．中国旅游文化[M]．北京：经济管理出版社，2014．

that time, the traditional craft industry was divided into two major systems, official craft and folk craft, but the two developed independently and worked well together. The official craft workshop brought together the best skilled craftsmen in the country. The products were well-selected and exquisitely crafted, representing the highest skill-levels of the times. The folk craft workshops all over cities and towns met the daily needs of society. Scattered across the nation, there were numerous well-known kilns with a variety of features, and porcelain was exported all over the world. Additionally, crafts made during the Liao and Jin dynasties were representative of ethnic minorities and also quite popular.

(4) Flourishing Period (1271-1911 AD)

During the Yuan, Ming and Qing dynasties, various craft industries flourished in China. The products were exquisite and diverse, all of which surpassed their predecessors and reached the level of "stunning". With the advancement of social economy and culture, the professional division of labor in the craft industries became more refined than before, and various crafts made significant technological and artistic achievements. Porcelain, cloisonne (Photograph 8.2), lacquerware, embroidery, gold and silverware, and ivory carving were all fine arts at that time. During the creation process, craftsmen sought sophistication and proficiency in their crafts. The structure and shape of various objects were becoming more refined, and craft specifications were also evolving toward a more structured and regularized development. Traditional Qing Dynasty craft products were no longer simple daily necessities, and some of them were transformed into works of art for people to appreciate and collect. In addition, some outstanding craftsmen of the Ming and Qing dynasties wrote special craft monographs to summarize their experience in the industry. Since then, related works have appeared one after another, promoting the inheritance and development of Chinese crafts.

Photograph 8.2 A Piece of Cloisonne work
(Source:https://pixabay.com/zh/photos/china-beijing-art-cloisonne-enamels-1269599/)

8.1.2 Features and Categories of Chinese Crafts

(1) Features of Chinese Crafts

In order to meet the diverse needs of various people, the design and production of Chinese crafts are based on the principles of economy, applicability, and beauty. First of all, Chinese crafts are both practical and artistic. When crafts are first created, they are necessities of life with practicality being the first goal. Once these necessary functions are fulfilled, through a process of continuous development the aim of craftsmanship gradually turns toward more aesthetic functions. Crafts begin to fill the needs of people's material and spiritual lives as productivity grows and improves. Second, Chinese crafts are still clearly influenced by national and regional culture. Craftsmen produce their crafts against the backdrop of traditional Chinese culture, and the aesthetics continue to be influenced by this cultural context. At the same time, many crafts are produced based on historical tales, myths, and legends, as well as traditions and folklore. People who utilize and appreciate these handicrafts experience the essence of traditional Chinese history and culture in addition to the beauty of the craftsmanship, materials, and concepts. Third, there are regional variations in Chinese crafts. Different regions have created unique cultures that have in turn given rise to many ways of thinking and many aesthetic variations. This development is due to the diversity of natural resources, national cultures, local customs, and climatic settings. Chinese crafts differ between the south and the north, the inland and the beach, for this reason.

(2) Categories of Chinese Crafts

According to the their distinct social classes, Chinese crafts can be divided into two categories: folk crafts and official or court crafts. Folk crafts are based on traditional crafts, which are integrated into the daily folk life of the people. Folk crafts include a large number of daily activities and necessities, such as weaving, ironing, oil-paper umbrellas, paper cuttings, and so on. These crafts are generally simple and rough, and folk artisans strive for exquisite craftsmanship under difficult conditions. Compared with folk crafts, official or court crafts are made under much better conditions. These bring together skilled and excellent craftsmen from all over the country, using high-quality raw materials regardless of cost, labor hours, and profit or loss in the manufacturing process. As a result, the majority of official handicrafts are more exquisite and quite often regarded as the pinnacle of Chinese crafts.

According to their function, Chinese crafts can be divided into three categories:

practical crafts, ornamental crafts, and religious and sacrificial crafts. Practical crafts are those that have a practical value in life, that is, daily necessities that have been decorated and processed such as daily ceramic crafts, furniture crafts, and some dyeing and weaving crafts. Since the primary goal of these crafts is to be useful and appropriate for daily use, practicality should come before shape and colour when creating such crafts. Ornamental crafts refer to crafts that are made to be appreciated by others and are used as point-level decorations for living spaces. This includes art works pasted on the wall, such as paper cutting and traditional New Year pictures, or interior furnishings such as ivory and jade carvings, decorative paintings, and weaving crafts. Ornamental crafts require unique styles and strong artistic composition in modeling and decoration, as well as a representation of harmony between objects and the environment. Religious and sacrificial crafts such as Buddha sculptures and papier-mâché offerings are usually used in religious and sacrificial festivals and activities like the Hungry Ghost Festival.

8.1.3 Chinese Crafts and Tourism

Chinese crafts have always played an important role in the country's tourism industry. It is not only this natural reflection of the working people's thoughts, feelings, and aesthetic tastes, but also the carrying of art and culture that strongly reflects unique Chinese nationality and locality. Some of these crafts, showing regional and ethnic characteristics of China and functioning as "ambassadors" of Chinese culture and civilization, "travel" to different parts of the world, showing their unique artistic beauty; others, functioning as tourism cultural products, enrich the tourism market in China.

Chinese crafts are being introduced into the tourism market for consumption and transformed from folk items into tourism commodities in order to meet the demands of the tourism market and increase the allure of travel to China. Creating tourist crafts that meet tourist needs and reflect the natural and cultural characteristics of tourist destinations can not only activate the tourist commodity market and promote the development of the tourist economy, but can also help to better protect and pass down traditional crafts and culture.

With the continuous advancement of cultural and tourism integration, Chinese crafts have quickly integrated into the cultural and tourism industry chain and formed a unique cultural ecology of crafts. They thrive in the tourism industry, traditional handicraft workshops, creative tourism markets, cultural exhibitions and other venues of presentation. The main presentations of these Chinese crafts mainly include on-site displays of craft culture in museums; intangible cultural heritage protection bases in tourist areas, cultural blocks and other places; exhibition and sale of tourism craft souvenirs in

Further reading

Eradicating Poverty: Traditional Tibetan crafts revive in NW China, helping locals (Excerpt)

tourist attractions; and hands-on experiences of making Chinese crafts during study tours. In addition, in recent years, many traditional tourism villages and towns have achieved the goal of poverty alleviation through craft production, helping villagers to become rich by developing rural tourism. At the same time, many craft cultures with unique regional characteristics have been widely publicized through tourism vlog platforms and tourism livestreaming platforms, which in turn has attracted a large number of tourists to these regions.

8.2 Chinese Paper Cutting

Paper cutting refers to using scissors or a knife to cut patterns on papers (Photograph 8.3). It is one of the most ancient and widely practiced traditional crafts in China, often used for daily decoration or in folk activities and festivals. On May 20, 2006, Chinese paper cutting was included in China's first batch of State-level Intangible Cultural Heritage List, and three years later, on September 28, 2009, it was included in UNESCO's *Representative List of the Intangible Cultural Heritage of Humanity*.

Photograph 8.3 A Piece of Chinese Paper Cutting Work
(Source:https://pixabay.com/zh/photos/culture-tradition-paper-cut-china-959225/)

8.2.1 The Origin and Development of Chinese Paper Cutting

Chinese paper cutting has a long history. According to archives, the art of paper cutting existed prior to the discovery of papermaking; the materials used to construct paper cutting works at the time were tough materials such as leaves and bamboo slips instead of paper. In the Western Han Dynasty, the invention of Chinese papermaking and the widespread use of paper greatly promoted the development of the art of paper cutting resulting in the true paper cutting. In the Southern and Northern Dynasties, paper cutting was connected to the customs of the time, enriching it and making it more extensive in subject matter. During the Tang and Song dynasties, the art of paper cutting was quite popular, and paper cutting works were marketed as memorable commodities. During the Ming and Qing dynasties, the art of paper cutting reached its peak and was used more widely in things such as floral decorations on folk lanterns, decorations on fans, patterns of embroidery. After the People's Republic of China was established, the art of paper cutting was used for the decoration of single paintings, comic strips, movies, cartoons, and numerous crafts, broadening the creative route of the paper cutting. Sheets and fabrics with paper cutting patterns have also appeared in modern times.

In addition, the art of paper cutting as a tourism resource is highly valued by the tourism businesses. In some cases, paper cutting souvenirs are evolving into high-quality artworks, and elements such as paper cutting patterns are gradually being employed in the design of different tourist products (travel postcard souvenir clothes, etc.). In other cases, some tourist sites set up live performances by folk paper cutting artists in tourist attractions so that tourists from all over the world can see, understand, experience, and learn, as well as share the delight that paper cutting brings.

Recommended Video

How relevant is traditional Chinese paper cutting art today

8.2.2 Categories and Themes of Chinese Paper Cutting

(1) Categories of Chinese Paper Cutting

Paper cutting has become the most popular folk art because of its simple materials and strong adaptability. Due to the influence of different regions and national cultures, paper cutting varieties with different styles have been produced. Paper cutting is classified into five categories based on their intended use. The first is for posting, and includes art meant to be immediately posted on doors, windows, walls, or coloured lights. The second is for decoration, and includes window grilles, wall flowers, ceiling flowers, and similar things. The third type is for lining and is used to decorate gifts, dowries, offerings, and so on, and features designs like joyful flowers that are generally used as decoration. The fourth category is embroidery bases, such as shoe flowers, pillow flowers, hat flowers, sleeve flowers, and the like. The fifth category is the printing and dyeing pattern, which is used for clothing, quilt surfaces, door curtains, head scarves, and such.

(2) Themes of Chinese Paper Cutting

In China, there are many distinct paper cutting themes, and each one displays the rich creativity and desires of the paper cutting makers. Paper cutting themes are always related to Chinese people's real lives and work, reflecting people's wonder at and gratitude to nature, as well as their pursuit of a better and happier life. Traditional Chinese paper cutting themes can be loosely split into the following categories.

a. People's Real Life and Work

Paper cutting works with the theme of "people's real life and work" express the simplicity and beauty of rural life. Most of the creators of paper cutting with this theme come from rural, pastoral, and forest areas, especially in places of an ethnic minority. The themes of their paper cutting include field labor, cattle and sheep herding, domestic animals, plants, flowers, vegetables, local architecture, local traditional festivals, and other folk activities.

b. Happiness and Good Fortune

Some of these paper cutting works use metaphors and symbols: for example, peonies symbolize "wealth", pines, evergreens, cranes, and peaches symbolize "longevity", peacocks, butterflies, and magpies symbolize "love". Other works express the meaning through homonyms and homophonic words. For example, the number "eight (bā)" has a similar pronunciation to the word "rich (fā)" meaning "wealthy life"; while "nine (jiǔ)" is pronounced similarly to the word "forever (jiǔ)" meaning "long life"; the word "fish (yú)" symbolizes prosperity and harvest, and shares its pronunciation with the word "surplus (yú)"; the phrase "Jujube (zǎo), peanut (shēng), longan (guì), and lotus seed (zǐ) shares pronunciation with the phrase, "May you two have a lovely baby! (zǎo shēng guì zǐ)". It is a commonly used greeting for newlyweds in China.

c. Opera Characters and Legend Stories

People use the paper cutting art form to express their feelings about the characters in Chinese operas, legends stories, historical stories, and also literary works. The classic characters and storylines in "Journey to the West" (《西游记》), "A Dream in Red Mansions" (《红楼梦》), "The Butterfly Lovers (the love story of Liang Shanbo and Zhu Yingtai" (《梁祝》), "Legend of the White Snake" (《白蛇传》), and "The Eight Immortals Crossing the Sea" (《八仙过海》) are some common themes.

d. Important Activities and Major Events

In recent years, people have a deeper understanding and pursuit of artistic creation. In addition to the traditional content, there are more and more trendy paper cutting works. These works are used to commemorate international and national activities, reflect practical problems, and express a good vision for the future life. These include the image of the China Pavilion at the 2010 Shanghai World Expo, and the "*Bing Dwen Dwen*" paper cutting specially created for the 2022 Beijing Winter Olympics.

8.2.3 Chinese Paper Cutting in Different Places

Paper cutting is a folk art with important regional components. In general, there are two styles of Chinese paper cutting: Northern and Southern. Different regions employ distinct materials and equipment, diverse techniques, and different topics and artistic styles. The following are representative areas of Chinese paper cutting.

(1) Zhejiang paper cutting

Zhejiang paper cutting is rich in themes, with dozens of patterns intertwined with distinct layers and strong regional characteristics, showing the unique charm of the seaside in the south of the Yangtze River. This is in stark contrast to the rough style of northern paper cutting. Flowers, fruits, birds, and fish are common Zhejiang paper cutting themes, and there are also dramatic plots that properly represent the beauty of the characters'forms.

(2) Yangzhou paper cutting

Yangzhou is one of the first areas in China where paper cutting became popular, and it is representative of the Southern style of Chinese paper cutting. In the Tang and Song Dynasties, an independent craft industry was formed, and professional artists were engaged in this work. Yangzhou paper cutting art has created a unique style over thousands of years, thanks to the meticulous study of generations of paper cutting artists. It is famous for the chrysanthemum paper cutting. Its works are generally dominated by plain colours, with smooth lines and attention to detailed description; they also have strict requirements including perfect shape, exquisite composition, and varied techniques.

(3) Foshan paper cutting

Foshan paper cutting was circulated in the Song Dynasty and flourished in the Ming and Qing dynasties. Its style has distinctive local characteristics, with the exaggerated and rich colours. Its works are cut and carved with scissors or knives on paper, or on special copper and silver foils. Foshan paper cutting holds a significant place in the traditional local folk culture. Paper cutting works are popular decorations for festivals, weddings, funerals, birthday sacrifices, social etiquette, and even people's daily demands.

(4) Fujian paper cutting

Fujian is also well-known for its paper cutting industry. Paper cutting in Fujian have distinct qualities with strong local folk customs and taste. There are many works in Nanping, Hua'an, and other regions that primarily portray mountain, poultry and cattle; in southern Fujian and Zhangpu paper cutting patterns frequently include aquatic creatures; and in Putian and Xianyou, gift flowers are the most commonly depicted.

(5) Yuxian paper cutting

Yuxian paper cutting originated in the Ming Dynasty and is a unique paper cutting art. At the end of the Qing Dynasty, Yuxian paper cutting tools were reformed from "cutting" to "carving". At the beginning of the 20th century, Yuxian paper cutting gradually formed its own unique artistic style in composition, shape, and colour, and created a unique new genre of folk paper cutting. Yuxian paper cutting contains a diverse spectrum of topics and a vibrant sense of life. Some are based on people's prayers for good fortune and happiness, some on historical legends and folklore, and still others on northern culture and folk customs. The colours used in these paper cutting works are primarily bright and pure. The vibrant colours are rich and vibrant and the contrast is high, implying prosperity and joy.

(6) Shandong paper cutting

There are many kinds of paper cutting in Shandong. According to the functions of folk customs, Shandong folk paper cutting can be divided into three categories: festival paper cutting, ritual paper cutting, and daily paper cutting. These can be roughly divided into two categories in terms of style. One is the rough and unrestrained style in the Bohai Bay area, and the other is the more characteristic delicate paper cutting in the coastal area of Jiaodong. Shandong paper cutting often employ symbolic and allegorical strategies in their creative conceptions, resulting in works that are both visually appealing and imaginative.

Recommended Video

The beauty of paper art in north China

8.3 Chinese Ceramics

Ceramics is a general term for pottery and porcelain, and it is also a genre of arts and crafts in China (Photograph 8.4). Traditional ceramics, also known as ordinary ceramics, are products fired from natural silicates such as clay as the main raw material. Modern ceramics are also called new ceramics, fine ceramics, or special ceramics. These commonly use non-silicate chemical raw materials or synthetic raw materials. Ceramics are widely employed in many sectors of the national economy and have several advantages, including excellent insulation, corrosion resistance, high temperature resistance, and high hardness. At the same time, ceramics are also a beautiful art for people to appreciate and collect.

Photograph 8.4　A photo of pottery making
(Source:https://pixabay.com/zh/photos/potter-pottery-vase-pot-art-craft-4682257/)

8.3.1 The Origin and Development of Chinese Ceramics

Ceramics were one of the great inventions in ancient China. The origin and development of ceramics was actually closely related to people's lives and production practices. The original pottery manufacturing process can be traced back to more than 14,000 years ago.① At that time, the pottery was hand-kneaded so its thickness was uneven, and because of the low firing temperature, the pottery was loose, high in water absorption, and easily broken. The pottery at that time was simple and rough in shape, mostly plants and animals closely related to human life (such as gourds, pumpkins, dogs, pigs).

In the 16th century BC, primitive celadon appeared, and in the Western Zhou Dynasty, primitive porcelain developed into porcelain, properly speaking. Pottery is a daily necessity and includes items made of clay as the main raw material after blanking, drying, and firing. It is divided into two categories: glazed (low temperature glaze, about 800℃ - 1000℃)② and unglazed. Due to the different components contained in the clay, the pottery can be white, green, brown, or other colours. The texture of the pottery is grainy

---

①朱晓晴. 中国旅游文化概览[M]. 西安:西北大学出版社, 2019.
②邵骥顺. 中国旅游历史文化概论[M]. 上海:上海三联书店, 1998.

and absorbent, and the sound it makes when percussed is not a clear tone. Porcelain is made of kaolin, feldspar, and quartz as raw materials, which are mixed, shaped, dried, and fired (about 1200℃ - 1300℃). After the porcelain body is sintered, it becomes non-absorbent or low in water absorption, and the sound is loud and crisp when struck. During the Eastern Han Dynasty, the obvious improvement in the quality of porcelain should be attributed to the transformation of the kiln. The invention of the elongated kiln enabled people to better control the furnace temperature and opened up a new era in the history of Chinese porcelain.

In the Tang Dynasty, the production technology and artistic prowess of ceramics reached a very high level. There are two major schools of porcelain: white porcelain from the Xing kiln(邢窑) in the North and celadon from the Yue kiln(越窑) in the South. At that time, porcelain production was skilled and exquisite. Porcelains were sold to neighboring countries such as Japan and India and went to the world through the Silk Road, playing an important role in international cultural exchanges. Since then China has been called "The Country of Porcelain. In the Ming and Qing Dynasties, the ceramics surpassed the previous generation in technique. In the Song Dynasty, porcelain products were very exquisite, and in addition to daily necessities, there were also display items. Kilns all over the country launched their own products of different styles, forming the five major kilns: Ru Kiln (汝窑), Guan Kiln (官窑), Ding Kiln (定窑), Ge Kiln (哥窑), and Jun Kiln (钧窑). In the Yuan Dynasty, on the foundation of the porcelain of the Tang and Song Dynasties, traditional Chinese painting and the porcelain-making process were more closely fused. A variety of coloured glaze products were fired, and the production process of blue and white porcelain matured.

8.3.2 Well-known "Capitals of Porcelain" in China

(1) Jingdezhen

Jingdezhen is one of the three major porcelain capitals in China, located in the eastern part of Jiangxi Province. There were ceramics here as early as the Han Dynasty, and during the Wei, Jin, and Southern and Northern Dynasties, the pottery developed into porcelain. Later, in the Tang Dynasty, ceramic whiteware appeared. Since the Song Dynasty, Jingdezhen has been designated as the official capital of porcelain and has become the center of Chinese porcelain production. In the Yuan, Ming, and Qing dynasties, Jingdezhen's colourful glazes, as well as emerging gold and red porcelain, began to be exported to Southeast Asia, Arabia, and European countries. Jingdezhen porcelain is beautiful in shape, extensive in variety, rich in decoration, and unique in style. Blue and white porcelain, rice-pattern decorated porcelain, and colour-glazed porcelain are three famous traditional porcelains of Jingdezhen.

a. Blue-and-White Porcelain

Jingdezhen blue-and-white porcelain is known as the "treasure of the world". It was created in the Yuan Dynasty and reached its peak in the Ming and Qing dynasties. The process uses cobalt oxide to draw patterns on the green body, after which the piece is glazed and then fired.

b. Rice-pattern Decorated Porcelain

The rice-pattern decorated porcelain was created and developed from the foundation of openwork carving during the Ming Dynasty, with a history of more than 500 years. According to records, the rice-pattern decorated porcelain produced in Jingdezhen in the Qing Dynasty had a high level of quality but the output was very small, sufficient only for the court's use. To make the rice-pattern decorations, porcelain workers use a blade to carve a little grain of rice on the green body, then fill it with glaze, decorate it in blue and white, and fire it in a kiln. This kind of porcelain is not only widely used in daily Chinese tea sets and wine sets, but also has been extended to various vases, chandeliers, wall lamps, and other lamps.

c. Color-glazed porcelain

Color-glazed porcelain usually adjusts the content of various trace elements in the glaze to achieve the purpose of changing the glaze colour to shades such as copper red, cobalt blue, iron black, lead green, and so on. Adding a particular oxidized metal to the glaze after firing will produce a certain colour.

Recommended Video

Reviving tradition in Jingdezhen, China's porcelain capital

(2) Dehua

Dehua is located in the central part of Fujian Province in southeastern China. It is rich in natural resources and densely distributed with porcelain clay minerals. Dehua porcelain originated in the Song Dynasty and has a history of more than 1,000 years. During the Ming and Qing Dynasties, it gradually formed its own techniques and styles and then made great progress. After the 1950s, Dehua porcelain continued to innovate while also inheriting traditional craftsmanship. The variety of traditional porcelain has developed to more than 390 kinds, and products with modern themes are also increasing day by day. Dehua is famous for its ceramic whiteware, which looks like jade due to its exceptional quality. Among the Dehua ceramic whitewares, the most famous is the Buddha statue sculpture.

(3) Liling

Liling is located in the eastern part of Hunan Province and is famous for its underglaze coloured porcelain. Underglaze is a traditional ceramic product with a unique decorative style. Porcelain workers first paint on the rough blank (green body), and then the piece is glazed and fired. The surface of this kind of porcelain is white as jade, and the patterns on the porcelain are non-fading, and durable. It can meet people's requirements for both aesthetic value and environmental awareness, and has higher collection and use value.

8.4 Chinese Carving

8.4.1 The Origins and Development of Chinese Carving

Chinese carving has a long history. In ancient times people kneaded and fired pottery, which activity is considered the origin of Chinese carving. The earliest known Chinese carving is a small pottery statue of a human head found in Mi County (密县), Henan (河南) Province, which is a relic of the Peiligang Cultural Site (裴李岗文化遗址) from more than 7,000 years ago. A large number of ceramics have been found in the Yangshao Cultural Site (仰韶文化遗址), which artifacts give insight into the origins of Chinese carving.

In the Shang and Zhou dynasties, the materials used for carving were more abundant than before and included bronze, clay, jade, and more①. The inclusion of animal figures in bronzes makes the bronzeware very vivid. During the Spring and Autumn Period and the Warring States Period, there were more kinds of materials, and the aesthetic priority turned to the pursuit of beauty. The main form of carving at that time was pottery figurines. Many lords and nobles purchased pottery figurines and pottery horses to be buried with them after their deaths. Therefore, during this period, the carving skill displayed in pottery figures and animals was greatly improved. The pottery figurines of this period are the earliest pottery figurines in China and are of great value for the study of the history of Chinese carving. During the Warring States period, there were also wooden figurines used as funeral objects, which were the earliest wooden figurines in China.

The development of Chinese carving in the Qin Dynasty brought outstanding achievements. In architectural decorations and burial objects, large stone carvings, bronze carvings, and pottery carvings appeared. In addition, the unearthed Terra Cotta Warriors (兵马俑) in the Qin Shi Huang Mausoleum (秦始皇陵) marked the achievement of

---

① 都大明, 金守郡. 中国旅游文化. 第3版[M]. 上海: 上海交通大学出版社, 2012.

Chinese carving in the Qin Dynasty. Its characteristics are tall shape, emphatic realism, and vivid imagery. The art of carving in the Han Dynasty improved on the foundations of the Qin Dynasty, and its new achievements were reflected in large-scale stone carvings. In the Wei, Jin(晋), and Southern and Northern Dynasties, the art of carving gained much inspiration and many elements from Buddhist art. Buddhist statues in grottoes became the mainstream of carving. "China's Four Grottoes"—Dunhuang Mogao Grottoes (敦煌莫高窟), Yungang Grottoes (云冈石窟)(Photograph 8.5), Longmen Grottoes (龙门石窟), and Maijishan Grottoes (麦积山石窟)—display a high level of stone and clay cravings.

During the Sui and Tang dynasties, tomb carvings and religious statue carvings created many works that can be passed down through the ages. The Buddha statues in this period mostly portrayed secular life in sympathetic terms, reducing the mysterious aura of religion. The art of carving in the Ming and Qing dynasties developed rapidly, especially architectural carving and display carving. The Forbidden City in Beijing is a representative of architectural palace carving. In addition, coloured glaze carving was also an important part of architectural palace carvings in the Qing Dynasty.

Photograph 8.5　Yungang Grottoes, Shanxi Province
(Source: https://pixabay.com/zh/photos/buddhism-yungang-grottos-878192/)

8.4.2 Features and Categories of Chinese Carving

The art of carving is a treasure of Chinese culture. Using skillful decoration and artistry, it reflects the spirit of ancient Chinese philosophy and culture. According to its form, it is generally divided into three categories: round carving, relief carving, and openwork carving. According to its function, it can be divided into monumental sculpture, garden sculpture or interior decoration carving, architectural decoration carving, and so on. According to its production materials, it can be divided into clay sculpture, wood carving, stone carving, copper carving, ice carving, sand carving, and so on.

(1) Jade Carving

China is a jade-producing country. Chinese jade carving has a history of over 4,000 years, which makes it one of the oldest carving varieties in China. Since ancient times, people have viewed jade ornaments and jade as emblems of nobility, honor, and auspiciousness. Due to the precious materials used in jade carving, Chinese masters make full use of the natural shape, colour, and texture of jade to design and create their works of art. Jade-carved jewelry and accessories are the most popular types of jade-carving crafts. From the perspective of the major schools, contemporary Chinese jade carving can be divided into two schools: Northern and Southern. The Northern school is represented by Beijing and covers Liaoning, Tianjin, Hebei, parts of Henan, Xinjiang, and so on, while the Southern school is divided into several branches, including Shanghai, Suzhou, Yangzhou, Guangdong, and Fujian jade carving.

a.Beijing Jade Carving

As a representative of the Northern school, Beijing jade carvings are very popular among collectors. When identifying Beijing jade carvings, collectors generally start by categorizing the colour, carving, and texture. Differing from the Southern style jade carvings, Beijing jade carvings are hard in texture and bright in colour. The carvings have the style of court art.

b.Shanghai Jade Carving (Haipai Jade Carving, 海派玉雕)

Shanghai jade carving is a jade carving art style represented by Shanghai. At the beginning of the 19th century, Shanghai became an important port for China's trade, and thus jade products from Suzhou, Yangzhou, and the surrounding areas were exported through Shanghai ports. This situation provided a broad development space for the jade carving industry in Shanghai. Formed at the end of the 19th century and beginning of the 20th century, Shanghai jade carving has a strong influence on the contemporary art of jade carving.

(2) Woodcarving

Woodcarving is a very practical traditional craft. In fact, as with other sculpture arts, the art of woodcarving is at first an unconsciously artistic behaviour, and it is not until people have developed a sense of aesthetics that woodcarving really becomes an art. The art of woodcarving originated in China in the Neolithic period, and a large number of woodcarvings were made in the Song Dynasty. During the Yuan and Ming Dynasties, due to the rapid development of overseas trade, the types of wood used increased and many hard-textured woods were imported from overseas, which led to the rapid development of woodcarving craftsmanship. The Ming and Qing Dynasties were a glorious period for woodcarving. Chinese woodcarvings are mostly used in architecture, religion, furniture, and furnishings, and play a decorative role. Most of the woodcarving works have an ethnic style and strong local characteristics(Photograph 8.6). Craftsmen generally choose tough, non-deformable materials for woodcarvings, such as nanmu, red sandalwood, camphor wood, cypress, ginkgo, agarwood, mahogany, and others. In addition, tree root carving is another traditional kind of woodcarving: this artform carves a vivid artistic image in a root without losing the root's unique shape.

Due to different folk customs, cultures, and resource conditions in different places, the materials and techniques used to make woodcarvings are different, forming many schools with strong local characteristics. These wood carving schools are very influential locally and even across the country. Among them, the most famous woodcarving schools are Quanzhou woodcarving, Dongyang woodcarving, Yueqing boxwood carving, Guangdong Chaozhou golden and lacquer woodcarving, and Fujian longan woodcarving. These five schools are called the "five major chinese woodcarving styles".

Photograph 8.6　A Piece of Woodcarving
(Source: https://pixabay.com/zh/photos/horse-woodcarving-gift-455922/)

a.Dongyang Woodcarving

Dongyang woodcarving has a history of more than 1,000 years. According to written records, Dongyang woodcarving began in the Tang Dynasty, developed in the Song Dynasty, and flourished in the Ming and Qing dynasties. In the Forbidden City in Beijing and Lingyin Temple in Hangzhou, ancient Dongyang woodcarving works are still preserved. Dongyang woodcarving is mainly based on relief techniques. The patterns often use the "full pattern" technique whereby pictures are covered with patterns, forming a unique artistic style. Dongyang woodcarving has a wide range of themes, including figures, landscapes, birds, beasts, flowers, fish, and insects; decorative content based on

Recommended Video

How modern woodcarving is rejuvenating ancient China

historical stories began to be represented.

b. Yueqing Boxwood Carving

Zhejiang Province is a traditional key production area for boxwood carvings, mainly in Yueqing and Wenzhou. Zhejiang boxwood carving originated in Yueqing County and developed into an artistic school during the late Qing Dynasty. It is named after the use of boxwood as a carving material. Boxwood grows slowly and has a tough and smooth texture with a warm yellow colour, which makes it suitable for carving small furnishings.

c. Guangdong Chaozhou Golden Lacquer Woodcarving

Golden lacquer woodcarving was originally an art of architectural decoration in ancient China. After it spread to the south, it was influenced by the artistic characteristics of places there and formed a distinct woodcarving school. This kind of woodcarving is made of hard-textured camphorwood. After carving, the wood needs to be coated with multiple layers of paint and finally pasted with gold foil. The pillars, rafters, door lintels, and furniture of houses and temples are decorated with gold lacquer wood carvings, which appear resplendent and give people a sense of grandeur.

(3) Shell Carving

Shell carving is a unique craft. It uses bright seashells as its raw materials, which are then carved or inlaid. There are many types of shells, works of nature with beautiful colours and textures, and some are quite reflective. Shell carving involves selecting these coloured shells and using their natural colour, texture, and shape to make various products through cutting, grinding, polishing, stacking, pasting, and other processes. Shell carvings mainly use flowers, birds, figures, landscapes, and similar things as themes. The types of shell carvings are divided into practical crafts such as wine utensils, necklaces, jewelry boxes and art appreciation products such as various types of screens. In addition, as tourist souvenirs shell carvings are small and easy to carry, with unique patterns that are very popular among tourists.

a. Dalian Shell Carving

Shell carving originated primarily in coastal provinces. Dalian (Liaoning Province) is recognised as the "The Cradle of Shell Carving" in China, and its works are exported to more than 50 nations and regions. The shell-carving artists in Dalian use local shells as raw materials. According to the colour and shape of each shell, artists use traditional carving techniques and traditional Chinese painting composition forms to create relief paintings of flowers, birds, landscapes, figures, and such.

b. Hainan Shell Carving

Hainan shell carving reached a high level in the Ming Dynasty, and gradually combined with the ancient art of coconut carving to form a unique artistic style. Most of the Hainan shell carvings are combined with coconut carvings, or are inlaid shells with coconut carvings as bases. The bright shell carving and the simple coconut carving form a strong contrast, with a unique artistic style and strong Hainan regional characteristics.

c. Beihai Shell Carving

Beihai shell carving is a traditional Guangxi handicraft with a long history, and its techniques matured in the late Ming and early Qing dynasties. Beihai shell carving is a handicraft using shells and conch shells, which are carved, ground, and stacked.

China Story

Liling, a New Ceramic Tourism Landmark

Chapter Summary

Chinese crafts play an important role in the country's tourism industry. They not only reflect the Chinese people's pursuit of refined aesthetics and a better life, but also are profound cultural repositories and have rich cultural connotations. Chinese crafts bring rich cultural resources and personalized experiences to tourism, making tourism more cultural and experiential. This chapter provides an overview of the origin and development of Chinese crafts, an awareness of features and categories of Chinese crafts, an insight into the importance of Chinese crafts to tourism culture and an introduction to the well-known Chinese crafts (including Chinese paper cutting, Chinese ceramics, and Chinese carving). All of these will help readers to further understand Chinese culture, and better think about the innovative and sustainable development of tourism in the context of cultural and tourism integration.

Exercises

Recommended Reading

Issues for Review and Discussion

1. How can Chinese crafts attract tourists? Give some advice to tourism destinations and tourism businesses.

2. Would a craft-related job be one of your employment options after your graduation? Why or why not?

3. Why are Chinese crafts facing a crisis of inheritance? How can Chinese crafts be effectively inherited?

Chapter 9
Chinese Food Culture

Learning Objectives

After reading this chapter, you should have a good understanding of
1. The history and development of Chinese food culture;
2. The relationship between food culture and tourism;
3. The introduction to the famous Chinese cuisines and Chinese tea;
4. The main characteristics of food culture and tea culture.

Technical Words

English Words	中文翻译
Chinese food culture	中国饮食文化
Neolithic Age	新石器时期
Spring and Autumn period	春秋战国时期
Land of Abundance	天府之国
Pearl River Delta	珠江三角洲
Zhang Qian	张骞
Western Regions	西域
Silk Road	丝绸之路
Monk Jian Zhen	鉴真和尚
Two Tax Laws	两税法
Imperial Examination	科举考试
Eight Cuisines	八大菜系
Book of History	《尚书》
Shen Nong	神农
Herbal Cuisine / Medicated Diet	中医药膳
Health preserving	养生
harmony of five flavors	五味调和

续表

English Words	中文翻译
Confucius	孔子
Mencius	孟子

Knowledge Graph

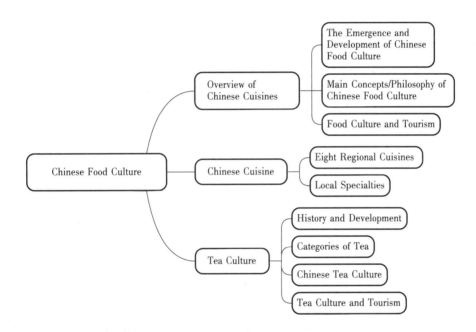

"Min Yi Shi Wei Tian (民以食为天)", which means food is always first and foremost for people, is a well-known Chinese saying, and has been spread from generation to generation for thousands of years. While the literal meaning of this sentence is simple and straightforward, it reflects the time-honoured and profound food culture in China, as well as Chinese people's strong feelings regarding food.

Throughout history, in order to survive and evolve, Chinese people have been constantly exploring food in their daily lives and work, and gradually this has developed into a system of food and dishes with distinctive local characteristics and flavours. When the quantity of food was sufficient to meet people's subsistence needs, Chinese people started to explore food further from cultural and aesthetic perspectives. In China, many famous dishes are full of historical and cultural connotations which attract and fascinate tourists. As a qualified tour guide, or tourism professional, one of the most important aspects of knowledge should be the characteristics of food culture in different parts of China, so as to be able to introduce local dishes to visitors or friends—such gourmet experiences can greatly enhance the joyfulness of travel!

9.1 Overview of Chinese Cuisines

Chinese Food Culture is an essential part of Chinese traditional culture, and one of the treasures of Chinese tourism culture. Chinese cuisine is one of the three great cuisine of the world, along with French and Turkish cuisines. Food culture refers to the development of relevant technology, science, art, dietary customs, traditions, thoughts and even philosophy of a particular social group, on the basis of which rest recognition and utilization of food materials, food production and food consumption. In other words, food culture involves all aspects of human beings' social development.

China has a long history in terms of food culture, and China is widely known as the "Kingdom of Cuisine". In China, food culture has the following five features: extensiveness, richness, consecutiveness, inclusiveness, and flexibility. All these features have made Chinese cuisine emphasise colour, aroma, taste, meaning and form. At the same time, the increasing diplomatic communication with neighbouring countries and western countries has influenced Chinese food culture to a wide extent.

9.1.1 The Emergence and Development of Chinese Food Culture

According to the research and records of archaeologists, people in ancient tribes four or five million years ago already knew how to cook food with fire. About ten thousand years ago, people learned to make fire artificially and cultivate livestock. In the Neolithic Age, people learned to plant rice and vegetables, and to extract salt from seawater. We have to acknowledge that these primitive cooking methods and sourcing of materials can simply be regarded as survival means to resist hunger, and therefore cannot be called "culture". It was not until the pre-Qin period, that is, during the Xia, Shang, and Zhou Dynasties that Chinese food culture formally originated.

(1) Phase Ⅰ Sprouting Period—pre-Qin

During the Spring and Autumn period, the ethnic groups of the north and south started to show respective features in terms of food preference, and these contributed to the original "four big cuisines". To be more specific, dietary habits in the north of China formed the earliest local specialties—Shandong Lu Cuisine (鲁菜)—whereas in the south, the Chu (楚) people, who occupied land producing large amounts of fish and rice, had the advantage of superior natural resources and created the embryonic form of Su Cuisine (苏菜). In the west, after Li Bing controlled the flood, the "Land of Abundance" (tiān fǔ zhī guó 天府之国), which refers to what is now Sichuan province, attracted a large number of immigrants, and they combined their dietary customs with those of the ancient Shu State (蜀) to form the prototype of Sichuan Cuisine (川菜). By contrast, Cantonese Cuisine (粤菜) appeared relatively late. Emperor Han Gaozu (汉高祖) established a political, economic, and cultural centre in Lingnan (which covered what are now Guangdong Province, Guangxi Province, the east of Yunnan Province, the west of Fujian Province, Hong Kong, and Macau) by taking advantage of the mild climate, abundant natural products, wide variety of edible plants and animals, and well-connected land and water transportation in the Pearl River Delta. The diversity of food here was more developed, including "flying(birds)", "diving(seafood)", "moving(land animals)", and planting (plants)" varieties, and these special dishes have lasted to today, forming the famous Cantonese cuisine.

(2) Phase Ⅱ Forming period—Qin and Han Dynasties

During the Qin and Han dynasties, the development of Chinese feudal society reached its peak, and China showed prosperous development in every aspect, including food culture. The increasingly frequent communication with other countries led to the introduction of food of a wide range of varieties. After Zhang Qian's historic mission to visit the Western Regions, through the Silk Road, he introduced fruits such as pomegranates, grapes, walnuts, and watermelons, as well as vegetables such as cucumbers, spinach, carrots, celery, lentils, and scallions, which enriched Chinese people's food choice. Tofu, interestingly known as "China's fifth invention", was also put on the table at this time. In addition, flavour enhancers that are commonly used nowadays, such as soy sauce, fermented black beans (豆豉, dòu chǐ)(Photograph 9.1), and vinegar, were all produced in this period. Fermented black beans began to be produced in large quantities during the Eastern Han Dynasty, and artificially brewed vinegar was also produced during the Han Dynasty, and was called "zuò" (酢) at that time. Soy sauce was called clear sauce (清酱, qīng jiàng).

In addition, during the Han Dynasty, with the improvement of brewing technology, people refined sugarcane into sugar and began to drink tea as a beverage. It can be seen that wine culture and tea culture also took shape in this period. Many food utensils, drinking utensils, and cooking utensils have been found in Qin Shi Huang Mausoleum Site Museum (also known as the Terracotta Warriors Museum), in Xi'an, China.

Photograph 9.1 Han Dynasty "Qi Lu dòu chǐ(齐鲁豆豉)"
(fermented black beans made in Shandong province, which were of high quality)

With the development of food, dining etiquettes were also established. For example, if a guest tried to add sauce into a dish or soup, the host needed to apologise immediately for not cooking to suit the guest's taste. If a guest kept drinking soup, the host was supposed to apologize for not preparing enough food. After dinner, the guest was supposed to stand up and offer to clean up the dishes, then the host was supposed to stand up to stop the guest and ask the servants to clean up. While Chinese people still follow some of these etiquettes on special occasions nowadays, most of the old traditions have been abandoned. For example, females and children could only eat after their husbands and fathers, and youngsters could not eat until the senior family members had finished, but in modern society, having meals together with families and friends is one of the most harmonious and happiest scenes in people's lives.

(3) Phase Ⅲ Flourishing Period—Tang and Song Dynasties

The Tang and Song dynasties are a period of time that all Chinese people feel the most proud. Along with the unprecedented progress in economic, political, and diplomatic fields, the prosperity, openness, and inclusiveness characteristic of this period nurtured the development of food culture.

The popularity of entertainment activities is seen as a major driver of food culture development during this period. Large-scale meals were always accompanied with musical and dancing performances, which significantly enhanced the atmosphere of meals, and made the demand for food diversity, quality, cooking style, and serving etiquette even higher. Accordingly, food processing technology become more and more exquisite.

Moreover, frequent exchanges between China and foreign countries during this period led to the introduction of western dietary technology in China, and some of China's technology also spread to foreign countries. For example, western wine-making techniques were introduced in the Central Plains of China from Gaochang (Xinjiang province now) in the west, while Chinese sauce-making and sugar-making techniques were introduced to Japan by the famous diplomat, Monk Jian Zhen(鉴真和尚).

During the Tang dynasty, the status of wheat and rice gradually rose. In the early Tang Dynasty, wheat as a staple food was relatively luxurious. After the middle period of the Tang Dynasty, the growth of urban populations and the popularization of wheaten food greatly promoted the development of wheat-making. The "Two tax laws" implemented during the reign of Emperor De Zong clearly made wheat an object of taxation, and this put wheat on a par with millet. The staple food of the Song Dynasty was much the same as that of the Tang Dynasty, except that rice became more and more important, eventually achieving its modern status as China's major grain. According to historical records, there were 41 kinds of food made from flour, 42 kinds of fruit, 21 kinds of vegetable, 9 kinds of congee, 19 kinds of cake and pastry, and 54 kinds of wine during the Song Dynasty.

(4) Phase Ⅳ Golden age of food culture—Yuan, Ming, and Qing Dynasties

Chinese food culture had its heyday during the last three feudal dynasties. Unlike previous phases, during this period, food culture was involved with specific political functions and therefore many forms of banquet were created for different purposes, such as the banquet awarded by the Emperor to hundreds of officials, the banquet for officials' farewell, the banquet for welcoming new officials, and the banquet for celebrating the top candidates from the imperial examination (Photograph 9.2).

At the same time, there were also many famous special food products, local specialties, and local snacks. As the prosperity of both national food culture and regional food culture increased, local cuisine gradually formed, as is often said, into "Eight Cuisines"(八大菜系): Lu(鲁菜), Sichuan(川菜), Guangdong(粤菜), Huaiyang(淮扬菜), Fujian(闽菜), Zhejiang(浙菜), Anhui(皖菜), and Hunan(湘菜).

Typical food for particular folk festivals was more distinctive. For example, on the Lantern Festival, people were supposed to eat sweet dumplings; when it came to the Dragon Boat Festival, rice dumplings were the must-have food; moon cakes were the representative food of the Mid-autumn Festival; tea eggs were for the summer solstice; and pastries were for the Double Ninth Festival (Chong Yang Festival). Folk cuisine has since become the foundational source of Chinese cuisine.

Tableware and stone tools appeared in large numbers during the Qing Dynasty. Made from porcelain, gold, and silver, they became an important part of Chinese food culture. In addition, Chinese tea was introduced to Europe, Brazil, and the United States, and in return, Western food was introduced to China.

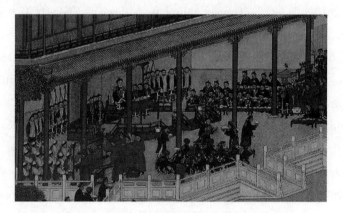

Photograph 9.2　Qing Dynasty Zi Guang Palace Banquet
(1761, Emperor Qianlong rewarded generals and solders with a banquet for winning a war)

9.1.2 Philosophy of Chinese Food Culture

(1) "Min Yi Shi Wei Tian" (民以食为天—Food is the first and foremost)

As mentioned at the beginning of this chapter, for thousands of years, Chinese people have always regarded food and eating food as the most important thing in life. This belief has to do with more than simply meeting the basic needs of survival; more importantly, eating has great social significance. Chinese people always treat others to have meals, as this is the best way to express their sincerity and warm hospitality. As the famous author Qian Zhongshu described in his book *Chifan*, "Eating has many social functions, such as promoting relationships, business cooperation" "To offer food to those who have food for themselves, this is a 'treat' (请客); we have food ourselves but we accept other's offer, this shows repect (赏面子) to the host—these are subtle interpersonal skills in China". This is true, Chinese people take every chance to have meals together: weddings, funerals, birthday celebrations, celebrations of newborns after one month (满月) and after one-hundred days (百天), welcoming guests, farewells, celebrations of children entering higher school and university, classmates' parties, colleagues' gatherings, friends' appointments, business negotiations, business deals, and so on. It is through eating that Chinese people promote interpersonal relations, resolve conflicts, achieve harmony and happiness, and extend ethics and morals. Compared with the western cultural practice of having meals alone, the social function of eating in China is unmatched and unique. There is an interesting saying: when a guest visits you, you must treat the guest with the best meal by all means, even if you are poor, you "carry the lid of the pot to sell along the street".

In China, food also tends to have a political function. In ancient China, the people's wellbeing was always the top priority for emperors. According to the earliest *Book of History*(《尚书》), providing food was the first of eight political policies; emperors were to regard the people as "heaven", and the people were to regard food as "heaven". This is seen as the original source of the saying "Min Yi Shi Wei Tian". In modern history, the greatest politicians, including Sun Yat-sen and Mao Zedong, advocated the belief: "what is the biggest problem in the world? Eating is the biggest problem." In order to realize a stable society, the first task is to provide people with sufficient and quality food.

It is interesting that there are many words in Chinese related to food, but that are used as metaphors. For example, people refer to a job as a "rice bowl"(饭碗), as without a job, there is no way of getting food; people call a job with higher security, such as that of a public servant, an "iron rice bowl"(铁饭碗), as those secure jobs are like bowls made of iron, stable and permanent, without the risk of decruitment; people call a high-paid or decent job a "golden rice bowl (金饭碗,), for the reason that only the rich or people with higher social status could afford a bowl made of gold. Of course, this is not to say that Chinese people live for work; instead, they work for life. As a typical agriculture-based society, China has a food culture that also reflects people's pursuit of carefree pastoral life, collective value, and higher spiritual life as opposed to material life. For thousands of years, the Chinese New Year, or Spring Festival, has been one of the happiest days of the year for Chinese people. A pot of liquor, several dishes of food, slaughtering pigs and chickens, making dumplings, reunion dinners; all the hard work throughout the year is worth it at the moment of this big reunion meal. People travel thousands of kilometres, hours and days, to get home on New Year's Eve for this big gathering based around food.

(2) Eating for Health

Chinese people believe that food and medicine come from the same source; all edible things are food and medicine, which can be used for both individual health and hygiene. Traditional Chinese medicine is nowadays not only widely used in China, but recognised in other parts of the world. Chinese medicine mainly uses medicinal plants, including roots, stems, leaves, and fruits. Shen Nong, who is believed to be the first person to discover tea as a drink, tasted hundreds of herbs and was poisoned up to seventy times during a single day. Such myths and legends reflect that during the early period when people had to continuously explore new foods by tasting them personally, the relationship between food and medicine was strengthened: food provided humans with basic nutrition, while medicine helped relieve the pain and cure the illnesses caused by inappropriate dieting. In response to this, "herbal cuisine", or the "medicated diet", came into existence.

Medicated diet is not a simple combination of food and Chinese medicine, but instead consists of special recipes prepared based on differentiation of symptoms and signs from traditional Chinese medicine. It has not only the efficiency of medicine but also the delicacy of food, and can be used to prevent and cure diseases as well as improve people's fitness level. For example, lotus-seed tea, with 30 lotus seeds and a little salt, is a recipe to strengthen heart function, relax the nerves, and treat insomnia. Steamed pears with rock sugar, prepared by peeling fresh pears, cutting them into pieces, applying rock sugar, and steaming them in a pot, is an excellent medicinal recipe for removing heat from the lungs, dissolving phlegm, and relieving coughing.

Gradually, people realized that medicated diet not only helped prevent disease, but also brought a number of other benefits, such as improving sleep quality, whitening and smoothing the skin, brightening the eyes, improving memory. Therefore, people started to integrate food with special medicinal functions into their daily diet, which is called health preserving. In other words, in order to keep healthy and achieve longevity, regardless of whether people were young or old, male or female, healthy or unhealthy, they were advised to follow a set of rules about food and exercise for a period of time or even their whole lives. During the Spring and Autumn period, people agreed that they would rather have healthy food every day than take medicine when feeling ill. Similarly, people during the Han Dynasty believed in the importance of controlling the amount of food they ate instead of eating too much and developing regular life habits rather than getting up or staying up too late. Chinese people also believe in the mantras: "don't eat until you are hungry, and don't finish until you feel full", and "don't drink until you feel thirsty, and don't drink overly". They believe all diseases can be attributed to eating habits, and eating the right amount of food, eating at the right time, eating at the right pace, and eating food with the least flavor and grease comprise the "regimen" we should follow. These principles are believed to be in line with the physical features of the Chinese people and the agriculture-oriented way of life, so they have been widely followed for thousands of years, even in modern society.

However, we should maintain a critical view of this, instead of taking it too far.

nowadays, due to commercial interests, the exaggerated effects of traditional Chinese medicine and health preserving may mislead people or even do harm to their health.

(3) Taste & the Harmony of Five Flavours

Chinese people pay great attention to the colour, smell, taste, and shape of food, and taste is regarded as the soul of Chinese food. Yuan Mei, a gourmand in the Qing Dynasty, said in his biography of Wang Xiaoyu, a cook, "It is difficult to know a soul mate, but it is especially difficult to appreciate a taste." It can be seen that Chinese food has always put taste aesthetics in the first place in the production and quality evaluation of dishes, and even consider delicious food as a source of enjoyment, style, and fun. Interestingly, the word taste, Wei in Chinese, is used in many other occasions in life; people use tasty to describe everything they find interesting, valuable, or worthy, while they use tasteless to show their negative feelings of anything they don't like. The concept of taste is therefore closely related to philosophy. Another interesting thing to share here is that someone once used three sensory organs to describe the difference between dishes from different countries, and concluded that French cuisine is for the nose (with pleasant flavour), Japanese cuisine is for the eyes (with delicate design), and Chinese cuisine is for the tongue (with charming taste).

Tastes of Chinese food are traditionally categorized into five flavours: sour, bitter, sweet, spicy, and salty. Over China's vast territory, the flavours of cuisine vary from one region to another, and usually one or two of the five flavours dominate. Flavour preferences can reflect features of geography, climate, agriculture, culture, and history.

Spicy — Central China, especially Sichuan Province and Hunan Province

Spiciness is also called the "pungent flavour" among the five flavours. It not only can whet the appetite, but also is said to have the functions of expelling wind and cold from the body, reducing internal dampness, moistening dryness, and promoting qi (气) and blood circulation.

Salty — Coastal Areas and Northern China

The salty flavour is important among the five flavours for its health benefits. Saltiness is said to help the body "dissolve stagnation". However, salty food should not be eaten too much, because eating too much salt is harmful to health.

Sweet — Eastern China

According to traditional Chinese medicine, the sweet flavour can "tone the body", alleviate illness, and improve one's mood. Sweet Chinese seasonings mainly include sugar, honey, and various jams, which can not only sweeten, but also enhance flavours and reduce fishiness and greasiness.

Sour — Southern Minorities and Shanxi Province

The sour flavour can reduce fishiness and greasiness, help digestion (including dissolving calcium in food), and whet the appetite. According to traditional Chinese medicine, it can constrict the intestines, stop diarrhea, promote salivation, and quench thirst.

Bitter — the Taste of Most Chinese Medicinal Food

The bitter flavour is said to clear "heat", strengthen the stomach, and promote salivation. Bitterness is used in Chinese cooking, but rarely alone. Slight bitterness can make dishes fresher and more delicious, greatly whetting the appetite. The bitter flavour is generally the taste of Chinese medicinal food, which is made by adding bitter medicinal herbs.

Which flavour is the best? None of them is. Chinese people emphasise the harmony of five flavours, which is called "Zhonghe (中和)". It is the highest aesthetic standard of food in China, so the charm of Zhong He is the charm of food. Zhong He represents harmony with the organic and natural integration of different flavours, just like the respectable harmony in nature, which includes Yin (阴) and Yang (阳), firm and soft, odd and even, positive and negative, big and small, and so on.

9.1.3 Food Culture and Tourism

The combination of food culture and tourism can be called "diet tourism", which refers to the integration of food culture and tourism activities: while tasting the local food, tea, and wine, tourists visit and appreciate the natural views and cultural landscapes of the place; in this way, eating and visiting best complement each other, as visitors acquire a sense of satisfaction for both taste buds and spirit. What a pleasant life! China's food culture has a long history, prosperous and profound. The unique and rich diet culture is a natural advantage and precious resource for developing tourism in various regions of our country. It is of great significance to explore the potential of regional and ethnic diet culture for promoting tourism and local economic development, and protecting ethnic and local culture. Food is the first of the six elements of tourism, which highlights the close relationship between food culture and tourism. Specifically, the relationship between food culture and tourism is reflected in the following two aspects.

First, food culture is the important foundation of tourism.

Food culture is an indispensable part of the tourism industry. In essence, tourism is a comprehensive activity with material and spiritual aspects. On the one hand, tourists' travel itineraries and sightseeing activities must include meals. One of the most satisfying moments during travel is enjoy a decent meal after a tiring journey; without quality food, travel can never be a perfect experience. Many travellers rate local food on social media after a trip, and this can largely affect the overall perception of a destination. For sure, positive evaluation of food will attract more travellers to long for a place. Therefore, the development of the catering service industry is very important for every tourist destination. On the other hand, local food culture is the embodiment of local culture in every aspect, and it provides insight for travellers to get to know more about the local culture. Just like cultural relics and historic sites, all kinds of special dishes and local snacks are distinct cultural markers of each destination, for they all demonstrate high aesthetic value and cultural value for tourists. For example, if you visit the author's city, Dalian, Liaoning Province, eating Dalian local snacks, such as grilled squid, men zi (焖子), and mini chicken kebabs must be top on your list.

More importantly, food culture can also bring tourist destinations huge economic benefits. Obtaining economic income has always been one of the main purposes of developing tourism. Unlike ordinary restaurants serving local people, those restaurants, hotels, or small food courts inside tourist attractions normally charge relatively higher price from tourists. Though this significantly increases economic benefits, and tourists seem to accept this kind of trade, the price should be regulated by local authorities instead of being unreasonable. At the same time, people's desire for higher food quality and better dining environment during their travel has boosted the development of other tourism-related industries, such as the hotel industry, the entertainment industry, and the media industry.

Second, tourism activities have a positive role in promoting the food industry.

In return, the prosperity of the tourism industry increases the demand for the food industry. Thanks to advertisements, posters, and brochures, the promotion of a tourism destination always consists of the promotion of local food, and therefore enhances the popularity and potential of local food: foodies see a place for trying new food, while smart businessmen see a chance to invest. For example, with the development of tourism in Yunnan Province, more and more local foods in Yunnan, such as rice noodles and floral pancakes, are becoming well known to tourists. In addition, the development of tourism promotes cultural exchange between a destination and the outside world, and frequent communication contributes to the diversity of food and enrichment of food culture.

It should be acknowledged that there is controversy over whether imported food should be embraced. China has a vast territory and numerous ethnic minorities, each of which has distinct characteristics in terms of food culture. However, as Han people make up the majority of the population in China, in the development of food culture tourism products, food culture from the Han group still dominates. So the dispute is about whether the minority ethnic regions should keep their original food culture or develop food diversity and absorb food culture from the mainstream to attract and cater for mass tourists. On the one hand, some hold the opinion that this blind pursuit of "common taste" will negatively affect the authentic local taste, and will eventually seriously affect the attraction of local food culture. What is worse, the influx of imported food will gradually change the eating habits of the local people, and precious traditional cooking skills will not survive. On the other hand, others feel that eating habits originated from genes, which are hardly expected to change, and that while it is a precious experience to taste new food, only food from people's home culture fits people's appetite and comfort tourists' homesickness. This explains why there is a "China Town" in most of the big western metropolitan cities like New York, London, and Paris. Likewise, this is also the reason why we see foreigners most in western restaurants and Starbucks in China.

After a period of development, China has formed four major forms of food culture tourism, the first of which is sightseeing tours in places where particular foods originated. For example, Hangzhou is home to the well-known Long Jing Tea. Long Jing grows near the West Lake in Hangzhou, and has a history of more than 1200 years, beginning during the Song Dynasty and flourishing during the Ming Dynasty. A popular tour in Hangzhou is to visit the West Lake District, appreciating the process of picking, frying, and making tea. Second is medicated food tours for health care. As mentioned in the last section, Chinese people have been continuously exploring the medicinal function of food and developing mature health care regimens. There is a city in Anhui, Bozhou, known as the "medicine capital". It is the hometown of the miracle doctor Hua Tuo. It has been the capital of traditional Chinese medicine since ancient times. Tourists who visit Bozhou always check out the local medicinal food, such as Da Bu Soup (soup with all precious medicinal ingredients, which is believed to strengthen health). Third is food culture-related museums. Museum tours are popular in those places with historical and famous tea culture and wine culture, such as the Chinese Tea Art Museum in Hangzhou and the Wuliangye Wine Culture Museum in Yibin. Fourth, some cities hold festivals and carnivals on a large scale to attract tourists. For example, the Guangzhou International Food Festival, the Dalian Beer Festival.

9.2 Chinese Cuisine

9.2.1 Eight Regional Cuisines

China covers a large territory and has 56 ethnic groups. Due to differences in climate, geography, history, resources, and eating customs within each region, a set of typical cooking styles, including particular ingredients, flavours, forms, and skills, have formed. These different cuisines can be roughly divided into eight regional cuisines, namely, Lu (Shandong), Chuan (Sichuan), Yue (Guangdong), Su (Jiangsu), Min (Fujian), Zhe (Zhejiang), Xiang (Hunan), and Wan (Anhui), which have been widely accepted all over China and the world. Certainly, there are also many other local cuisines that are famous, such as Beijing cuisine and Shanghai cuisine, as well as local snacks.

(1) Lu (Shandong) Cuisine

Shandong is the birthplace of many famous ancient figures such as Confucius and Mencius. And much of Shandong cuisine's history is as old as Confucius himself, making it the oldest existing major cuisine in China. Historically speaking, since the Song Dynasty, Shandong cuisine has been the main representative of northern food. During the Ming and Qing Dynasties, Shandong cuisine became the main food for the royal banquets and emperors' daily diet. Therefore, most people consider Shandong cuisine to be the first of the eight major cuisines. Shandong cuisine is considered the most influential cuisine in China, and many cuisines have developed from it. Nowadays, the food of northern cities, such as Tianjin, Beijing, and cities in the northeast, can always be categorized under Shandong Cuisine.

Consisting of Jinan cuisine and Jiaodong cuisine, Shandong cuisine, in general, is known for its pure and plain taste, rather than a mixed taste or having much grease. It is characterised by its emphasis on aroma, freshness, crispness, and tenderness. Shandong Cuisine is known for its excellent seafood dishes and delicious soup: the plain soup tastes clear and fresh, while the greasy soup features thickness and strength. Shandong is a large peninsula surrounded by the sea to the East and with the Yellow River meandering through the centre. As a result, seafood is a major ingredient of Shandong cuisine. In terms of cooking style, Jinan cuisine mainly depends on frying, deep-frying, stir-frying, and grilling, while Jiaodong style is famous for its seafood with fresh and light flavour.

Famous dishes: Stir Fried Prawns, Fried Sea Cucumbers with Onions, Sweet and Sour Carp, Large Jiaodong Chicken Wings, Mount Tai Fish with Red Scales, Jiuzhuan Dachang (九转大肠, braised pork intestines in brown sauce).

(2) Chuan (Sichuan) Cuisine

Talking about Sichuan Cuisine, most people find it mouth-watering and cannot resist the temptation of its "spiciness". Sichuan cuisine is one of the most famous Chinese cuisines, known by people all over the world. Characterized by its spicy and pungent flavour, Sichuan cuisine emphasises the use of chilli. Chinese pepper and Chinese prickly ash are considered as the best spices for this, producing thrilling, exciting, and durable tastes. In addition, garlic, ginger, and fermented soybeans are also used in the cooking process. The main ingredients include both vegetables and meat, and frying, frying without oil, pickling, and boiling are basic cooking techniques.

Sichuan Hotpot must be the most famous hotpot known by foreigners, as in every Chinatown there must be a Sichuan Hotpot restaurant. Unlike other types of dishes, which are served complete and ready to eat, the unique charm of the hotpot is cooking while eating; when eating, the food is still steaming hot. For this reason, hotpot is especially popular in cold areas and mountain climates. The greatest hotpot invention is the "double-flavour" hotpot, which is also known as the Yuanyang (鸳鸯) hotpot. Yuanyang is a species of bird that are extremely loyal to their partners; Yuanyang always stick with each other and never separate. This is used as a metaphor to describe the best combination of two tastes of soup for boiling vegetables and meat, usually one is light flavor, like cream-coloured chicken soup, or even more plain mushroom soup, and the other strong, the fiery-red oil full of chilli peppers and numbing Sichuan peppercorns. This unique design is meant to cater for different tastes, and to enable people to taste as much as possible. Deriving from this, nowadays, people have increased the number of flavours from two to four, or even up to nine, by dividing the pot into small squared sections.

Famous dishes: Double Cooked Pork Slice, Kung Pao Chicken, Sliced Beef in Hot Chilli Oil, Mapo Tofu.

(3) Yue (Guangdong/Cantonese) Cuisine

Guangdong, located on the southeast coast of China, has a mild climate and abundant resources. Due to its geographical location and accelerating commercial development, a number of Cantonese travelled abroad and settled down in the 20th century, so Cantonese food, originating from Guangdong, is perhaps the most widely available Chinese regional cuisine outside of China.

Famous dishes: Roast Suckling Pig, Black Tea with Condensed Milk（港式奶茶）, Shrimp Wonton Noodle Soup（鲜虾云吞面）, BBQ pork with a red outer colouring（叉烧）, Steamed Shrimp Dumplings（虾饺）.

(4) Su (Jiangsu) Cuisine

Jiangsu cuisine, also called Huaiyang（淮阳）cuisine, developed from the local recipes of Yangzhou（扬州）, Suzhou（苏州）, and Nanjing（南京）. Jiangsu, an eastern province in China, has over 1000 kilometres (620 miles) of coastline along the Yellow Sea. There are two great rivers flowing through the whole province—the Yangtze River from west to east and the Beijing-Hangzhou Grand Canal from north to south—which bring Jiangsu abundant natural resources. It has been called "Yu Mi Hometown（鱼米之乡）", which means home to fish and rice.

Its main cooking techniques are braising and stewing, which preserve the original flavour. The flavour is light, fresh, and sweet, with a delicate and elegant colour. Jiangsu cuisine is known for its duck recipes. One of the most highly recommended courses is known as three sets of ducks, a complex dish with three kinds of ducks.

Famous dishes: Sweet and Sour Mandarin Fish, Pork Balls.

(5) Min (Fujian) Cuisine

Fujian province has a favourable geographical location, with mountains in the north and the sea to the south. Its economy and culture began flourishing after the Southern Song Dynasty. During the middle Qing Dynasty, around the 18th century, famous officials and scholars promoted Fujian cuisine, so it gradually spread to other parts of China. Consisting of Fuzhou（福州）cuisine, South Fujian cuisine and West Fujian cuisine, Fujian cuisine is distinguished for its choice seafood, beautiful colour, and magic combination of sweet, sour, salty, and savoury tastes. South Fujian cuisine, popular in Xiamen（厦门）, Quanzhou（泉州）, and Zhangzhou（漳州）, is more fresh and delicious, and less salty, sweet, and sour; West Fujian dishes are salty and hot, prevailing in the Hakka region and with strong local flavour. As Fujian people emigrated overseas, their cuisine become popular in Taiwan and abroad.

In terms of ingredients, seafood and food from mountain areas are mainly used in Fujian cuisine. The coastal area produces nearly 200 varieties of fish, turtles, and shellfish, and common foods from the mountains include mushrooms, bamboo shoots, and tremella. The local people are good at cooking seafood, with their cooking featuring methods of stewing, boiling, braising, quick-boiling（生烫）, and steaming. There are also a number of great chefs who can cut sliced ingredients as thin as paper and as slim as hairs, as they believe that such exquisite slicing can best present the aroma and texture of the food. More importantly, they also put special emphasis on food processing, from selecting ingredients and mixing flavours to timing the cooking and controlling the heat. They have a good mastery of sauce: when a dish is less salty, it tastes more delicious; sweetness makes a dish tastier, while sourness helps remove the seafood smell.

Buddha-jumping-over-the-wall might be the most representative dish of Fujian cuisine, and contains 18 precious and expensive ingredients. All of these ingredients are simmered together over a low fire for hours with premium Shaoxing rice wine. The name of this dish implies it is so delicious that even the Buddha would jump over a wall to have a taste once he smelled it.

(6) Zhe (Zhejiang) Cuisine

Hangzhou used to be the capital city during the Southern Song Dynasty, when a number of famous chefs from other parts of China gathered there, contributing to the prosperity and reputation of Zhejiang cuisine. Together with Suzhou, Hangzhou is one of the two "paradise cities" of China, and Zhejiang cuisine shares some similar characteristics with Suzhou cuisine, with both of them taking advantage of nearby seafood resources and featuring freshness, tenderness, softness, and smoothness.

Zhejiang cuisine's dishes generally belong to one of three categories. The first category is influenced by northern(particularly Beijing)cuisine, with the main ingredients being of high quality, and roast suckling pig, roast duck (Beijing Roast Duck). The second category is greatly influenced by Anhui cuisine, which is famous for the process of braising in soy sauce. The dishes have strong taste, rich oil, and fancy colour. The other category is that of local dishes, the real native cuisine. The famous Hang cuisine restaurant, "West Lake Lou wai lou", opened in the reign of Emperor Daoguang in the Qing Dynasty, and is widely known for dishes like West Lake vinegar fish and stir-fried prawn with Longjing tea leaves.

Famous dishes: West Lake Carp in Vinegar, Dongpo Braised Pork, Braised Bamboo Shoots.

(7) Xiang (Hunan) Cuisine

Xiang cuisine originates from the area along the Xiang River, Dongting Lake, and the mountain areas of the west of Hunan province, and can be best represented by Changsha cuisine. Like some eastern regions mentioned earlier, Hunan province is also known as "the land of fish and rice", due to its advantageous geographical place and humid climate.

Very similar to Sichuan cuisine, Hunan cuisine is also characterised by its hot, spicy, strong, and pungent flavour. Chilli, pepper, and shallots are used frequently in cooking. It's not hard to find that both Sichuan and Hunan are characterised by humid climates, so local people eat hot and spicy food to help remove dampness and cold from the body, which reflects the close relationship between regional food and natural features. However, what makes Hunan cuisine different from Sichuan cuisine is that it also incorporates sour and sweet flavours, as it uses distinctive sauces, like "strange-flavour sauce", to enliven the taste of some dishes, and uses honey in its unique desserts.

Additionally, like most of the cuisines in the south of China, the main cooking methods for Hunan dishes are braising, double-boiling, steaming, and stewing. It is also renowned for its frequent use of preserved meat in cooking. Rice is the staple food, though northern-style side dishes and fillers are also popular, such as bean curd "bread" rolls or dumplings and savory buns. Hunan is therefore one of China's culinary heartlands, incorporating many flavors and regional influences.

Famous dishes: Dong'an Chicken; Peppery and Hot Chicken, Lotus Seeds with Rock Sugar, Steamed Pickled Meat.

(8) Wan (Anhui) Cuisine

Anhui cuisine, which shares some similarities with Jiangsu and Hangzhou cuisine, developed from the local cooking styles of the Huangshan Mountain(黄山). This region's uncultivated fields and forests provide various wild ingredients for this region's cuisine.

It is also worth noting that the development of Anhui cuisine was enhanced greatly by a group of businessmen in history, namely the famous "Hui Shang (徽商)" or Huizhou merchants. The long period from the middle period of the Ming Dynasty until the end of the Qing Dynasty was the golden age of the Huizhou merchants; in such aspects as number of businessmen, scope of activities and business sectors, and amount capital, Huizhou merchants ranked first among all the merchant groups in China. They mainly traded in salt, tea, and wood, and engaged in a wide range of commercial activities in all parts of China. Importantly, though Huizhou merchants were extremely rich in capital and experience, they still favoured their home cuisine, so their demands for luxurious banquets and high-quality dishes promoted the development of Anhui cuisine.

Anhui cuisine is known for simple methods of preparation and cooking. Frying and stir-frying are used much less frequently; instead, braising and stewing are the main cooking methods, and specific attention is paid to the temperature while cooking. Dry cured meat and sugar are always used in sauces to improve the taste and freshness. A must-try dish is red-braised fermented mandarin fish, which has a pungent odour, much like stinky tofu. However, just as passionate lovers of stinky tofu describe, while it smells stinky, it tastes wonderful and unique.

Main dishes: Fermented Bean Chicken, Mushrooms and Chestnuts.

9.2.2 Local Specialties

People all over the world are attracted by Chinese food: not only the traditional food introduced in the last section, but also various local snacks. Local snacks, also called local specialties or refreshments, generally refer to food that can be eaten for breakfast or as night snacks, or between formal meals. Unlike main dishes, which can be served on the table for formal meals and occasions, local snacks are normally not served before or after main meals, as starters, or as kinds of "decorations" for entertainment purposes. Local snacks have a wider variety of types, flavours, and ingredients, including staple foods like wheat and rice, all kinds of meat, vegetables, and even fruit and milk products. However, compared with the traditional eight cuisines, Chinese local snacks have gained more popularity in some sense due to their fresh ingredients from local areas, unique styles of cooking, interesting presentation in street markets, and most importantly, being economical and common.

Chinese local snacks are multifarious. It is almost impossible to cover all local delicacies of our country. This section takes several Beijing snacks as examples, and selects a number of the most popular local snacks from all parts of China, to present an overview to readers.

The most famous Beijing food is Peking Duck, which consists of a small, round, thin pancake wrapped around three to four pieces of duck meat and greasy duck skin, with several sliced onions, cucumbers, and a sweet soybean paste (a sweet sauce made of fermented flour) as a flavour enhancer—amazing! It's said that in the past, a foreign ambassador visited Beijing and was served Peking Duck; after trying it, he was deeply immersed by the unique flavour, and made a joke: "After a dinner of Peking Duck, I'll agree to sign any document." More surprisingly, in the USA, the Manhattan Peking Duck restaurant has 440 seats, but a reservation still has to be made two weeks in advance!

Peking Noodles are prepared by draining boiled, hand-pulled wheat noodles until no soup is left, then topping them with minced pork in a smoky yellow soybean sauce and laying fresh vegetables (sliced cucumber, crunchy radish) to the side to balance the addictive saltiness of the soybean sauce. The diner is meant to stir the noodles with their chopsticks until each string of the noodles dips into the flavourful meat and sauce on the top—then it is ready to eat!

Love or hate it, one of Beijing's most famous and unique flavours is a grey-green drink that locals have proudly adored since the Liao Dynasty. Sometimes translated as "soymilk", Beijing's douzhi(豆汁) is actually made from mung beans, has a mild sourness to it, and isn't sweet like soymilk. Beijing people believe that this drink is rich in protein, and whether you have a chilled one in summer or a hot one in winter, it benefits your health. You'll find douzhi throughout the city, from street stalls to restaurants, and it warrants a taste to find out if you are a douzhilover or hater.

Animal liver and tripe are especially favoured by Beijing people, who have famous snacks like quick-fried pork liver and tripe. Fried liver is served with salty mushroom soup and raw garlic on top, and people have it for breakfast. Tripe is the stomachs of bulls or lambs. After being washed very clean, it is then cut into pieces, put into a pot of boiling water, and fired quickly. After adding cooking oil, sesame sauce, Chinese vinegar, chilli oil, bean paste, and small pieces of vegetables, the dish is ready to serve.

Let's introduce a few sweet snacks. Jiaoquan(焦圈), which can be translated as "fried ring", is made of wheat. The right type of wheat must be chosen to ensure that after deep frying, it tastes crispy. This is thought to be the best accompaniment for douzhi. Pea flour cake is made by grinding peas, taking off the skins, cleaning them, boiling them until soft, freezing them, and then finally cutting the big blocks into pieces. It is said that pea flour cake was favoured by Empress Cixi(慈禧), making it even more famous. Sugar-coated haws(糖葫芦) are a typical snack in northern China, especially in Beijing.

Chinese people, especially those who live overseas, claim the most unforgettable tastes in China are neither those from five-star restaurants nor meals that can be found at local restaurants, but are always the "not very clean" but delicious foods found in noisy, crowded corners in the cities. The foods discussed below are a selection of local sacks from China, north to south and west to east. It is these foods that always provoke Chinese people to feel homesick and nostalgic.

Harbin, one of the biggest cites in the northeast of China, is the capital of Heilongjiang Province. Harbin red sausage is a hugely popular cold cut in China. People get it from deli shops and eat it on its own as a snack, with bread as a picnic food, or cook it with vegetables or eggs. Compared with western sausages, the texture is firmer and drier, with a salty and smoked flavour.

Proper street kebabs, originating from the Islamic lamb kebabs with cumin in Xinjiang province, have now developed into a rich variety in all parts of China. The ingredients are no longer limited to lamb; according to local resources, nowadays we see street barbeques of seafood like squid and oysters, chicken wings, vegetables, and so on. Normally, different sauces are served and customers can choose the sauce and level of spiciness according to their individual tastes. The smell of street-side kebabs always provides the best comfort and relief from the hustle and bustle of life.

Spicy crayfish, originally from Hunan, is now favoured by people all over the country. The fresh crayfish is stewed in a broth with chilli and abundant spices.

Suitable for all seasons and regions, the most pleasant thing in life might be inviting a group of friends to a jam-packed stall, sitting on tiny plastic stools, and ordering a huge bucket of bright red crayfish: no chopsticks needed, holding crayfishs with the hands, dipping thoroughly into the strong-flavoured soup, taking off the shell, and finally eating the food—all worth it! The preferred beverage to go with these tasty freshwater lobsters is ice-cold Chinese beer.

Guilin, located in southern China among clear rivers and the Karst Mountains, is famous not only for its heavenly landscape, but its bowls of rice noodles. There are noodles sold everywhere in Guilin and the surrounding areas. In recent years, another similar rice noodle from Liuzhou in Guangxi Province, called Liuzhou river snails rice noodle (螺蛳粉), has gained great popularity. Unlike other rice noodles, the flavour of Liuzhou river snails rice noodle is uniquely created by river snails, pork bones, and many other spices, and pickled vegetables, dried beancurd sticks, fresh green vegetables, peanuts, and chilli are usually added. There is a joke that if you boil Luosifen, people from thousands of miles away will smell it!

Lanzhou hand-pulled noodles, unlike Beijing noodles, can be served without soup, with soup, or quick-fried. Also, unlike rice noodles, which are made of rice and hard to digest for children and seniors, Lanzhou noodles suit everyone. Almost everywhere in China, when people, feel hungry and tired, they are attracted by this flagship halal food, with its clean, fresh, and hot soup with slices of beef on top.

Stinky tofu must be the most famous "dark cuisine" known to foreigners. It is made from fermented bean curd: fried, braised, steamed, or grilled. For its passionate lovers, stinky tofu is delicious no matter how it's prepared. Stinky tofu is most popular in Hunan Province in central China, the Yangtze River Delta region (especially Shaoxing).

9.3 Tea Culture

Tea, coffee, and cocoa are the three major hot beverages in the world today, among which tea is respected as the top one. It is widely recognised that coffee was first discovered by Africans, and the Maya in America began to cultivate cacao trees about 3,

000 years ago. Tea is thought to have originated from Asia, in particular, China. Almost all the tea producing countries directly or indirectly imported tea from China, and tea drinking customs around the world are also derived from China. Therefore, just like porcelain, silk, and so on, tea has become a remarkable symbol of China worldwide. At the same time, tea culture has also become an essential part of Chinese food and tourism culture.

9.3.1 History and Development

Tea culture remained in China for a few centuries before it spread to other parts of the world. The character, sound, and meaning of the word "tea" was first agreed on in China. As early as 1610, tea was exported to the Netherlands and Portugal, then it spread to England in 1638, then Russia and America in 1664 and 1674 respectively. In some Chinese dialects, such as that of Fujian people, tea is called "te", and this sound was introduced to western counties: for example, in English it is "tea" and in German it is "tee".

Chinese tea culture has a time-honoured history. As mentioned in the first section of this chapter, Shen Nong was a legendary figure who tasted thousands of plants in his life and thus poisoned himself hundreds of times. He believed that water was only safe to drink after being boiled. One day he noticed some leaves had fallen into his boiling water. He took a sip of the brew and was pleasantly surprised by its flavour, and even more miraculously, it helped him get rid of the poisoning effects of plants he had tasted. Later, the ancient Chinese got to know more and more about tea: as they needed to work in the fields for many hours, even during the scorching hot summer, tea was found not only to relieve people's thirst, but to lower their temperature and make them feel more refreshed and energetic after drinking it, and so it gradually became a popular drink. Tea culture reached its zenith during Tang Dynasty, with the book named *The Classic of Tea* by Lu Yu as the milestone of this golden age. This book contains the comprehensive history of tea production, along with descriptions of tea's origin, evolvement, present situation, and production technology, tea drinking skills, and tea ceremony principles. It is not only a natural science book of tea, but also a monograph of tea culture.

Nowadays, tea is mostly produced in the south of China, and Chinese tea contributes to a great amount of the tea enjoyed by people all over the world. Though China is the original tea-producing nation and its tea products are of outstanding quality, today Chinese tea must compete against foreign teas from many other places in the world. However, Chinese tea still dominates the worldwide tea market due to its numerous advantages. Of

Case Study

Chinese Food at the Beijing Winter Olympics Cheered up the Athletes

particular note is the fact that Chinese rituals for preparing and drinking tea have been studied, simulated, and performed as an art in every part of the world.

9.3.2 Categories of Tea

Chinese tea has the most complex categories and classifications. In general, there are six categories: green tea, black tea, dark green tea, oolong tea, yellow tea, and white tea. For each kind of tea, there are more specific divisions according to place of origin, duration of growing, flavour, appearance, etc.

Green tea is the most common one, and the highest output. It is known for its freshness. Without being fermented, simply after being dried, tealeaves are directly fried in the pot over the heat, to maintain its green features. Famous green tea varieties include Longjing (龙井), Biluochun (碧螺春), Huangshan Maofeng (黄山毛峰), and Putuo Buddha (普陀佛). Green tea is the best option for most people, as they have to work for hours during the day, and green tea helps prevent computer radiation and supplement the moisture content of the human body.

Unlike green tea, black tea is made after being fermented. Black tea is named after the colour of the liquid it produces when brewed. In fact, in Chinese, black tea is translated as "Hongcha" (红茶, its literal meaning is red tea). Precious varieties of black tea include Dianhong tea (滇红茶) from Yunnan, Qimen tea (祁门茶) from Anhui, and Ninghong tea(宁红茶) from Jiangxi. Black tea is known for its effects including cleaning grease from body, promoting digestion, enhancing appetite, and accelerating the blood circulation.

Dark green tea is also fermented, in a particularly long process, until the tealeaves turn black. Dark green tea can be made into "brick tea", after being pressed tightly. Brick tea can be stored for a long time, and some brick tea is specially shaped and designed to make delicate works of art. The most famous dark green tea is Puer tea (普洱茶) from Yunnan. Dark green tea is good for softening the blood vessels, preventing cardiovascular diseases.

Oolong tea (乌龙茶) is semi-fermented, kind of between green tea and black tea. Of the six types of tea, oolong tea has the most complex and time-consuming production process, and the best techniques are required when brewing the tea. Famous varieties include Tieguanyin tea (铁观音茶), Wuyi tea (武夷茶), and Taiwan tea. Oolong tea is favoured by females as it helps to keep a good body figure and smooth the skin.

Yellow tea is a lightly fermented tea, with a very similar production process to that of green tea, except that it needs to be braised. People discovered it in the process of making green tea; by adding some innovative technology, yellow tea is produced. Yellow tea is characterised by its refined taste and yellow leaves. Its rare varieties include Junshan Silver Needle (君山银针), Mengding Huangya (蒙顶黄芽), and Huoshan Huangya (霍山黄芽).

White tea is also a kind of slightly fermented tea, with special and delicate processing by only withering and drying. The buds and tea leaves are covered with white hairs, so it is named "white tea". The name also describes the colour of the tea liquid, which is snowy and silver. White tea is known as the "aristocrat" among the six kinds of tea, and is regarded as the healthiest tea. Famous varieties include White Peony (白牡丹), Baihao Yinzhen (白毫银针), Gongmei (贡眉), and Shoumei (寿眉).

It should be noted here that despite the multiple flavours and benefits, people should take some common-sense precautions when drinking tea. For example, people should not drink tea on an empty stomach, when they have a fever, or immediately after meals, and it is advisable to choose different types of tea according to one's physical features, the seasons, and so on.

9.3.3 Chinese Tea Culture

Generations of growers and producers have perfected ways of manufacturing tea, and tea culture has become an important part of Chinese traditional culture. This tea culture is not only reflected in the taste and colour of tea, but also in the presentation of tea sets and the process of serving of tea. In other words, tea has become more than a kind of beverage; rather, in many ways, it is a symbol of Chinese people and culture.

Serving tea is also seen as the way for Chinese people to treat their guests with the warmest hospitality. Whenever guests visit, it is a tradition to make and serve tea. The host should first ask the guests for their preferences—green, black, or any other kind of tea—and then serve the tea in the most appropriate and exquisite teacups. During the tea serving, the host should always take careful note of how much water remains in their guests' cups and fill them with hot tea in a timely manner. This way, their cups are kept filled and the tea retains the same flavour. Of course, snacks, sweets, and other side dishes may be served at tea time to complement the fragrance of the tea and to allay hunger.

Chinese people's attitudes towards tea reflect their attitudes towards life. Given one has a sufficient tea set and mature tea preparation and serving skills, it is always a pleasure to perform a tea ceremony in front of guests, or simply with family. The ceremony should be carried out in a leisurely, quiet, and peaceful atmosphere, normally accompanied with some traditional Chinese instrument (such as Guzheng) playing music, using fresh and clean water, delicate tea sets, and elegant handling. While tasting tea, Chinese people enjoy not only the delight brought by the brew, but also achieving spiritual peace and joy and being in an aesthetic realm. Therefore, tea is not just for satisfying physiological thirst; the calm, peaceful, and slow sips people take show their desire for a comfortable, refreshing, and tranquil life.

9.3.4 Tea Culture and Tourism

As mentioned earlier in this chapter, just as Chinese food culture plays an essential role in tourism development and regional tourism activities promote the local food industry in turn, Chinese tea culture is also regarded as an indispensable part of Chinese tourism culture.

For many decades, tea tourism has been a unique feature of Chinese tourism culture. In the past, tea tourism was usually an organic combination of cultural tourism, sightseeing tourism and folk tourism. In the current era, tea tourism usually uses an outdoor tea garden as a landscape background, which is then decorated and embellished to cater for the tourists. For example, Meijiawu (梅家坞) Tea Village in Hangzhou is well known for its Longjing tea plantation. Longjing tea (literally translated as "Dragon Well Tea") was once granted the status of the Gong Cha (贡茶), or imperial tea, for the Emperors of the Qing Dynasty. Meijiawu has a history of over 600 years and is home to 160 teahouses. Here, visitors can learn more about the region's rich tea culture, as well as try their hands at picking tea leaves (under the guidance of the Meijiawu experts).

Nowadays, with the improvement of material life, people are no longer contented with traditional tea tourism: instead, they have begun to pursue healthcare, cultural taste, and the most natural and pure surroundings for their tea tourism. Tea is not only a commodity but also a healthcare product. Tea is considered the healthiest beverage of the 21st century. Its nutritional value and use in healthcare are recognised and accepted by more and more people. To cater for people's healthcare needs, an increasing number of tea baths, tea restaurants, tea bars and teahouses have been set up in combination with other regional tourism resources. Furthermore, tourists today are also eager to understand and learn more comprehensive and systematic knowledge of tea culture through their tea tourism. To expand tourists' knowledge of tea culture, a series of tea-related cultural activities have been organised in some "hometowns" of tea, including reading tea poems, appreciating tea paintings, reading tea books, and so on.

Our country owns rich natural resources related to tea culture, and thanks to the accumulation of tea culture for thousands of years, today, the resources of tea tourism include the abovementioned natural scenic spots where famous tea originated, tea cultural and historical landscapes, teahouses, tea ceremony performances, and economic zones of factories and shops associated with tea industries. The best tea tourism destinations include Lincang (临沧), Yunnan Province, where the famous Dianhong tea is produced; Zhangjiajie (张家界), Hunan Province, which is not only the place of filming for the blockbuster movie *Avatar*, but is also home to the most precious category of tea—Junshanyinzhen; Fanjing (梵净) Mountain, Guizhou (贵州) Province, which is home to green tea and is well‐known for its precious natural resources, historical Buddhist mountain, unique natural scenery, and large number of cultural and historical sites (which led to it being ranked as one of the top 10 tourist attractions of "Beautiful China" in 2013).

China is a country with an enormous production of tea, and tea is produced in more than 20 provinces. The development and utilization of these natural tea‐production landscapes plays a key role in tourism and cultural exchange, will greatly promote economic expansion and can improve the life quality of regional people.

Chapter Summary

This chapter starts with the emergence and development of Chinese food culture, dating back to before the Qin Dynasty. Then, it introduces the three main concepts of Chinese food culture, and the relationship between food culture and the tourism industry. More specifically, it illustrates the two most essential elements of Chinese food culture: Chinese cuisine and Chinese tea. As China covers a large territory, the different regional ingredients and cooking styles have formed eight well-known regional cuisines. This chapter introduces the origin, typical characteristics and famous dishes of each regional cuisine, as well as many other local cuisines and famous local snacks. The last section introduces Chinese tea culture, which, with a time-honoured history, complex categories and classifications, and sophisticated serving etiquette, plays an important role in the Chinese tourism industry today.

Issues for Review and Discussion

1. Can you introduce the history and development of Chinese food culture?
2. What is the relationship between food culture and regional tourism?
3. What are the main concepts of Chinese food culture?
4. Can you name the eight regional cuisines and briefly describe each of them?
5. What are the main categories of Chinese tea?
6. What are the typical and popular forms of tea tourism nowadays?

China Story

Rice noodle has promoted local tourism

Exercises

Chapter 10
Martial Arts

Learning Objectives

After reading this chapter, you should have a good understanding of
1. The development of Chinese martial arts;
2. Well-known styles of Chinese martial arts;
3. The philosophical notions of Chinese martial arts;
4. Martial arts-related tourist attractions.

Technical Words

English words	中文翻译
routine	套路
chisel	凿子
the Middle Pleistocene	中更新世
Peking man	北京猿人
petroglyph	岩画
The Neolithic Age	新石器时代
counter-attack	反攻
feint attack	佯攻
Jiaodi play	角抵戏
sword dance	剑舞
broadsword dance	刀舞
double halberd dance	双戟舞
Macaque Dance	沐猴舞
Dog Fighting Dance	狗斗舞
Drunken Dance	醉舞
Five-Animal Exercise	五禽戏
martial art form	武术程式

续表

English words	中文翻译
imperial examination system	科举制
the martial art examination	武举
the literary examination	文举
art of archery	射术
spear techniques	枪术
New Treatise on Disciplined Service	《纪效新书》
boxing style	拳势
Emei-Style Spear Techniques	《峨嵋枪法》
Taijiquan Theory	《太极拳论》
Techniques of Neijia Boxing	《内家拳法》
school	流派
Eight Diagrams	八卦
Five Elements	五行
combat sports	搏击运动
push hands	推手
National Martial Art Performance Competition	全国武术表演竞赛大会
Excavation and Sorting Movement	挖掘整理运动
UNESCO's List of the Intangible Cultural Heritage	联合国教科文组织非物质文化遗产名录
National Intangible Cultural Heritage List	国家级非物质文化遗产名录
Xi Ci	《系辞》
theory of yin-yang	阴阳理论
Chen-style Taijiquan	陈式太极拳
Shaolin Kung Fu	少林功夫
soldier-monk	僧兵
staff technique	棍术
Seven Star Fist	七星拳
Arhat Fist	罗汉拳
Iron Palm Fist	铁砂掌
Dragon Claw Fist	龙爪掌
harmony	和合
Dragon Fist	龙拳
Tiger Fist	虎拳

续表

English words	中文翻译
Leopard Fist	豹拳
Snake Fist	蛇拳
Crane Fist	鹤拳
combining hardness and softness	刚柔并济
using softness to overcome hardness	以柔克刚
harmony between internal and external parts	内外合一
essence	精
qi	气
spirit	神
judging the opponent's force	听劲
dispersing force	化劲
Zen	禅宗
World Cultural Heritage List	世界遗产名录
The Book of Tao and Teh	《道德经》

Knowledge Graph

- Martial Arts
  - The origins and development of Chinese martial arts
    - Origin
    - The formative stage
    - The mature stage
    - The modern stage
  - Influential Chinese martial arts styles
    - Taijiquan
    - Shaolin Kung Fu
  - The philosophy of Chinese martial arts
    - Harmony
    - Yin-yang
  - Martial art-related tourist attractions
    - Shaolin Temple
    - Wudang Mountains

Chapter 10   Martial Arts

Chinese martial arts have a history spanning thousands of years. The ancestors of the Chinese people first created them as individual combat skills for survival in both the natural and social environments. After centuries of development, they now have a well-established system, building from routines and combat techniques to develop forms for tactical action. The martial arts serve diverse functions including physical exercise, competitive sports, and combat. Moreover, they have become one of the most well-known symbols of Chinese culture and an important channel through which China communicates with the world.

10.1 The origins and development of Chinese martial arts

10.1.1 Origin

(1) The original fighting skills in hunting

In the primitive society of the ancestors of the Chinese people, production was underdeveloped and the level of production was extremely low. Individuals had to fight a range of rivals including predators and enemies from different tribes to survive and reproduce in their harsh environment. In the competition for survival, the ancestors used not only their own bodies to punch, kick and dodge, but also gradually learned the use of simple wooden and/or stone tools, such as sticks, stone hammers, and chisels to fight their enemies. Through practice, they accumulated knowledge and skills in stabbing, hitting, slashing, and splitting.

Before learning to grow crops, hunting was an important means for the ancestors to obtain food and clothing. The knowledge and skills they had acquired in beating wild animals with tools of stone and wood for survival were gradually applied to their hunting activities. Some Chinese classics record such hunting activities: *Our Lord Goes Hunting* (《郑风·大叔于田》) in *The Book of Odes* (《诗经》), the first anthology of verse in China, portrays ancient Chinese people fighting tigers with their bare hands.

Historic sites also demonstrate the fighting skills and primitive weapons used by the Chinese ancestors in their hunting activities. Many stone hammers, stone knives and other stone tools, and a smaller number of sharp bone tools, were found at Zhoukoudian Cave of northern China, occupied by Peking Man (Homo erectus pekinensis) during the Middle

Pleistocene. In addition, hunting petroglyphs of various styles and content survive in Western China. These rock paintings vividly depict scenes of ancient Chinese people hunting wild animals during the period of the primitive hunting culture, providing an important basis for the study of early martial arts activities. The petroglyphs at Cangyuan (沧源) in Yunnan and Helan Mountain (贺兰山) in Ningxia are two well-preserved examples. Hunting prompted the ancestors to form and hone the fighting skills of attacking and defending with their bare hands or simple weapons, with movements including punching, kicking, jumping, dodging, smashing, hacking, slashing, and stabbing. These instinctive, spontaneous, and random body movements occurred both in the ancestors' fights for survival and their hunting activities and are the original forms of the Chinese martial arts, laying an important foundation for the formation of their fighting skills.

(2) The original fighting skills in the battlefield

During the Neolithic Age, stone tools including axes, knives, spearheads, and mallets, as well as bone tools such as fishbone forks, were used widely. By the end of the Neolithic period, the production of tools made more rapid progress due to copper mining, and the use of bronze tools greatly improved productivity. These advances in tool making laid a material foundation for the gradual formation of skills such as splitting, stabbing, cutting, and piercing in later martial arts techniques. It also ameliorated living standards, leading to a surplus of material resources for subsistence and thus to the emergence of private property.

During this period, primitive wars frequently broke out between clans and tribes as they fought for their own interests in conflicts over resources and wealth. The use of force became an important means of plundering resources and wealth. Primitive warfare facilitated the formation of martial arts, which started to emerge from the skills that had developed through fighting and hunting wild animals and through military combat. Many of the combat actions using bare hands or wooden and stone instruments were formed naturally during these wars. At the same time, to aid their survival and that of their tribes, people combined all the combat skills acquired in war, separated them from production skills, gradually standardized and stylized them, and passed them on to younger generations together with production skills such as hunting. Thus, the primitive martial arts were formed.

10.1.2 The formative stage

(1) The Spring and Autumn Period and the Warring States Period

An important work in the history of Chinese martial arts was created in the early Western Zhou Dynasty; it is named *Zhou Yi* (《周易》), also known as *The Book of Changes*. It introduced two significant philosophical ideas: "one *yin* (阴) and one *yang* (阳) are the dao (一阴一阳为之道)," and "in (the system of) the *Yi* there is the taiji, which led to the two elementary Forms. These two Forms produced the Four emblematic Symbols, which again produced the eight Trigrams."(易有太极，是生两仪，两仪生四象，四象生八卦。)

During the Eastern Zhou Dynasty, the states in the kingdom of Zhou frequently waged wars with each other in their competition for hegemony. The five hundred years of this dynasty are divided into the Spring and Autumn Period and the Warring States Period. Years of war led to combat skills from the battlefield developing rapidly and becoming highly valued among both the army and the civilian population. The emergence of iron tools and the rise of infantry and cavalry in these periods led to the diversification of weapons, which had varied lengths and forms. The quality of the weapons was also substantially improved. At the same time, the art of fighting was further highlighted, and the effect of martial arts on health and fitness was also valued. At this time, martial arts contests, in which offensive and defensive skills were stressed, became very common. Attack, defence, counter-attack, feint attack, and so on began to appear in styles of boxing.

(2) The Qin Dynasty and the Han Dynasty

In 221 BC, the State of Qin defeated the other six states and its king proclaimed himself emperor, known as the first emperor of Qin. To prevent the remnants of the six states and their civilians from rebelling, he ordered that the practice martial arts should be forbidden. This led to some fighting skills which were previously practiced in the army, for instance hand-to-hand combat, to gradually break away from combat and develop into civilian entertainment, for example the original form of wrestling, which was turned into Jiaodi play.

The great period of development of the martial arts took place in the Han Dynasty. Sword dances, broadsword dances, and double halberd dances in the form of single, pair, or group dances were often performed at court banquets. Freehand boxing performances and competitions were also highly valued by the rulers. The emperors of the Han Dynasty also used martial arts as a means of demonstrating national strength to foreign guests, which accelerated the spread of martial arts overseas. Broadsword play, sword play, and wrestling began to spread to Japan during the Han Dynasty and had a profound impact on the development of Japanese martial arts. In addition to the practical techniques of defending oneself and defeating enemies, boxing began to acquire alternative functions, developing into Xiangxing dances for entertainment and for maintaining health and fitness. The Macaque Dance, Dog Fighting Dance, and Drunken Dance are examples of this which might be considered early pictographic boxing. Among these, the Five-Animal Exercise, which was created by Hua Tuo, provided a template for the creation of Xiangxing boxing in later generations.

(3) The Jin (晋) Dynasty and the Southern & Northern Dynasties

The Jin, Southern, and Northern Dynasties was the period of most frequent regime change in Chinese history and a number of states under different emperors' rule co-existed at this time. The long-term separatist regime and continuous wars had a particular influence on the development of Chinese martial arts in this period.

During this period, martial arts performances were officially listed as court entertainment. Wrestling was popular among civilians in both the north and south, and wrestling exchange activities were often held between different regions. At the same time, martial arts competitions were often held between different states, with archery contests as one of the main events. These developments demonstrate that national and ethnic awareness was attached to recreational martial arts competitions, endowing martial arts with deeper and broader meanings.

In the historical era therefore, regime change occurred on average every few years. Years of war led to boxing being highly valued by armies, and many soldiers were well-known for their agility and their barehanded combat skills. As the nomadic and Han cultures developed and became more integrated during this period, there was a long term development of boxing skills in the north towards a strong and vigorous style. At the same time, civilians faced a struggle to survive in the face of wars and exploitation by the ruling class. They were frequently forced to question whether they would still be alive tomorrow. Learning the skills of boxing therefore became a necessity for many civilians during this chaotic era. The development of martial arts among civilians largely took the form of barehanded combat, this being their last resort for survival. Thus, the practice of martial arts among civilians, in contrast to the era of the Han Dynasty, was no longer only for entertainment, but part of the struggle for survival.

By the time of the Jin Dynasty, a wealth of martial arts experience had been accumulated. Important movements were linked together, making it easier to memorize and practice them. The Forms and routines of martial arts were created. Martial artists introduced many spoken instructions and essential techniques, developments which signified a great advancement in Chinese martial arts. The drills of these martial arts forms, routines, and techniques were for both combat training and entertainment performances, the latter being a combination of combat and entertainment in martial arts techniques. Performing martial arts and practical martial arts were thus closely related during this period.

10.1.3 The mature stage

(1) The Sui and Tang Dynasties

An unprecedentedly prosperous society and economy prevailed during the Sui and Tang Dynasties, and the increasing frequency of cultural exchange between these dynasties and foreign countries provided a broader platform for the development of Chinese martial arts. Both the ruling class and the civilian population had a great enthusiasm for martial arts during this historical period.

The development of martial arts in the Sui Dynasty was dominated by the ruling class selecting martial artists and dictating who could practice martial arts skills. The rulers strictly prohibited civilians from practicing martial arts and confiscated their weapons, while selecting martial art talents according to their own needs. These practices developed into the unofficial martial arts examination used by the Sui Dynasty.

Empress Wu in the Tang Dynasty established the martial arts examination as part of the Imperial Examination System, officially assessing martial arts practitioners and selecting talents from among them. This had significant implications for the history of Chinese martial arts; even though the martial arts examination was far less developed than the literary examination in the Imperial Examination System, and its influence was far smaller, it was a necessary supplement to the literary examination. The establishment of the martial arts examination was the result of the refinement and standardization of the martial arts. Not only did it improve the social status of martial arts practitioners, but it also provided them with a pathway for social advancement; it was of great significance to the promotion and development of the martial arts. This method of selecting martial arts talents from across the social classes laid the foundation for the establishment and development of martial arts in the Song Dynasty and was also inherited by the subsequent dynasties.

It should also be noted that China during the Tang Dynasty was the political, economic, and cultural centre of the world and there were frequent exchange activities with neighbouring countries., Most of the cultural exchange relating to martial arts at this time were with Japan, Korea, India, and the Eastern Roman Empire. Exchange activities with Japan focused on the art of archery; those with Korea were largely about spear techniques; the activities with India were mainly about integrating martial arts with health preserving; wrestling competitions were often held with the Eastern Roman Empire. All of these activities promoted the development of techniques, skills, principles, and theories in the Chinese martial arts.

(2) The Song Dynasty

The formal system of Chinese martial arts was established during the Song Dynasty. Firstly, this was an important period for the development of Chinese martial arts among civilians; this being mainly reflected in the unprecedented popularity of military martial arts in rural areas and the rapid development of martial arts routines in urban areas. Amid the acute ethnic and class conflicts of the time, more peasants gathered to practice martial arts in many different areas and more martial artists taught their skills than ever before.

Secondly, martial arts changed significantly in the army, under strong military pressure from the nomadic peoples of the north. This is manifested in the stylization of military training and the further standardization of weapon techniques. Standard training codes were introduced, and the central government assigned skilled martial artists to military units for coaching. These measures further improved soldiers' martial arts levels and promoted the popularity of martial arts among them. The coaches were responsible for martial arts training but they had no command over military operations and could therefore devote their energy to the study of martial arts, further promoting their development. Civilian martial arts organizations flourished.

(3) The Ming and Qing Dynasties

Threats from the Mongolian cavalry in the north and Japanese pirates along the southeast coast during the Ming Dynasty reinforced the importance of military training and led to the government frequently recruiting martial art practitioners from around the country. More than 40 Shaolin monks were recruited, who succeeded in winning many battles. Commander-in-chief Qi Jiguang's actions to defeat Japanese pirates are a good example: he recruited local warriors and gave them systematic military training, including striking and stabbing techniques and the use of both long and short weapons. This method of recruiting martial arts practitioners and soldiers not only promoted the development of local characteristics in the martial arts, but also curbed corruption in the army.

Important developments in the martial arts also occurred in the Ming Dynasty, mostly during the Jiajing period. This phenomenon had a direct relationship with the war against Japanese pirates which was taking place at that time. For example, Qi Jiguang's *New Treatise on Disciplined Service* (《纪效新书》) is a summary of his many years of experience fighting Japanese pirates along the coast of Zhejiang, as well as being a textbook for training Qi's army. Recording 32 boxing styles as well as weapon techniques, it has great practical value and is a precious martial arts book.

The theory of Chinese martial arts was further enriched and developed during the Qing Dynasty, when many martial arts books were published, expounding instructions, techniques, and principles. Examples of this include Cheng Zhenru's *Emei-style Spear Techniques* (《峨眉枪法》), Wang Zongyue's *Taijiquan Theory* (《太极拳论》), and Huang Baijia's *Techniques of Neijia Boxing* (《内家拳法》).

Most of the styles, or schools, of Chinese martial arts were also formed in the Qing Dynasty. There were more than 100 boxing styles, or schools, each with well-recorded origins and development, clear boxing theory, a unique style and coherent system. Martial arts routines thus reached completion in this period. In addition, boxing techniques and schools appeared that were named after traditional philosophical terms, and interpreted boxing using philosophical principles. Examples include: Taijiquan based on the Taiji theory, Baguazhang based on the Eight Diagrams theory, and Xingyiquan based on the Five Elements theory. It would be fair to argue that Chinese martial arts reached a peak of historical development during the Qing Dynasty.

10.1.4 The modern stage

From the founding of People's Republic of China to the 1970s, martial arts were classified according to the characteristics of boxing and weapon techniques. In the context of the development of martial arts, their practice was limited to routine sports at this time, but the fighting function was resurrected in the form of combat sports in the late 1970s. This brought changes to the classification of martial arts, with a move towards classification according to categories and sport forms. Chinese martial arts categories are divided into individual exercise, pair exercise, group exercise, Sanda (散打), and push hands. In terms of sport forms, the classifications divide them into routine sports, combat sports, and exercises

The National Martial Art Performance Competition in the 1950s, and the Excavation and Sorting Movement of martial arts in the 1980s were both of vital importance in promoting the development of martial arts after the founding of the People's Republic of

China (PRC). In the context of Reform and Opening up, martial arts have also begun to be integrated into the development of the socialist market economy, with the martial arts economy and martial arts industrialization gaining increasing attention. Martial arts athletic competitions and the popularization of martial arts reflect the influence of the socialist market economy and a macro situation of martial art market economy has therefore been created since the 1980s.

The World Martial Arts Festival, starting in 2004, serves to disseminate and promote Chinese martial arts and traditional culture to the world. Taijiquan was included in China's first National Intangible Cultural Heritage list, published in 2006, and in 2020, UNESCO also recognised Taijiquan in its List of Intangible Cultural Heritage. The Beijing Olympic Games once again showcased the charm of Chinese martial arts to the world. The Taijiquan performance at the opening ceremony, as well as the Routine Contest of Chinese Martial Arts, an Olympic Games special event, demonstrated Chinese martial arts to athletes and sports fans all over the world. The then President of the International Olympic Committee, Mr. Rogge, presented medals to the contest winners. The Beijing Olympics were a great encouragement to the development of Chinese martial arts, and also highlighted and demonstrated respect for them. These events constitute a striking symbol of martial arts during this period.

10.2 Influential Chinese martial arts styles

10.2.1 Taijiquan

As one of China's most renowned traditional martial arts forms, with its focus on edifying the temperament and building the body, Taijiquan was included on *China's first National Intangible Cultural Heritage List*, published in 2006. Taijiquan is not only a symbol of eastern culture but is also the most popular form of martial arts in the world. It has now spread worldwide to more than 150 countries and regions, with around 300 million Taijiquan practitioners across the globe.

Taiji (太极) comes from "in (the system of) the Yi (易) there is the Grand Terminus, which produced the two elementary Forms," in *Zhou Yi·Xi Ci*(《周易·系辞》). Tai (太) means grand and ji (极) means terminus. Taiji is a significant term in Chinese traditional philosophy. In the Song Dynasty, the Neo‑Confucianist Zhou Dunyi wrote the book *Explanations of Taiji Diagram*(《太极图说》), and draws Taiji into the shape of circle in his Taiji Picture. Enlightened by the philosophical ideas in Zhou's work and illustration, martial arts practitioners at the end of the Ming Dynasty began to integrate these concepts with the skills of guiding the breath with the will, using stillness to control motion in the traditional qigong and Taoist breathing exercises, together with boxing skills in other schools of martial arts. A new style of martial arts, with a continuous movement of drawing circles in the air was then invented and developed. This new style gained the name Taijiquan after the book titled *Taijiquan Theory*, written by Wang Zongyue, was published during the reign of Emperor Qianlong in the Qing Dynasty.

Photograph 10.1　A Taijiquan Practitioner
(Source: https://pixabay.com/zh/photos/tai-chi-taiji-martial-qi-gong-1678125/)

A range of styles of Taijiquan have been formed and developed over its long period of evolution (Photograph 10.1). Five major styles have become widespread, and these are named after the Chinese families who invented them. They are the Chen style, the Yang style, the Wu style, the Wu style and the Sun style. Among these, the Chen style is believed to be the oldest, and all the styles are thought to trace their historical origin to Chen Village (陈家沟村), Wenxian (温县), in central China's Henan Province.

Nearly 400 years ago, the founder of the village, Chen Bu, brought his family to the village from Shanxi Province. In the ninth generation of his family, Chen Wangting transformed the pre‑existing Chen style training practice into a new martial art. He integrated it with the dialectical ideas of yin-yang (阴阳) theory in *The Book of Changes*, Confucianism and Taoism and, after countless trials, he created Chen-style Taijiquan. In the Qing dynasty, the sixth-generation inheritor, Chen Changxing, taught Yang Luchan, who was not a member of Chen Village, to practice Chen-style Taiji, and this led to the development of other schools of Taiji.

Chen‑style Taijiquan is characterised by its "twining" movement, in which the alternation between speed and slowness combines with the explosion of power to form a

Further reading

Taiji centre launched in Greek university

free-flowing motion. Taijiquan is classified into two types according to its functions. One is for fighting and self-defence, while the other is for health and longevity. When both forms are integrated into one, this allows the practitioner to "combining hardness with softness" through Taiji. Younger people who learn Taijiquan are often encouraged to focus its techniques and toughness, whereas older learners are usually guided to focus on exercising the body and the gentleness of the practice. This is the principle of "utilizing the toughness and nurturing the gentleness" in Taijiquan.

10.2.2 Shaolin Kung Fu

The culture of Chinese martial arts is broad and deep, with many schools of boxing. Shaolin Kung Fu is one of the most influential and most long-standing martial art styles in China; it is an general name for various kinds of martial arts practiced by the Shaolin monks.

The trend for monks to practice martial arts developed in Buddhist temples during the Northern Wei Dynasty. In the nineteenth year of the reign of Emperor Xiaowen of the Northern Wei Dynasty, a prominent monk named Bata, from the Western Regions, built Shaolin Temple at Mount Song. From then on, Shaolin Kung Fu gradually developed through the monks' long-term martial arts practice.

Shaolin Kung Fu flourished in the early Tang Dynasty. At the end of the Sui Dynasty, insurrections and wars broke out frequently. In the war between Wang Shichong who had proclaimed himself emperor and Li Shimin who became the second emperor of the Tang Dynasty, the Shaolin monks were invited to support Li Shimin. After Li Shimin was crowned emperor, he rewarded the monks and granted Shaolin Temple the right to train soldier-monks. Shaolin Temple thus established a relationship with the royal family, gained an eminent reputation and earned the title of "the Number One Temple under Heaven".

Shaolin Kung Fu flourished after Li Shimin granted the temple permission to train soldier monks. Martial arts trainings at Shaolin Temple were directly linked to combat, which provided favourable conditions for the development of Shaolin Kung Fu. The monks practiced boxing skills, cudgel techniques, qigong, and tactics to improve their combat skills and abilities martial arts masters were often invited to the temple from all over the country to teach the monks. In this way, Shaolin Temple became a national centre for martial arts practitioners, earning itself the opportunity to assimilate the strengths of a range of martial art schools. Simultaneously, Shaolin Kung Fu itself also became widespread.

Shaolin-style boxing and Shaolin cudgel techniques stand out among the martial arts practiced at the Shaolin Temple. Among the boxing skills, the Seven Star Fist (七星拳), Arhat Fist (罗汉拳), and Iron Palm Fist (铁砂掌) are well known; they consist of only a small number of moves but are powerful and practical. The main hand position in Shaolin Kung Fu is the Dragon Claw (龙爪手). The cudgel is the Shaolin monks' preferred weapon because of its bluntness; using the cudgel thus echoes Buddhism's tenet of being merciful and Shaolin monks can defeat their opponents without killing them. The process of learning weapon techniques usually starts with mastering the cudgel play. Shaolin cudgel techniques include more than 80 forms, including: Six Harmony Cudgel (六合棍), Stove Cudgel (烧火棍), Mountain-Shaking Cudgel (震山棍), and Two-Section Cudgel (梢子棍).

Shaolin Kung Fu has a unique style and notable features: all the upward, downward, forward, and backward movements are in straight lines. This is because it is based on combat and engaging the enemy requires either attack or defence from the front. Circular movements are unnecessary and consume a lot of energy. This element of Shaolin Kung Fu is known as engaging the enemy is a matter of moving only two or three steps forward or back (Photograph 10.2). Therefore, practicing Shaolin Kung Fu is not limited by the venue or the weapon, and this flexibility has created favourable conditions for its popularization.

Photograph 10.2   Martial Arts Training at Shaolin Temple
(Source: https://unsplash.com/photos/qzc4wuyUbYs)

10.3 The philosophy of Chinese martial arts

The Chinese martial arts are nurtured, produced, and developed as a model of traditional Chinese culture. They are thus influenced by various ideas, viewpoints, and propositions found in traditional Chinese philosophy, and Chinese martial arts are also known as "techniques with philosophy". The fundamental reason for this is that the martial arts are rooted in the fertile soil of Chinese culture, with thousands of years of history, and contain profound Chinese philosophical thoughts. It can be said that Chinese martial arts have incorporated the excellent ideological essence of traditional Chinese philosophy and thus demonstrate its unique philosophical spirit.

10.3.1 Harmony

The concept of harmony is one of the basic principles of traditional Chinese culture, with an extensive and long-lasting influence on the development of Chinese civilization and traditional culture. The concept of harmony encompasses meanings of peace, cooperation, combination, and integration.

Harmony is the essential cultural spirit of Chinese martial arts. The concept of harmony is the value orientation running through both the mental approach and practical norms of martial arts culture. Harmony is therefore the unique value orientation of martial arts culture. The means by which to fully realize the multi-faceted functions of martial arts culture such as combat, the cultivation of health and quality is through harmony. It could be argued that the ultimate goal pursued by Chinese martial arts culture is harmony. The harmony between human body and mind is regarded as true; interpersonal harmony is regarded as goodness; the harmony between nature and man is regarded as beauty. Harmony constitutes the foundation of the development of martial arts culture and is also its special beauty.

(1) Following nature's course and achieving harmony between man and nature

Traditional Chinese culture originates from farming culture, and the development and shaping of it was significantly impacted by farming production. The so-called farming culture, in short, is a cultural system established from the social context in which agricultural production is the main way of life. Therefore, Chinese people have advocated since ancient times that "people regard food as all-important, and people regard land as all-important". People rely on their land to obtain the most important necessities of life before they can participate any other social activities. Therefore, ancient Chinese people had a deep and great reverence towards nature, praying for abundant harvests to bring food and clothing. It is from this social background of self-sufficiency and natural economy that the cultural spirit of "man follows the laws of land, the land follows the laws of heaven, the heaven follows the laws of Tao, and the Tao follows the course of nature" was formed.

As one of the cultural achievements of ancient Chinese people, the Chinese martial arts developed under the influence of this unique perception of the connection between nature and man. During the initial stages of the development of Chinese martial arts, Chinese ancestors gained enlightenment by observing the movements and activities of wild animals in nature and were inspired by their hunting and fighting methods. They gradually formed their own simple hunting skills. Ancient Chinese people acquired and accumulated a range of fighting and combat skills both from experience and from continuous practice and consolidation. It could be argued that Chinese martial arts maintain the cultural spirit from the very beginning of civilization, of imitating nature, learning from it, and integrating human activities with it.

In the development of Chinese martial arts, practitioners took imitating and learning from nature to be the law. They advocated learning from all things, learning from the world, gaining inspiration and enlightenment from generation, development, and evolution in nature. They took a range of birds' and beasts' figures, movements, attack, and defence methods and integrated them into the forms and techniques of boxing. While it enriched boxing skills, this practice also shows an appreciation and worship for nature. For example, in the Eastern Han Dynasty, Hua Tuo created the Five Animal Exercise by imitating the features of five animals, tiger, deer, bear, ape, and bird. The Dragon Fist, Tiger Fist, Leopard Fist, Snake Fist, and Crane Fist in Shaolin Kung Fu also exemplify this practice.

Taijiquan is a model that illustrates both the belief and practice that man learns from nature, and through it man can realize unity with nature. According to *The IllustratedCanon of Chen-style Taijiquan* (《陈氏太极拳图说》) written by Chen Xin, boxing is just skills but the Tao of Taiji exists within it. Its essence is closely related to the characteristics of water. The rhythms of its movements are slow, soft, relaxing, and flexible, with an affinity to the soothing and calm nature of water. By contrast, when force is exerted, it shows rapid and immediate movements and changes, resembling the unstoppable force of the current. The structure of the forces in Taiji emphasises the combination of hardness and softness, using softness to overcome hardness, taking advantage of the force received, using the weak to vanquish the strong, and striking first while drawing upon force later. These are like the characteristics of water; breaking hard objects despite its softness, having no fixed shape, changing unexpectedly, and turning potential energy into kinetic energy.

Under the influence of traditional Chinese philosophy, practitioners of Chinese martial arts have inherited the approach of the ancient people to learning about nature, man, and the connection between them, advocating for nature and Taoism. This way of thinking has formed unique cognitive habits in Chinese martial arts, acquiring knowledge through perceiving and consolidating natural patterns and applying it to the practice of martial arts. The creation of boxing techniques, understanding of techniques and principles, and the practice of skills are always guided by the laws of nature. They make efforts to integrate nature, objects, and themselves into one, simultaneously expressing and advocating for both life and nature. They constantly pursue the supreme philosophical level; unity between nature and man.

(2) Achieving harmony between internal and external elements

The ideas of "cultivating both internal and external parts" and "strengthening both body and spirit" are advocated as important motivations for the practice of Chinese martial arts. Practitioners of Chinese martial arts should pursue not only physical fitness but also mental strength. Harmony between body and spirit is one of the most fundamental characteristics of Chinese martial arts culture.

Spirit is the essence which is embodied in body. In Chinese martial arts culture human life is regarded as a unified system, and a person is regarded as a whole. Overall harmony between the spirit and body is pursued as an essential goal, demanding the exercise of both body and will. Chinese martial arts skills require the body to move, thus promoting physical exercise and firstly cultivating strength in the body. This physical exercise promotes the circulation of essence, qi (气) and blood within body, helping to strengthen the internal dimension, which is spirit. Practitioners must repair their spirit before strengthening their body. Great importance is attached to the leading role of spirit and mind in Chinese martial arts, which highlights essence, qi (气), and spirit, and emphasises the principles of cultivating both form and spirit, unifying the mind. These are the philosophical approaches to the practice of Chinese martial arts.

(3) Strengthening both skills and virtues

Virtues are intrinsic to Chinese martial arts and the idea that virtues are contained within the martial arts is vital to the philosophy of Chinese martial arts culture. Following that concept, the principles of cultivating virtue together with refining skills, as well as admiring excellent skills and extolling good moral qualities, are highly valued. Practitioners should both practice martial arts skills and demonstrate moral qualities including humility, friendliness, and harmony in their interpersonal relationships.

As early as the text *Zuo Zhuan* (《左传》), written in the pre-Qin period, King Zhuang of Chu put forward the proposition of "the seven virtues of martial arts:" "martial arts prohibits violence, ceases wars, keeps the state strong, consolidates the foundation of the state, stabilizes the people, unites the public, and increases wealth."("禁果、戢兵、保大、定功、安民、和众、丰财者也。") Therefore, in addition to its combat and military functions, martial arts also have moral values oriented towards the maintenance of peace and harmony.

The combat techniques of different boxing styles demonstrate the idea that virtues are contained within the martial arts. Many techniques in Taijiquan reflect the unity of martial arts and virtue; for example, the technique of listening to force and transforming force involves the idea of caring and showing sympathy, which in turn guides Taijiquan practitioners to make friends by learning skills from others, give precedence to virtues, and take forceful measures only after courteous ones fail. Shaolin's Ten Commandments of Bunta lists ten rules, six of which are regulations on virtue. They emphasise that martial arts practitioners should be benevolent, observant, loyal, faithful, humble, and generous. Value is placed on using techniques, harmony, equilibrium, and the learning of combat skills to seek to avoid conflict. Practitioners should adopt a rational approach to the timing of fighting or not fighting. Subduing the enemy without fighting (defeating the enemy without fighting them) is the principle of "using force", which demonstrates noble principles and cultivation.

The ideas of cultivating noble moral qualities and maintaining harmony with others shows that, although combat is an essential part of martial arts, equal importance is attached to cultivating virtue and moral qualities. This is of vital importance in Chinese martial arts.

10.3.2 Yin-yang

The theory of yin-yang (阴阳) is the most representative dialectical concept in traditional Chinese philosophical thought. Yin (阴) and yang (阳) originally referred to man's front and back sides respectively, as they were oriented toward the sun. Ancient Chinese people called the side facing the sun "yang" (阳) and the side facing away "yin" (阴). Later, yin-yang was extended to other paired concepts, such as cold and warm, up and down, left and right, inside and outside, restlessness, and tranquillity. As a result, the ancient philosophers realized that all phenomena in nature could be explained by the theory of yin-yang, and learned that there was a relationship between yin and yang, that they opposed each other while also interacting with each other.

The theory of yin-yang has a deep influence on Chinese martial arts. It profoundly affects both their principles and techniques, and the ideological essence of the theory of yin-yang is reflected in how Chinese martial arts have developed. In terms of techniques, when creating boxing skills, Chinese martial artists divided the movements into two systems: attack and defence. They also adhered to the centrality of yin-yang in developing the forms. For example, the spatial structure of boxing comprises high and low order, using movements that include both jumping in the air and standing or crouching on the ground. The rhythm of the techniques is formed of both movements as well as steady postures. Furthermore, some movements are fast and powerful, while some are gentle and slow. The use of force is approached as a combination of hardness and softness. The range of motion reflects yin-yang through the appropriate degree of either opening or closing motions; there are both striking actions that are quite extended, and those of accumulating force. The methods of tactical strike consist of feints and strikes; practitioners achieve the goal of knocking down their opponents with one hit by shifting between feint and strike. Therefore, the dialectical relationship between movement and stillness, fast and slow, feint and strike, following and reversing and inhaling and exhaling can all be regarded as specific manifestations of yin and yang in martial arts. These reciprocal pairs, each of which contains complementary and mutually-transformational components, present styles of Chinese martial arts to the world.

The idea of yin-yang is evident in various martial arts styles in that they do not go to the extremes of harness or softness. Instead, they value the coordination of movement and stillness as well as the change between yin and yang. Wang Zongyue, in his "*Taijiquan Theory*", stated that yin and yang are not separated from each other but interact with and complement each other. Shaolin-style Kung Fu has similar ideas, using yin to confront yang and using yang to confront yin.

It could be argued that almost all boxing and weapon techniques in Chinese martial arts contain the unity and transformation of yin and yang embodied in harness and softness, feint and strike, and movement and stillness.

10.4 Martial art-related tourist attractions

10.4.1 Shaolin Temple

Founded in AD 495, Shaolin Temple is one of the first national 5A-level tourist attractions in China. It is located at the southern foot of Mount Song (嵩山) to the northwest of Dengfeng City (登封市) in Henan Province. Its name derives from its location in the dense forest of Shaoshi Mountain (少室山). Shaolin Temple is known as the Ancestral Monastery of the Zen Sect and the Principal Temple in the World.

Over a history of more than 1,500 years Shaolin Temple has gradually formed a system of "Shaolin culture", which comprises the three major components of Zen, martial arts, and medicine. Shaolin-style Kung Fu has a history spanning more than 1,000 years and has formed an extensive martial arts system including boxing, cudgel, sword, and broadsword. Shaolin Temple's 72 unique techniques are well-known both domestically and internationally. In addition to its martial arts, Shaolin Temple has integrated Buddhist culture with Taoist culture and Confucian culture over its long history and developed it into a Buddhist sect with Chinese characteristics, Zen. Shaolin Zen medicine takes meditation as the fundamental dharma-gate, using breath, visualization, vital energy and blood, meridians, pulse condition, and others as the basic theory. It uses vaporization, guidance, the massage of acupuncture points, and other basic methods for the diagnosis, treatment, and nursing of health conditions. Shaolin Zen medicine is a priceless treasure of traditional Chinese medicine.

However, its traditional qualities of purity and peace have been impacted by rapid development in recent years. Furthermore, incessant media attention has put Shaolin Temple under scrutiny while also making it a popular tourist attraction.

To sum up, while Shaolin Temple is famous for its beautiful scenery and culture, years of commercialization have led to a highly developed system of tourism that has resulted in a detrimental impact on its purity and peace.

10.4.2 Wudang Mountains

Wudang Mountains are a national 5A-level tourist attraction, located in Danjiangkou City (丹江口市) in the northwest of Hubei Province. It is famous for its splendid natural landscapes, large-scale ancient building complex, long-standing Taoist culture, and extensive and profound Wudang martial arts. In 1994, the ancient building complex in the Wudang Mountains was included in UNESCO's World Cultural Heritage List. Its tourism slogan was "exploring Taoism at the Wudang Mountains, nurturing health at the Taiji Lake".

Tourism at Wudang mainly focuses on Taoist health and cultural heritage. Taoist health tourism integrates experiencing health and wellness alongside sightseeing. The Wudang Martial Arts Summer Camp, for teenagers to learn Taijiquan, is an exemplar of

Further reading

Excavation begins at UNESCO World Heritage Site in Wudang Mountains

Recommended Video

Chinese Martial Art: The Swordsmanship of Wudang Style

China Story

Wudang Martial Art Tourism

this type of tourism. Wudang-style Taijiquan is an important component of Wudang martial arts, which is a major school of the Chinese martial arts.

Wudang martial arts has the two functions of promoting health and self-defence. It was invented and developed by the ancestors of the Wudang School, who practiced longevity in the Wudang Mountains by observing and imitating the offensive and defensive movements of animals and birds in nature. Their system is based on the Taoist classic *The Book of Tao and Teh*《道德经》, combined with *The Book of Changes* and traditional Chinese medicine. In 2006, Wudang martial arts was included in the National Intangible Cultural Heritage List.

Wudang tourism disseminates the essence of traditional Taoism and Taoist health culture. The essence of Taoism includes the philosophical concept of harmony (physical and mental harmony, interpersonal harmony, social harmony, harmony between man and nature), the appeal for "following the will of civilians", the appeal for equality between everyone, the virtue of "holding simplicity and abandoning fraud," and the spirit of "being kind and tender without engaging in disputes". These are in line with the core values of socialism.

An important mission of Wudang tourism is to spread the essence of traditional Taoist thought and realize the dissemination its cultural value through Taoist cultural and health tourism.

Chapter Summary

Created as individual combat skills for survival, Chinese martial arts have developed for thousands of years. They now have a well-established system consisting of routines, competitive sports and combat techniques, and a variety of categories in which Taijiquan and Shaolin Kung Fu have earned high reputation. Chinese martial arts are known as "techniques with philosophy", influenced by various traditional Chinese philosophical ideas of which harmony and yin-yang are of particular importance. Tourism incorporating Chinese martial arts has been promoted recently and a number of martial art-related tourist attractions in China have become increasingly well-known domestically and internationally. They have become one of the most well-known symbols of Chinese culture and an important channel through which China communicates with the world.

Issues for Review and Discussion

1. Can you introduce the history and development of Chinese food culture?
2. What is the relationship between food culture and regional tourism?
3. What are the main concepts of Chinese food culture?
4. Can you name the eight regional cuisines and briefly describe each of them?
5. What are the main categories of Chinese tea?
6. What are the typical and popular forms of tea tourism nowadays?

Exercises

Recommended Reading

Chapter 11
Traditional Chinese Medicine

Learning Objectives

After reading this chapter, you should have a good understanding of
1. The two major theories of traditional Chinese medicine;
2. Diagnosis and treatments in traditional Chinese medicine;
3. Health maintenance and promotion in traditional Chinese medicine;
4. Tourism related to traditional Chinese medicine.

Technical Words

English word	中文翻译
viscera	脏腑
meridians	经脉
collaterals	络脉
essence	精
wind	风
cold	寒
Summer-heat	暑
dampness	湿
dryness	燥
internal heat	火
yang deficiency	阳虚
yin deficiency	阴虚
qi	气
theory of five elements	五行理论
metal	金
wood	木
water	水

续表

English word	中文翻译
fire	火
earth	土
The Medical Classic of the Yellow Emperor	《黄帝内经》
observation	望
auscultation and olfaction	闻
interrogation	问
palpation and pulse feeling	切
five internal organs	五脏
six hollow organs	六腑
sanjiao	三焦
normal pulse	平脉
abnormal pulse	病脉
acupuncture	针法
"Ling Shu"	"灵枢"
acupuncture point	穴位
surgical anaesthesia	手术麻醉
cancer chemotherapy	化疗
TCM massage	中医按摩
manipulation	推拿
microcirculation	微循环
Hypercoagulable of blood	血液高凝的
cerebral circulation	脑循环
meridian belonging	归经
medicated diet	药膳
Solar Term	节气
Su Wen	《素问》
Bei Ji Qian Jin Yao Fang	《备急千金要方》
health nurturing	养生
TCM physiotherapy	中医理疗

Knowledge Graph

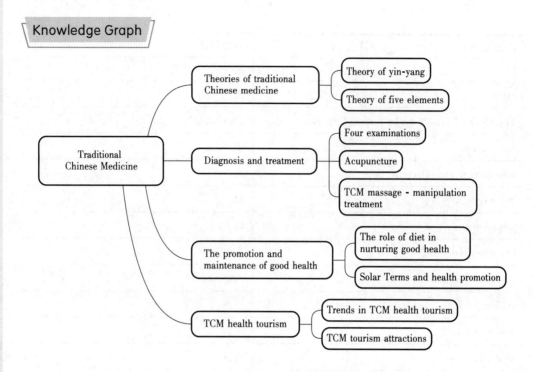

11.1 Theories of traditional Chinese medicine

Traditional Chinese medicine (TCM) is a scientific knowledge system concerning human life, health, and disease. It has been developed through long-term medical practice by integrating traditional Chinese philosophy, with the natural sciences, humanities, and social sciences. Guided by a scientific mode of thought, it consists of a systematic knowledge of the differentiation between conditions, treatment methods, prescriptions, herbs, and clinical experience.

11.1.1 Theory of yin-yang

The theory of yin-yang in TCM is derived from one of the most representative dialectical concepts in traditional Chinese philosophy. Ancient Chinese philosophers believed that the universe was a whole into which all different kinds of things were integrated, and which could be divided into yin and yang. They also believed that yin and yang existed not only inside of natural phenomena, but in their development and transformation.

The theory of yin-yang in TCM stems from the interaction between this traditional Chinese philosophical theory and TCM, originating from a proposition made by the famous doctor Yi He during the Spring and Autumn Period (770 BC - 476 BC). In contrast to the theory of yin-yang in philosophy, the theory of yin-yang in TCM is less concerned with philosophical dialectic, but gives greater emphasis to specific ideas related to medicine. As the core concept underpinning the theoretical system of TCM, it permeates all levels of its ideology, including the analysis of tissue structures, physiological functions and pathological changes in the human body, and gives guidance for the diagnosis and prevention of disease.

As a whole constituted by viscera (脏腑), meridians and collaterals and their constituent parts, the human body can be divided into yin and yangfrom various perspectives using the principles of yin-yang theory. For example, from the perspective of anatomical location, the upper body is yang, while the lower body is yin (; the exterior is yan, while the interior is yin ; the back is yang, while the abdomen is yin. From the perspective of the functions of viscera, six hollow organs including the stomach, small intestine, large intestine, gallbladder, bladder and sanjiao (三焦) digest and transport food downward and they are classified as yang. Five internalorgans including the heart, liver, spleen, lung and kidney produce and store essence inside the human body and they are classified as yin.

In addition to explaining the human body, the theory of yin-yang in TCM is also used to examine the occurrence, development, and progression of diseases. TCM takes the view that damage to the harmony and coordination between yin and yang, caused by pathogenic factors, leads to pathological changes in the human body. The pathogenic factors, for example wind, cold, summer heat, dampness, dryness, and internal heat, can also be divided into yin and yang. Cold and dampness are classified as yin pathogenic agents, while wind, summer heat, internal heat, and dryness are classified as yang pathogenic agents. Yin pathogens lead to yin excess in the human body, while yang pathogens lead to yang excess. Both types of excess energy consume healthy qi (气), and can lead to the development of complex pathological changes such as yin or yang deficiency.

Medical interventions to restore the harmony and coordination between yin and yang heal diseases, and following the natural rules of yin and yang, contribute to the nurturing of health. For example, in spring and summer when yang qi (阳气) is dominant, the human body's yang should be protected to prevent it from being damaged. Likewise, in autumn and winter when yin qi (阴气) is dominant, the human body's yin should be protected to prevent it from being damaged. In this way the goal of preventing diseases and prolonging life can be achieved.

11.1.2 Theory of five elements

The theory of five elements is an ancient philosophical theory stemming from early Chinese people's perceptions of and thoughts about nature. According to this theory, the internal systems of many natural entities can be divided into five elements: wood, fire, earth, metal, and water. The five elements represent five functional states and dispositions within living things as well as the overall dynamics between them. The theory of five elements therefore studies and describes the relationships within things and between things.

The essential idea of the theory of five elements is harmony and coordination between heaven, earth, and man. The great classic of traditional Chinese medicine *The Medical Classic of the Yellow Emperor* (《黄帝内经》) gives a systematic explanation of the influence of weather and changes in climate on the human body, as well as the relationship between blood, qi (气), and viscera (脏腑) within the body and the seasonal factors affecting it. The theory of five elements and the relationship between nature and man is therefore a central concept running throughout *The Medical Classic of the Yellow Emperor*.

The current interpretation of the theory of five elements in TCM is that living creatures proactively adapt to nature, and it therefore focuses on their dynamic states under the five climatic conditions described below.

Spring is associated with wood. The climate gets warmer with the arrival of spring and many living creatures emerge from hibernation. Animals start to move around more widely in search of food, while plants take root and sprout. All living things are moving and expanding in spring. The movement characteristics of wood are rooting downward and sprouting upward, which is an apt description for the condition of living creatures.

Summer is associated with fire. Summer brings hot weather and plants and animals grow more quickly, becoming bigger and taller. Fire flares upwards. The connotations of flaring are hot, upwards, and ascending; fire thus is used to represent the climate and the growth of living creatures in summer.

The period covering late summer and early autumn (the sixth month in Chinese lunar calendar) is associated with earth. Ancient Chinese people called this period "long summer". The climate during this period is characterised by high temperatures and rain, animals are indolent on sultry days, and the growth of plants stagnates. Earth connotes stability, and it thus describes the relatively static state of living creatures in this period.

Autumn is associated with metal. In autumn, the state of living creatures turns into intake and storage. Animals consume large quantities of food and drink to store fat in preparation for scarcity in the approaching winter. The temperate monsoon climate is characterised by cold, dry winters, so plants need to shed their leaves and flowers to reduce water loss. The characteristics of metal are convergence and condensation, so it is used to refer to living creatures' state of intake and storage in this season.

Winter is associated with water and the state of hibernation. Animals move around less or hibernate to preserve heat, while plants hide deep underground preserve water. Water has the characteristic of flowing down; it is thus used to describe the descending state of living creatures in this season.

In TCM, the theory of five elements is applied to explain the main physiological functions of the organs. For example, fire connotes warm and hot; the heart is classified as internal heat (in Chinese, the internal heat is the same Chinese character of fire, 火) because heart *yang* can warm the body. Water conveys the meaning of moisture and flowing downwards; the kidney stores essence and has the characteristics of closure and concealment, so it is classified as water. The theory is also applied to the analysis of pathological changes in the human body and as a guide to the diagnosis and treatment of disease.

The theory of five elements in TCM regards the human body as a whole in which the components attributed to different elements should maintain a dynamic harmony. It also guides man's adaptation to natural changes, such as variation in the climate, stating that appropriate and proactive adaptation will maintain the principle of harmony between man and nature. Health can thus be nurtured and maintained.

11.2 Diagnosis and treatment

11.2.1 Four examinations

observation, auscultation and olfaction, interrogation, palpation and pulse feeling, often referred to as the "four medical examinations" of TCM, are the main methods of diagnosis and they are recorded extensively in *The Medical Classic of the Yellow Emperor*.

Observation is a diagnostic method with which TCM doctorscheck pathological symptoms by observing the patient's spirit, colour, shape, figure, facial features, tongue coating, fingerprints, and excrement and other physical signs. TCM regards a person as an organic whole, in which the exterior and interior are interconnected. Yin and yang can be measured by observing various external manifestations and changes in the body, the strength of the visceral functions, the rising and falling of the qi and blood. For example, important information such as a person's mental state, physical strength, facial colour and complexion can be obtained from observation. There is no substitute for careful observation, and it is therefore central to the diagnosis of disease.

The auscultation and olfaction diagnostic method that identifies pathological symptoms through sound and odour. Listening techniques include listening to and identifying a patient's voice, language, breathing, coughing, vomiting, snoring, bowel sounds, and other sounds. Attention to odour includes abnormal odours emitted by a patient, the odour of their excrement, and the odour of hospital wards. The various sounds and smells of the human body are products of its physiological functions and pathological changes in the viscera. The theory of using five tones (五音) to respond to the five internal organs was put forward as early as the publication of *The Medical Classic of the Yellow Emperor*. The physiological or pathological conditions of the organs can be assessed through abnormal changes in their corresponding sounds and smells, thereby providing a basis for the diagnosis of disease.

Interrogation is a diagnostic tool used by TCM doctors to understand disease through purposeful questioning of patients or their companions. It is also the most fundamental method employed by TCM doctors with their patients. Interrogation may seem simple, but it is not easy; an experienced TCM doctor can generally grasp a patient's condition using this method within two or three minutes. First, TCM doctors need to have a holistic understanding of the patient's aetiology, pathology, clinical symptoms, and physical signs as well as the occurrence and development of the disease. Detailed and comprehensive inquiry can thus help them grasp the key points. Secondly, the TCM doctor uses interrogation as a process through which to apply critical thinking to make a diagnosis; asking and thinking at the same time. Information provided by the patient is the basis for an initial judgement of what syndrome or disease is present.

Palpation and pulse feeling diagnosis is divided into two parts, pulse feeling diagnosis (Photograph 11.1) and pressing diagnosis, in which TCM doctors touch and press certain parts of a patient's body with their hands to obtain pathological information. In ancient times, pulse feeling diagnosis is one of the most well-known characteristics of TCM diagnosis. In taking the pulse, the performance or condition of the pulse is diagnosed. The performance is divided into normal or abnormal pulse. A normal pulse is calm and gentle, the rhythm is neat, and it adapts normally to physiological activities and climatic environments. All other pulse conditions are considered diseased.

Photograph 11.1 Pulse feeling Diagnosis
(Source: https://pixabay.com/zh/photos/chinese-medicine-diagnosis-3666183/)

11.2.2 Acupuncture

Acupuncture is the practice of penetrating the skin with thin, solid, metal needles which are then activated through gentle and specific movements of the practitioner's hands, or with electrical stimulation.

Acupuncture is part of the ancient therapy method of TCM. A complete meridian system was introduced in *The Medical Classic of the Yellow Emperor*, the earliest complete classic of TCM in the existing literature. It articulates a system of meridians and collaterals: the former are distributed deep among the muscles and are difficult to find, while the latter are shallow and hence more easily found on the superficial parts of the body. Meridians mainly run vertically while collaterals run across the whole body. Meridians and collaterals connect the internal organs, hollow organs , sense organs, orifices, and tissues such as the skin, muscles, tendons, and bones; they thus make the body an organic whole. *The Medical Classic of the Yellow Emperor*, especially the section titled "Ling Shu"(《灵枢》) systematically discusses acupuncture theory, methods, indications, and contraindications. "Ling Shu" ("灵枢") provides the earliest summary of acupuncture, and remains the core content of acupuncture practice to this day.

TCM practitioners believe that meridians and collaterals create an energy flow, or qi (气), through the body that is responsible for overall health and that disruption to the energy flow can cause disease. Applying acupuncture to certain points (Photograph 11.2), acupuncture points, is thought to improve the flow of qi (气), thereby improving health. Acupuncture is practiced using hair-thin needles and most people report feeling minimal pain as they are inserted. The needle is inserted to an acupuncture point producing a sensation of pressure, ache, soreness, numbness, or bloating. Needles may be heated during the treatment, or a mild electric current may be applied to them. Some people report acupuncture makes them feel energized, while others say it relaxes them.

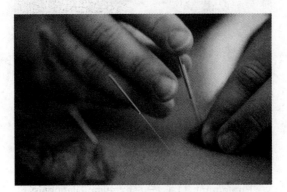

Photograph 11.2　Acupuncture Treatment
(Source: https://unsplash.com/photos/QgcdtM9rA5s)

Acupuncture points are believed to stimulate the central nervous system and this in turn releases chemicals into the muscles, spinal cord, and brain. These biochemical changes may stimulate the body's natural healing abilities and promote physical and emotional well-being. Studies have shown that acupuncture is an effective treatment, either alone or in combination with conventional therapies, in the management of pain and treatment of nausea caused by interventions including surgical anaesthesia, cancer chemotherapy, asthma, and addiction.

In November 2010, acupuncture and moxibustion, both TCM modalities, were included in the United Nations Educational, Scientific and Cultural Organization (UNESCO) Representative List of the Intangible Cultural Heritage of Humanity. In February 2017, a bronze acupuncture statue was erected in the lobby of the WHO, signifying the globalization of Chinese acupuncture.

11.2.3 TCM massage - manipulation treatment

TCM massage is defined as using finger skills to continuously press skin and muscle tissue and move over it to cure disease.

Massage is one of the oldest medical practices known to humanity history. When a person inadvertently damages part of their body, or experiences pain due to disease, they will instinctively use their hands to protect or caress the place where the disease or pain occurs. In winter, people generate heat to maintain body temperature by repeatedly rubbing parts of the body with their palms. These instinctive practices of caressing or rubbing the body with the palms are the prototypes of the original massage technique.

From the Han Dynasty to the Ming Dynasty, this treatment was called massage, following the Ming Dynasty, it became known as manipulation. Nowadays, it is called massage in the south of China while in the north it is known as manipulation.

The treatment mechanisms of massage and acupuncture share a similar source ; both rely on acupoints on the body's surface to deliver stimulation. Both cure disease by adjusting the balance of yin and yang in the viscera by promoting the circulation of qi (气) through the meridians and collaterals. The only difference is the means of treatment, one using the palm while the other uses the needle. The therapeutic effect of applying massage to meridian points or other specific points can help either enhance a certain tissue function, eliminate pathogens, or inhibit the hyperfunction of tissues and organs.

Both clinical practice and experimental studies have shown that TCM massage has effects on various systems of the human body. It can accelerate blood flow and change the hypercoagulable state of blood, improving microcirculation and cerebral circulation to prevent the occurrence of cerebrovascular diseases. For example, massage of the head, face, and neck, increases cerebral blood flow significantly, making people feel refreshed and full of energy. Rubbing the Feishu (肺俞), Dingchuan (定喘), Fengmen (风门), and other acupoints can improve the ventilation function of the respiratory system; regular massage of these acupoints can prevent chronic bronchitis and improve the symptoms of emphysema. Rubbing the Zusanli (足三里) acupoint and massaging the abdomen can promote digestion and absorption. Massage also significantly improves and affects the motor nervous system of the human body. Frequent facial massage can remove secretions from the surface of the skin, promote the shedding of dead epidermal cells, prolong the aging process of epidermal cells, and improve the nutritional status of the skin, thereby increasing the complexion and elasticity of the skin (Photograph 11.3).

Photograph 11.3　Manipulation Treatment
(Source: https://pixabay.com/zh/photos/chinese-medicine-massage-techniques-3666269/)

11.3 The promotion and maintenance of good health

Nurturing good health through the prevention of disease and maintenance of health is an important component of TCM. The goal of improving health, delaying aging, prolonging life, and preventing disease is achieved through a combination of health care methods based on self-adjustment and self-regulation.

11.3.1 The role of diet in nurturing good health

TCM theory is used as a guide to achieve a diet balanced according to the nature, flavour, meridional alignment, and function of food. TCM thus studies the properties of food and diet in maintaining health, strengthening the body, and preventing aging.

The role of diet in health preservation began to emerge in TCM during the Spring and Autumn Period. During the Warring States Period, the earliest medical classic existing in our country, *The Medical Classic of the Yellow Emperor*, further enriched knowledge of diet and health. It describes human activities as composed of basic substances: essence, qi, bodily fluid, blood, and the meridians, and that these substances all originate from daily dietary intake. Over the long-term development of TCM, diet and health promotion has formed one of its unique characteristics.

The understanding of drugs in TCM stems from the understanding of food. TCM takes the view that medicine, drugs, and food share the same origin in certain aspects. To some extent, the health-preserving and therapeutic effect of food is the origin of medicine.

The properties of food in TCM include its nature, taste, meridional alignment, and function. The theory of food in TCM shares similar origins with those of the wider Chinese materia medica. Food has five properties, cold, cool, warm, hot, and neutral. Most cold and cool food, for example lotus root and eggplant respectively, have the effect of clearing heat and irritability, and thus are suitable for hot climate. Most warm food, for example hot pepper and ginger, have the effect of improving yang in the body to keep out the cold, and thus are suitable for cold climate. Food of neutral nature, for example corn and tomato, is suitable for all four seasons.

Food is further classified into five flavours, sour, bitter, sweet, pungent, and salty. Food of sour flavour, such as hawthorn fruits, can increase appetite and prevent sweating and diarrhoea. Food of bitter flavour, for example bitter melon, has the effect of clearing heat, strengthening the stomach and promoting salivation. Food of sweet flavour, such as longan, has the effect of nourishing the spleen. Food of pungent flavour, for example ginger, has the functions of facilitating the circulation of qi and blood in the body, expelling cold from the body and reducing dampness in the body. When we get caught in the rain or have a cold, we may feel more comfortable after having a bowl of hot ginger soup. Food of salty flavour, such as seaweed, has the function of nourishing the kidneys and bone marrow.

Due to their shared theoretical origins, food is combined with Chinese medicine under the guidance of TCM to create a medicated diet. This diet has a long history in TCM and there is large variety within it. Each element has a special function, strict recipe, and unique flavour. The ingredients generally vary from person to person and different medicines are applied on the basis of the physiological conditions present in each person, so as to achieve physical fitness and healing.

Health tourism involving the medicated diet has been promoted in several places in China, among which Huanren (桓仁) (in the City of Benxi, Liaoning Province) and Pu'er (普洱) (in Yunnan Province) are two examples. The Huanren Manchu Autonomous County Government has built Huanren into a "Northern International Health-promotion City". It has actively advocated for local special medicated meals and medicated diet brands such as "Huanren Ice Wine", "Huanren Rice", "Huanren Mountain Ginseng", and thus combined tourism with health promotion. Pu'er has grown rapidly in the fields of health care, leisure, health preservation, and health tourism. During every Dragon Boat Festival, the Baicao Roots Food Culture and Tourism Festival is held there, the promotion of which has increased since 2017. At each of the tourism festivals, the Dragon Boat Festival International Forum of Ethnic Medicated Diet and Health Promotion is held. The theme of the forum is "Nurture in Pu'er, Healthy Life". It plays an important role in promoting the heritage, innovation, and development of ethnic medicine in Pu'er City, and the integration of ethnic medicine with health preservation, thus creating a large health care brand in Pu'er.

Recommended Video

Frost's Descent

11.3.2 Solar Terms and health promotion

Adapting to achieve harmony between man and nature is a major principle of TCM. This means that, to nurture good health, people should adapt to changes in the climate, time period, geographical environment, and living conditions and avoid any disturbance these changes may cause, so as to achieve a long and healthy life.

Acclimatizing to seasonal changes is the most important and basic way of adapting to nature. The ancient Chinese divided the sun's annual circular motion into 24 segments and each segment was called a specific 'Solar Term' (inscribed in 2016 on UNESCO's Representative List of the Intangible Cultural Heritage of Humanity). The criteria for their formulation were developed through the observation of changes in the seasons, astronomy, and other natural phenomena in the Yellow River reaches of China and this system has been progressively applied nationwide. Under the influence of the progress through the Solar Terms, people should adjust their bodies to the varying climate.

"Su Wen" ("素问") in *The Medical Classic of the Yellow Empero*, the earliest medical classic in China, proposes the principle of "nourishing yang in spring and summer, and nourishing *yin* in autumn and winter". Through health promotion, TCM guides the adaption of the human body to the alternation of the seasons and the cycles of the sun and the moon. The nurturing of good health through diet should follow the changes of four seasons as well, choosing foods of a type and flavour appropriate to the time of year. Sun Simiao in his *"Bei Ji Qian Jin Yao Fang"* (《备急千金要方》) set out the dietary choices that should be made according to seasonal changes. In spring, sour food should be avoided while sweet foods should be increased to nourish spleen qi. In summer, bitter food should be reduced while pungent food should be increased to nourish lung qi. During the late summer and the early autumn, sweet food should be avoided, salty food should be increased to nourish kidney qi. In autumn, pungent foods should be reduced while sour flavours should be increased to nourish liver qi. In winter, salty food should be reduced while bitter food should be increased to nourish heart qi. Food for spring includes Chinese chives, Chinese yam, Chinese water chestnut, and spinach. Summer foods include watermelon, winter melon, tomato, and mung bean. Foods for autumn include pear, tremella, pig's lung, ginkgo nut, and lemon. Foods for winter include mutton, chicken, chestnuts, walnuts, longan, and sweet potatoes.

Taking trips according to seasonal changes with the aim of adjusting the physical and mental state is known as four-season health tourism, which is seen as an extension of both health care and tourism. From the medical perspective, tourism has a direct effect on eyesight, heart and lung function, the coordination of limbs, fat burning, and delaying aging. Solar Term health tourism in line with seasonal changes can not only relieve physical fatigue, but also play a role in mental health and the treatment of disease.

Case Study

Four Seasons Health Tourism Products of the Poyang Lake Ecological Economic Zone

Further Reading

Chinese 24 Solar Terms: The Chinese wisdom of dividing time

Note

11.4 TCM health tourism

TCM health tourism is a new model integrating tourism, vacation, rest, health care, recuperation, and popular science.

11.4.1 Trends in TCM health tourism

In February 2016, the State Council issued the *Outline of the Strategic Plan for the Development of Traditional Chinese Medicine (2016-2030)*(《中医药发展战略规划纲要（2016—2030年）》). The plan set out the development of TCM health tourism services, promoting the integration of TCM health care services with the tourism industry, developing TCM health tourism to disseminate the experience of TCM culture, and integrating tourism with TCM recuperation, rehabilitation, health preservation, cultural communication, business exhibitions, and scientific research into Chinese medicinal materials. In July 2016, the Ministry of Culture and Tourism and the National Administration of Traditional Chinese Medicine of the People's Republic of China issued the *Notice on the Establishment of National Traditional Chinese Medicine Health Tourism Demonstration Areas (Bases, Projects)*(《关于开展国家中医药健康旅游示范区（基地、项目）创建工作的通知》). It proposed the construction of 10 demonstration areas, 100 demonstration bases and 1,000 demonstration projects across the country over three years. In March 2018, the first batch of 73 demonstration bases was announced; China's TCM health tourism has a bright and promising future.

Many places in China have launched TCM culture and health tourism, including Beijing, Heilongjiang, Hainan, Gansu, Sichuan, Henan, which have all piloted TCM tourism areas or projects. For example, China's first medical tourism pilot area was initiated in Qionghai (琼海), Hainan Province in 2013. In 2016, Hainan launched the flight route from Almaty (阿拉木图) to Sanya (三亚), initiating the tourist experience of TCM to Russian-speaking visitors. Nowadays, Hainan's tourism has been transformed from the earlier scenic and folk tours to a comprehensive and three-dimensional "health care plus tourism" model combining TCM physiotherapy, thermal spring health care, climate health care, and rainforest oxygen inhalation. From 2015 to 2016, Changzhou (常州) in Jiangsu Province and Shangrao (上饶) in Jiangxi Province successively became medical tourism pilot areas approved by the State Council.

The development of TCM health tourism, is still in its infancy however, especially faced with the challenge of increasing its attractiveness. In the context of numerous competing tourism products, TCM culture must develop a distinct development path to enhance its attractiveness to enable health tourism to stand out from the crowd. Diversified TCM cultural tourism products should be developed, and TCM tourism brands established to enhance publicity. It would be beneficial in the competitive tourism market to adopt a holistic approach by jointly developing tourism for TCM health promotion, healthcare, traditional cultural experience, and sightseeing while also promoting the interconnection of the six major elements (food, travel, shopping, housing, transportation, and entertainment) within the industry. Further products of TCM tourism, such as tonics, medicated food, traditional medical tools, beauty products, and cultural souvenirs should also be developed. The integration of medical and dietary care, recuperation, and sports and health programs including Taijiquan and Five-Animal Exercise would enable comprehensive new TCM tourism projects to be developed. Such an approach would facilitate tourists' enjoyment of the full range of TCM tourism services. At the same time, brands typifying local TCM culture should be set up to enhance the value of TCM health tourism products, strengthen publicity, and stimulate positive responses.

TCM health tourism should also be promoted internationally. The *Outline of the Strategic Plan for the Development of Traditional Chinese Medicine (2016-2030)* (《中医药发展战略规划纲要（2016—2030年）》) explicitly supports the participation of TCM institutions in the construction of the "Belt and Road". In January 2017, the National Administration of Traditional Chinese Medicine and the National Development and Reform Commission jointly issued the *Traditional Chinese Medicine Belt and Road Development Plan (2016-2020)* (《中医药"一带一路"发展规划（2016-2020年）》). As a health tourism resource, TCM plays an important role in the "One Belt, One Road" strategy to build a shared future for mankind. Local governments should fully explore and develop their TCM cultural resources to achieve a high international reputation. One approach would be to form new tourism brands by combining TCM with famous attractions, such as Shaolin medicine and the Prescription Cave (药方洞) at Longmen Grottoes (龙门石窟). Alternatively, TCM's own cultural tourism brands might be developed around well-known TCM tourist attractions. A good case in point is the Memorial Temple to the Medical Sage (医圣祠) in Nanyang (南阳), a major cultural site protected at the national level, which is an important global symbol of TCM and the roots of its culture.

The strategic advantages of the Belt and Road Initiative will enable tourism routes to be developed along the Silk Road. A regional integration strategy would further advance the development of the TCM health tourism industry. Shaanxi would act as the centre for Gansu, Qinghai, Ningxia, Sichuan, and other provinces in the west, while Xi'an (西安) would be the centre for surrounding areas such as Xianyang (咸阳), Baoji (宝鸡), Tongchuan (铜川), Shangluo (商洛), Hanzhong (汉中), and Ankang (安康). The integration of medical culture and tourism will enable the multi-level development of

TCM health tourism industry to be realized in these regions. TCM health experience tourism products could be developed to showcase the qualities of various locations in Shanxi, including the pedicure zone at Xianyang, the thermal spring base at Lantian (蓝田), and tourism routes at Yaozhou District (耀州区) (the hometown of Sun Simiao, one of the most significant TCM pharmacists). Another example is Lingtai County (灵台县) in Gansu Province, which is a section of the ancient Silk Road rich in the history of Huangfu Mi's (the author of the first book on acupuncture) life and work. Tourism companies along the route could work together to transform these opportunities into real productivity, developing TCM cultural tourism brands and products reflecting unique local characteristics.

In 2020, some places in China effectively promoted the early, comprehensive, and in-depth involvement of TCM in epidemic prevention and control, with Hangzhou being a good example. Medical teams from Hangzhou (杭州) were delegated to support overseas regions in the international fight against the pandemic. In the post-pandemic era, places like Hangzhou can further strengthen exchange and cooperation with international travel agencies and foreign health care institutions to build international TCM tourism brands that reflect local characteristics. Hangzhou can offer TCM-based physiotherapy services by combining methods including its TCM ointment, acupuncture, and moxibustion.

Further Reading

Health tourism from Chinese mainland on the rise

Tourism 4.0 will see the tourism industry become integrated with the mobile internet. With the continuous development and innovation of mobile applications, customized and personalized travel are becoming more and more popular both domestically and internationally. Mobile apps can also deliver telemedicine, mobile medical care, and the real-time download of electronic prescriptions. Alongside this prominent feature of tourism 4.0 people are also paying more and more attention to health promotion. Customized personal health travel plans can lead to the creation of integrated medical information services for visits to health care cultural bases, the online purchase of health care products, and convenient access to electronic prescriptions. The construction of TCM network information platforms must catch up with this trend rapidly, and the relevant mobile apps will need to be developed.

Further Reading

TCM health tourism expected to boom due to favourable policies

11.4.2 TCM tourism attractions

(1) Medicine Capital – Bozhou (亳州)

Bozhou is a famous national historical and cultural city known both as "the Medicine Capital of China" and "the cradle of traditional Chinese medicine culture". The development of the medicated diet has a history spanning thousands of years; as early as the Spring and Autumn Period and the Warring States Period, Lao Tzu, who was born in Guoyang (涡阳), thought deeply about health and his writings were regarded as a classic of health preservation. During the Eastern Han Dynasty, another Bozhou native, Hua Tuo, known as the "sacred doctor", cleverly combined food and health promotion with physical fitness, thus creating a precedent for the maintenance of good health among ordinary. This gradually evolved into the combination of Chinese cuisine and TCM which is now known as Chinese medicated food.

The Bozhou medicated diet, as the original template for the TCM medicated diet, has always been widely appreciated. It has become one of the main attractions bringing tourists to Bozhou with the rise of modern tourism and its development as a famous tourist city.

Bozhou currently has a concentrated planting area of 1.16 million mu of Chinese herbal medicines, with 100,000 pharmaceutical traders and millions of pharmaceutical farmers. It is the world's largest trading centre for Chinese herbal medicines, with activity encompassing planting, processing, circulation, scientific research, and derivatives. The city is thus home to a complete system of traditional Chinese medicine development, industry, and cultural dissemination. The idea that medicine and food are of the same origin is an important theory advocated by TCM for the maintenance of good health; the Bozhou folk medicated diet, medicinal tea, medicinal porridge, medicinal drink, and other varieties of food therapy are thus innovating on the basis of a long history. The local signature medicated meal is Cao Cao Fish Head (曹操鱼头), which is said to be a medicated dish used by Cao Cao to treat diseases of the head.

The people of Bozhou have always valued medicated meals; even if they do not have a thorough understanding of the theory of TCM, every household can make one or two medicinal dishes, such as nepeta salad, crystal mint, or platycodon. Traditional Chinese medicines such as red dates, lotus seeds, wolfberry, and lily are also added to daily cooking in the city.

During the 2017 Bozhou Cultural Tourism Year, ten gold medals were launched for medicated meals on sale in 20 of the city's hotels, offering tourists delicious medicated food. In the same year, Bozhou was awarded the title "National Medicated Food Capital" and "World Medicine Capital, Health Bozhou" has become the city's slogan. In 2018, the specifications for the Medicated Diet Competition were raised to even higher levels, and the 2018 World Medicated Diet Culture and Food Festival and China (Bozhou) Medicinal

Diet Competition was held. In 2019, the "Hua Tuo Cup" China (Bozhou) Medicated Food Competition was held to promote the development of the Bozhou medicated diet.

(2) Lingnan TCM Cultural Expo Park

Lingnan Traditional Chinese Medicine Cultural Expo Park (岭南中医药文化博览园), also known as Traditional Chinese Medicine Town (国医小镇), is located in Guangzhou (广州). It promotes the heritage and history of TCM culture. This comprehensive project integrates TCM culture and tourism, production and processing, products and technology, commerce and circulation, education and scientific research. Lingnan has a strong cultural atmosphere of TCM and reflects the unique characteristics of local culture.

The Expo Park is the main section of the Traditional Chinese Medicine Town. The Lingnan Chinese Herbal Medicine Germplasm Seedling Breeding Base (岭南中草药种质种苗基地) has been completed, and it has collected more than 1,300 southern medicinal seeds. A range wide range of projects have been completed: the Chinese Medicine Garden (国医园), Hundreds species of Herbs Garden (百草园), Sea of Four Seasons Materia Medica (四季本草花海), and Chinese Medicine Cultural Expo Center (中医药文化博览中心). Lingnan Traditional Chinese Medicine Cultural Expo Park (岭南中医药文化博览园) is currently the national base for TCM publicity and education.

The Maliu Mountain Southern Medicine Forest Park (马骝山南药森林公园) is across town from Lingnan, it brings together tourism, resource cultivation, scientific research, and education. The purpose of the park is to protect the forest and medicinal resources of the Tropic of Cancer. It was established under the guidance of TCM culture, providing tourists with a TCM health promotion experience. It is aimed at creating a system of planting and manufacturing Chinese herbal medicine by combining agricultural production with forest resources. The park will give full play to the advantages of TCM resources, effectively combining tourism, commercial service industry and TCM resources to form a high quality TCM health tourism product and service system with broad appeal. Targeting the demand side of the tourism market, it will vigorously develop TCM tourism, cultural experience, health promotion, health care, rehabilitation, beauty care and exhibitions.

Further Reading

Jilin Province to be home to UN health tourism project

China Story

The Development of TCM Tourism at Emei Banshan Qiliping (峨眉半山七里坪)

Exercises

Recommended Reading

Chapter Summary

This chapter introduces the theory of yin-yang (阴阳) and theory of five elements, which are two fundamental theories in TCM. The "four examinations", which include observation, auscultation and olfaction, interrogation, palpation and pulse feeling, are the signature diagnosis methods of TCM. Based on the two theories and diagnosis, TCM doctors may employ a range of treatment methods including two well-known techniques, acupuncture and manipulation treatment. Nurturing good health through the prevention of disease and maintenance of health is an important component of TCM, in which having an appropriate diet and acclimatizing to seasonal changes both play important roles. As TCM has been being promoted, it has been integrated with tourism, vacation, rest, health care, recuperation, and popular science. TCM tourism is developed and launched in a number of places in China, among which Bozhou and Lingnan Traditional Chinese Medicine Cultural Expo Park (岭南中医药文化博览园) are exemplars.

 Issues for Review and Discussion

1. How to understand the relativity between yin and yang?
2. What role does diet play in nurturing good health?
3. What are the trends of TCM health tourism?

教学支持说明

为了改善教学效果,提高教材的使用效率,满足高校授课教师的教学需求,本套教材备有与纸质教材配套的教学课件(PPT电子教案)和拓展资源(案例库、习题库等)。

为保证本教学课件及相关教学资料仅为教材使用者所得,我们将向使用本套教材的高校授课教师赠送教学课件或者相关教学资料,烦请授课教师通过电话、邮件或加入旅游专家俱乐部QQ群等方式与我们联系,获取"电子资源申请表"文档并认真准确填写后发给我们,我们的联系方式如下:

地址:湖北省武汉市东湖新技术开发区华工科技园华工园六路

邮编:430223

电话:027-81321911

E-mail:lyzjjlb@163.com

旅游专家俱乐部QQ群号:758712998

旅游专家俱乐部QQ群二维码:

电子资源申请表

填表时间：_____年___月___日

1. 以下内容请教师按实际情况写，★为必填项。
2. 根据个人情况如实填写，相关内容可以酌情调整提交。

★姓名		★性别	□男 □女	出生年月		★职务	
						★职称	□教授 □副教授 □讲师 □助教

★学校		★院/系	
★教研室		★专业	
★办公电话		家庭电话		★移动电话	
★E-mail（请填写清晰）			★QQ号/微信号	
★联系地址		★邮编	

★现在主授课程情况	学生人数	教材所属出版社	教材满意度
课程一			□满意 □一般 □不满意
课程二			□满意 □一般 □不满意
课程三			□满意 □一般 □不满意
其 他			□满意 □一般 □不满意

教材出版信息						
方向一	□准备写	□写作中	□已成稿	□已出版待修订	□有讲义
方向二	□准备写	□写作中	□已成稿	□已出版待修订	□有讲义
方向三	□准备写	□写作中	□已成稿	□已出版待修订	□有讲义

请教师认真填写表格下列内容，提供索取课件配套教材的相关信息，我社根据每位教师填表信息的完整性、授课情况与索取课件的相关性，以及教材使用的情况赠送教材的配套课件及相关教学资源。

ISBN（书号）	书名	作者	索取课件简要说明	学生人数（如选作教材）
			□教学 □参考	
			□教学 □参考	

★您对与课件配套的纸质教材的意见和建议，希望提供哪些配套教学资源：